THE CATHOLIC BIBLICAL QUARTERLY

MONOGRAPH SERIES

3

THE USE OF *tôrâ* BY ISAIAH

HIS DEBATE WITH THE WISDOM TRADITION

THE USE OF *tôrâ* BY ISAIAH

HIS DEBATE WITH THE WISDOM TRADITION

BY

JOSEPH JENSEN, O.S.B.

Department of Religion and Religious Education
School of Religious Studies
The Catholic University of America

The Catholic Biblical Association of America
Washington, D.C. 20017
1973

Nihil Obstat
REVEREND MONSIGNOR PATRICK W. SKEHAN
Censor Deputatus

Imprimatur
THE MOST REVEREND WILLIAM V. BAUM
Archbishop of Washington
May 23, 1973

THE USE OF *tôrâ* BY ISAIAH:
HIS DEBATE WITH THE WISDOM TRADITION
by Joseph Jensen, O.S.B.

PRODUCED IN THE UNITED STATES
by Information Products & Services Corporation
5315 Lee Highway, Arlington, Va. 22207

LIBRARY OF CONGRESS CATALOGUE CARD NUMBER: 73-83134

TO MY MOTHER

Table of Contents

Preface ix
Introduction 1
Chapter 1. ETYMOLOGY, MEANING, AND KINDS OF *tôrâ* 3
Etymology 3
The Meaning of *tôrâ* 5
Priestly *tôrâ* 6
Priestly *tôrâ* and Divination 7
Priestly *tôrâ* as *Responsum* 9
Ritual Distinctions and Priestly *tôrâ* 9
Priestly *tôrâ* in Hosea 10
Thesis of Begrich 12
tôrâ as a "Legal" Term 14
Prophetic *tôrâ* 18
Eighth Century Prophets:
Amos, Hosea, Micah 19
Seventh Century Prophets:
Zephaniah, Habakkuk, Jeremiah, Nahum 19
Exilic Prophets:
Ezekiel and Deutero-Isaiah 22
Post-Exilic Prophets:
Haggai, Zechariah, Malachi 24
Prophetic *tôrâ* as a
Literary (Liturgical) Form 25
Conclusions 26
Chapter 2. ANTIQUITY OF *tôrâ* AS WISDOM TERMINOLOGY 28
"Instruction" in Ancient Near Eastern
Wisdom Tradition 29
tôrâ in the Collections of Proverbs 35
Proverbs 13:14 37
Proverbs 28:4 37
Proverbs 28:7 38
Proverbs 28:9 39
Proverbs 29:18 40
Proverbs 31:26 41
tôrâ in Proverbs 1-9 41
Chapter 3. YAHWEH AND WISDOM IN ISAIAH 45
Wisdom Influence in Isaiah 45
Isaiah's Polemic against "The Wise" 51
Yahweh as Imparter of *tôrâ* 58

Chapter 4. *tôrâ* IN ISAIAH 65
Isaiah 1:10 68
Formal Elements:
Aufmerkruf; Rhetorical Question 69
Content and Terminology 73
Isaiah 1:10-17 and Psalm 50 83
Isaiah 2:3 84
Authenticity 85
Yahweh the Wise King;
Wisdom Terminology 89
Isaiah 5:24B 95
Authenticity 95
Isaiah 5:24b Considered Apart
from its Context 97
Isaiah 5:24b and its Context 100
Isaiah 8:16.20 104
Preliminary Problems 105
The Context 107
Interpretation 110
Isaiah 30:9 112
Summary 120
Chapter 5. CONCLUSIONS 122
Bibliography 136
Index of Modern Authors 147
Index of Scripture References 149

PREFACE

The basic argument of this study was first set forth in brief and preliminary form as a research report at the Thirty-third General Meeting of the Catholic Biblical Association in September, 1970; it was elaborated more fully in my dissertation, "The Use of *tôrâ* by Isaiah," submitted to the School of Sacred Theology of The Catholic University of America in 1971. The present monograph is based on that dissertation, though the text has been considerably shortened and has been revised in other ways.

I would like to express my heartfelt gratitude to Patrick W. Skehan for directing the dissertation, for his many valuable suggestions and criticisms, and for his unfailing support and help at every stage in the development of this study; a fuller account of my debt to him would include earlier years of classroom instruction and continuing contacts since then. I owe him thanks also for the help which he, as new Chairman of the *CBQMS* Editorial Board, has given in bringing this study to publication. My thanks go also to Joseph A. Fitzmyer, S.J., the former Chairman of the *CBQMS* Editorial Board, under whom this study was accepted for the series and from whom I received valuable advice for its final preparation. I also thank Peter Kearney and Alexa Suelzer, readers of the original dissertation, for useful cricitisms and suggestions. Needless to say, the deficiencies of this study are attributable to me, not to any of them. An expression of gratitude is due also to Robert E. Coughlan of Information Products & Services Corporation for his painstaking work in producing the printed text, for his cheerful willingness to make last minute changes, and for his resolute concern for both quality and economy. Finally, I thank my mother, Annette Jensen, and Mr. and Mrs. James Miller, for their work on the indexes.

The translation used throughout this study is *The New American Bible*, though I have occasionally departed from it in the interests of a more literal rendering. Hebrew and Greek words have been transliterated throughout, even when set in the original alphabets in the source cited or quoted. For the conventions of transliteration, citations of Scripture, and abbreviations, see *The Catholic Biblical Quarterly* 33 (1971) 85-88. Most of this information is given also in any recent volume of *CBQ*. To those lists note the following addition: BHS=Biblica Hebraica Stuttgartensia.

INTRODUCTION

The position argued in this study is that Isaiah's use of the term *tôrâ* reflects wisdom usage ("wise instruction"). This is a difficult position to argue because of the almost universal tendency of commentators to see in Isaiah's various *tôrâ* passages either priestly, prophetic, or legal terminology and because of the wide-spread persuasion that *tôrâ* as wisdom terminology is late. If the position is to be argued at all, therefore, it is necessary to investigate some of the earlier, often generally accepted, assertions concerning the meaning of the term and its use in priestly, legal, prophetic, and wisdom traditions. Only then is one prepared to approach the question of Isaiah's use of it; and this requires both situating Isaiah in his relationship to contemporary wisdom circles and investigating the individual texts in which he uses the term. Thus it does not seem possible to present the case in anything short of a full-length study.

I am convinced that the matter deserves full treatment not simply for the sake of the five Isaiah texts involved, but also because of the implications that flow from this use of *tôrâ*. Ever since the seminal study of Johannes Fichtner, "Jesaja unter den Weisen," *TLZ* 74 (1949) 75-80, a discernible relationship of Isaiah to wisdom circles has been widely recognized and accepted, but there has not been complete agreement concerning the nature of that relationship. If the position I am arguing is correct, I believe that it helps define this relationship more closely and points, moreover, to indications of Isaiah's long-term influence on the wisdom tradition.

I

ETYMOLOGY, MEANING, AND KINDS OF *tôrâ*

The purpose of this chapter is to discuss certain general notions connected with the term *tôrâ* and to challenge certain assumptions or conclusions that, though widely held, are based on very little solid evidence. A discussion of these matters will smooth the way for the arguments of later chapters.

Etymology

As recently as 1905 at least one author felt able to speak with assurance of the derivation of *tôrâ*:

> We need not delay over the derivation of the word. It comes from *yarah*, which denotes the act of shooting arrows or hurling a javelin. All that we need attend to at this point is that *torah* is from the hiphil of the stem, and that the verb in the hiphil is strictly cognate in use to the noun, so that the two ought to be studied together.[1]

Few today would wish to speak so confidently. Barnabas Lindars, for example, in approaching the question of the use of *tôrâ* in Deuteronomy does not feel that much help can be expected from etymology, "the more so as this in fact remains an unsolved problem."[2]

Explanations for the derivation of *tôrâ* have been offered, but none of them rest on compelling arguments, and none of them have been accorded general acceptance. The three basic theories on the etymology of *tôrâ* are connected with the names of Gesenius, Wellhausen, and Delitzsch.[3]

Wilhelm Gesenius derives *tôrâ* from *yrh*, presumably from the hiphil. The development is: to throw, to throw the hand, i.e., to point, to show, to instruct; other authors follow the same derivation.[4]

[1]Willis J. Beecher, "*Torah*: A Word-study in the Old Testament," *JBL* 24 (1905) 2.

[2]Barnabas Lindars, "Torah in Deuteronomy," in *Words and Meanings: Essays Presented to David Winton Thomas*, ed. P. R. Ackroyd and B. Lindars (Cambridge: Cambridge University Press, 1968), 117-36. A similar view is expressed by Walter Gutbrod, "*nomos*," in *TDNT*, IV; the section on "The Meaning of *tôrâ*" is found on pp. 1044-47.

[3]Thus Ivan Engnell, *Israel and the Law* (Uppsala: Wretmans Boktryckeri A.-B., 1954), 2; Gunnar Östborn, *Tōrā in the Old Testament: A Semantic Study* (Lund: Håkan Ohlssoms Boktryckeri, 1945), 6-12; and Lindars (following Engnell), "Torah in Deuteronomy," 118f.

[4]Wilhelm Gesenius, *Thesaurus philologicus criticus linguae hebraeae et chaldaeae Veteris Testamenti* (2nd ed.; Leipzig: F. C. W. Vogel, 1840), II, 626f. See also Auguste Gampert, *La thora; Étude historique sur ses origines et son développement* (Geneva: Imprimerie Romet, 1895), 15; S. R. Driver, *An Introduction to the Literature of the Old Testament* (Cleveland: The World Publishing Company, 1956 [c1897]), seems to follow the same derivation; see p. 31 (on Ex 18) and p. 153n. (on Dt 33:10).

Julius Wellhausen is the originator of the second position. In his earlier works he retained the idea of "throwing" in the hiphil of *yrh*, from which he derived *tôrâ*, but related it to the act of casting lots.[5] Later, however, Wellhausen changed his opinion on this,[6] though this is often not noted.[7]

Friedrich Delitzsch equates *tôrâ* with Akkadian *têrtu*, which he derives from (*w*)*arû* (=Heb. *yrh*), whose meaning in Form I he gives as "bringen, führen, wegführen" and in Form III as "zubringen lassen, überliefern . . ., spez. Wissen und Üben von etw., jem. darin unterweisen."[8] Albright[9] also sees *tôrâ* (of which *hôrâ* is a denominative) as the equivalent of *têrtu*,[10], both forms being derived from the same Akkadian root; but he derives them from

[5]Julius Wellhausen, *Prolegomena to the History of Ancient Israel*, tr. A. Menzies and J. S. Black (Edinburgh: A. & C. Clark, 1885), 394; the German original was published in 1878. Against the derivations of both Gesenius and the earlier Wellhausen it may be noted that it is by no means clear that the meaning "to instruct" for *hôrâ* ought to be developed from the idea of throwing or casting—whether lots, fingers, or anything else. Roland Murphy, in an unpublished M.A. dissertation, *A Study of the Hebrew Root yrh* (Washington, D.C.: The Catholic University of America, 1948), following Mayer Lambert, holds that *yrh* is properly a *primae waw* verb and the qal imperfect has been mistaken by lexicographers for a hiphil. (The participles, clearly hiphil, and one hiphil perfect that occur in the meaning "to throw" can be explained as secondary formations out of the "pseudo-hiphil"; the one apparent occurrence of a niphal in Ex 19:13 is taken for an error—a mistaken reading of yod in place of waw.) If this thesis is accepted, the idea of throwing disappears from the authentic hiphil forms. Murphy asserts that the meaning "to show, to teach" cannot be explained with any certainty from the root idea of *yrh*, "to throw," and allows the possibility that the meaning "to teach" may come from a different root.

[6]The relevant text is in *Reste arabischen Heidentumes*, Vol. III of *Skizzen und Vorarbeiten* (Berlin: Druck und Verlag von Georg Reimer, 1887), 167.

[7]E.g., Engnell, *Israel and the Law*, 2.

[8]For the equation of *tôrâ* and *têrtu*, see Friedrich Delitzsch, *Prolegomena eines neuen hebräisch-aramäischen Wörterbuchs zum Alten Testament* (Leipzig: J. C. Hinrichs'sche Buchhandlung, 1886), 47 (and p. 41n. for the equation of *yrh* with (*w*)*arû*); since his intent in listing *tôrâ* and *têrtu* together (along with forty-five other pairs) is to demonstrate the "innige Verwandschaft des Hebräischen mit dem Assyrischen, die weit innige Zusammengehörigkeit dieser beiden Sprachen . . .," it does not seem proper to say that Delitzsch considered *tôrâ* a loan word, as some (e.g., Engnell, p. 2) do. For his derivation of *têrtu* from (*w*)*arû*, see *Assyrische Grammatik* (Berlin: H. Reuther's Verlagsbuchhandlung, 1889), 146; for the meanings assigned to (*w*)*arû*, see *Assyrisches Handwörterbuch* (Leipzig: J. C. Hinrichs'sche Buchhandlung, 1896), 241. Much of this must be considered doubtful, however. Delitzsch derived *têrtu* from (*w*)*arû* and treated the Akkadian root as *wrh* (and therefore equivalent to Heb. *yrh*, taken to be originally *primae waw*), but Wolfram von Soden, *Grundriss der akkadischen Grammatik* (Rome: Pontifical Biblical Institute, 1952), 68, derives it from (*w*)*âru* representing *w'r*; see also *The Assyrian Dictionary of the Oriental Institute of the University of Chicago*, Vol. I, Part II (Chicago: Oriental Institute, 1968), 318; Murphy, *A Study* . . ., 27; Engnell, 2f.

[9]W. F. Albright, "The Names 'Israel' and 'Judah' with an Excursus on the Etymology of *TÔDÂH* and *TÔRÂH*," *JBL* 46 (1927) 151-85.

[10]The meanings he gives for *têrtu* are "commission, command, oracle, especially of hepatoscopy (the oracle *par excellence*)" (p. 180). Alfred Haldar, *Associations of Cult Prophets among the Ancient Semites* (Uppsala: Almqvist & Wikells Boktryckeri A.-B., 1945), 99, also relates *tôrâ*, which "originally signified the decision of the oracle," to *têrtu*.

(w)âru (which he specifies as *wa'âru*), rather than the *(w)arû* favored by Delitzsch.[11]

None of these views imposes itself with irrefutable force. It is quite possible that Wellhausen's earlier derivation and that of Albright have been somewhat influenced by the widely held conviction that *tôrâ* has a primitive connection with the giving of oracular response,[12] a matter which will be discussed later on.

The Meaning of *tôrâ*

In view of the contradictory and uncertain nature of the opinions outlined above, it would be extremely risky to attempt to arrive at basic or derived meanings of *tôrâ* on the basis of etymology. A safer course would be through the examination of OT usage. Even this course is fraught with difficulties if it is a question of the evolution or development of the meaning of the term. It is fairly well agreed that the general meaning of *tôrâ* is "teaching, instruction," but this general meaning takes on varying nuances depending on the particular circle or milieu in which the word is used; or possibly we should think of a more specific meaning within a particular circle as the starting point of development to a more general sense, as some hold.[13]

The circles within which *tôrâ* was formulated and passed down are generally given as three: priestly, prophetic, and wisdom.[14] Whatever chronological development can be discerned would also be reflected in this listing, in

[11]Roland de Vaux, *Ancient Israel, Its Life and Institutions*, tr. J. McHugh (New York: McGraw-Hill Book Company, Inc., 1961), 354, rejects this explanation, deriving *tôrâ* rather from *yrh*, "which is frequently employed in the factitive form with the meaning 'to show,' 'to teach.' " Murphy, *A Study* . . ., 27-29, commenting on the theory of Delitzsch, finds the evidence for an Akkadian cognate of Hebrew *yrh* dubious.

[12]Östborn, too, connects *tôrâ* with the giving of oracles, though he works from the etymology proposed by Gesenius. In his Chapter 2, "The Deity as Imparter of Tora," he works from the concept of tree oracles. He finds the most compelling argument in Gen 12:6, where an oak (?) tree is given the epithet *môreh*, which he takes to be the participle of *hôrâ* and renders "to impart *tōrā*," in the sense of oracle-giving (*Tōrā in the Old Testament*, 25). The majority of scholars seem to share this view; on this text see, e.g., John Skinner, *A Critical and Exegetical Commentary on Genesis* (New York: Charles Scribner's Sons, 1910); A. Clamer, *La Genèse traduite et commentée* (Paris: Letouzey et Ané, Éditeurs, 1953); E. A. Speiser, *Genesis* (*AB* 1; Garden City, New York: Doubleday & Company, Inc., 1964); and *The Oxford Annotated Bible*, ed. H. G. May and B. M. Metzger (New York: Oxford University Press, 1962); Roland de Vaux, *Ancient Israel*, 279, seems to hesitate.

[13]Cf. Lindars, "Torah in Deuteronomy," 119: "Although 'instruction' frequently seems to be an adequate rendering, it would be a mistake to take this in a general sense. If an oracle is involved, *twrh* (which can denote both the action of giving a message, and the content of it, i.e., the message itself) is primarily a specific direction in response to a query, and the broader notion of instruction is to be regarded as a result of the generalizing tendency common in semantic development."

[14]See Lindars, *ibid.* Joachim Begrich, "Die priesterliche Tora," *BZAW* 66 (1936) 63-88, refers primarily to priestly *tôrâ*, but sees it imparted also by elders, prophets, wisdom teachers, and laymen (p. 64).

that *tôrâ* is generally thought to have originated in priestly circles, while use of the term in the wisdom tradition is usually considered to be a late development; the designation of prophetic words as *tôrâ* would take its origin somewhere between. Priestly *tôrâ* and *tôrâ* as a designation for "law" are often not distinguished at all. Much attention will be given in a later chapter to the question of whether *tôrâ* enters the wisdom tradition only at a late period. At present it is necessary to investigate these other currents at least briefly, for our understanding of what is meant by "priestly *tôrâ*," "*tôrâ* as law," and "prophetic *tôrâ*" will have an important bearing on later discussion.

Priestly *tôrâ*

The conviction is virtually universal that giving *tôrâ* is originally and primarily a priestly function.[15] This is based on a number of OT texts, most especially Dt 33:10; Hos 4:6; Mic 3:11; Jer 18:18; and Ezek 7:26. This conviction is almost certainly correct, though the early evidence is not as abundant as might be wished. Lindars and Gutbrod both remark that *tôrâ* is comparatively rare in early OT literature; the latter finds it not all in J and only rarely, if at all, in E.[16] There is an abundance of references in P which *may* reflect very early traditions, but the evidence is difficult to assess. Of the texts mentioned above, Hosea, Micah, Jeremiah, and Ezekiel date from the eighth to the sixth centuries, of course, while the one in Dt (surely non-Deuteronomic in origin) may be considerably older, or possibly considerably younger.[17] Although there is a strong tendency among scholars to date this Blessing of Moses (Dt 33) early, as a whole, special difficulties are sometimes found precisely with the passage which deals with Levi (vss. 8-11). On the basis of more recent evidence for ancient Northwest Semitic orthography, poetic style, and metrical forms, Cross and Freedman essayed a new investigation and reconstruction of the Blessing of Moses.[18] They concluded that the poem as a whole was composed, most probably, in the eleventh century. But their reconstruction contains only vs. 11 of the section on Levi, and their note on vss. 8-10, after alluding to problems of style, meter,

[15]See especially Begrich, "Die priesterliche Tora," 64; Gutbrod, "The Meaning of *tôrâ*," 1045. Those who hold that *tôrâ* terminology comes from the manipulation of sacred lots necessarily attribute *tôrâ* first of all to priests. By way of exception Beecher, "*Torah*: A Word-study in the Old Testament," 5, puts the prophets in the first place.

[16]Lindars, "Torah in Deuteronomy," 117. Gutbrod, "The Meaning of *tôrâ*," 1044f. He lists as disputable Ex 13:9; 16:4; 18:16.20; 24:12.

[17]Authors differ widely on the dating of Dt 33. See S. R. Driver, *A Critical and Exegetical Commentary on Deuteronomy* (New York: Charles Scribner's Sons, 1902), 387; Otto Eissfeldt, *The Old Testament: An Introduction*, tr. P. R. Ackroyd (New York: Harper and Row, Publishers, 1965), 228. Cross and Freedman date the Blessing to the eleventh century in its oral form (see following note).

[18]Frank M. Cross, Jr., and David N. Freedman, "The Blessing of Moses," *JBL* 67 (1948) 191-210.

content, syntax, and orthography, leaves open the question of whether anything of these verses pertained to the original Blessing. No secure arguments for ancient *tôrâ* practice can be built on this text.

Thus, though the view that *tôrâ* is originally and primarily priestly in origin is probably correct, the early evidence is not overwhelming. But three frequently made assumptions concerning the *nature* of early priestly *tôrâ* need to be questioned, namely, that it is obtained by divination, that it is given by way of response to a question, and that it deals primarily with distinctions between the clean and unclean, the sacred and profane. These may possibly be true assumptions, but the argument here will be that they do not harmonize well with what Hosea has to say about priestly *tôrâ*, and his words are the earliest clear evidence we have.

Priestly *tôrâ* and Divination

We have already seen that the earlier Wellhausen derived *tôrâ*, in its etymology and practice, from the casting of lots; though he later thought better of the suggestion, others have continued to adhere to the position abandoned by him.[19] Now, there is no question that divination was practiced in Israel, most especially through the use of sacred lots; but it may be asked whether this ought to be related specifically to *tôrâ*. There are many OT texts that refer to divination by sacred lot,[20] but *tôrâ* does not figure in any of them[21] except Dt 33:8-10 (on which see below). In the two texts which use a specific term for the oracular reply, Num 27:21 and Prov 16:33, it is not *tôrâ* but *mišpāṭ*.

It might be possible to argue from the reference to *'ēlôn môreh* in Gen 12:6 (especially in view of the probably similar term *'ēlôn mᵉ'ônᵉnîm* in Jgs 9:37)

[19]E.g., Louise Pettibone Smith, "The Use of the Word *twrh* in Isaiah, Chapters 1-39," *AJSL* 46 (1929) 1-21, especially p. 1; Ludwig Köhler, *Theologie des Altens Testaments* (3rd ed.; Tübingen: J.C.B. Mohr, 1953), 195; Aage Bentzen, *Introduction to the Old Testament* (2nd ed.; Copenhagen: G.E.C. Gad, Publisher, 1952), I, 185, 189; H. W. Robinson *Inspiration and Revelation*, 202; Lindars, "Torah in Deuteronomy," 120, after referring to Dt 33:8-11 as the classic *locus* for priestly *tôrâ*, goes on to say that the possibility that this function includes some oracular method is suggested by Ex 18:13-23. But it may be pointed out that, aside from the mention of "consulting God" (*lidrōš 'ĕlōhîm*) in vs. 15 and of "bringing to God whatever they have to say" in vs. 19, there is nothing here that suggests an oracular method of arriving at decisions. On the contrary, the decision is reached by judging (*šāpaṭ*—vs. 16) and "making known to them God's decisions and regulations (*'et ḥuqqê hā'ĕlōhîm wᵉ'et tôrōtāyw*)" (vs. 16). Since it is a question of civil disputes (between a man and his neighbor—vs. 16), it is not surprising to find them settled by reference to the established rules of behavior. The fact that *tôrôt* is the second of the two terms argues against Lindars' suggestion, for the idea of oracular method nowhere attaches itself to *ḥuqqîm*. It may also be argued that it is not necessarily a question of *priestly tôrâ* here; although the priests seem often to have administered Israel's customary law, Martin Noth, *Exodus: A Commentary*, J.S. Bowden (Philadelphia: The Westminster Press, 1962), 150, sees in the passage a description of Israel's practice after the time of the settlement and names the Minor Judges (Jgs 10:1-5; 12:7-15) as those who filled the office here attributed to Moses.

[20]E.g., Lev 16:8; Num 26:55f.; 27:21; 33:54; 34:13; 36:2f.; Jos 7:14-18; 14:2; 15:1; 17:1; 18:6ff. (etc.); Jgs 18:5f.; 20:9; 1 Sam 14:36-42; 23:6-12; 28:6; 30:7f.; Ezra 2:63; Neh 7:65.

that *hôrâ* (and therefore *tôrâ*) is connected with divination, simply because it is difficult to assign any other meaning than "soothsayer's (or: soothsaying) oak," or something similar, to the expression. But, even disregarding the possibility (which cannot be excluded) that *môreh* is here a proper name with no connection with divination, these words tell us nothing about priestly practice in Israel; at best the title may say something about Canaanite practice and possibly preserve a hint on the etymology of *hôrâ*.

Again, *hôrâ*, probably, though not certainly, refers to divination in Hab 2:19 (see below, p. 27). It is a late text and would thus provide only a very weak argument for any essential connection between *tôrâ* and divination, quite aside from the fact that the passage deals with a pagan, reprobate concept, while *tôrâ* often expresses Israel's loftiest thoughts.

We have already seen that in a long series of texts relating to the sacred lot, *tôrâ* does not occur.[22] An exception to the rule may be Dt 33:8-11, with its reference to urim and thummim (vs. 8) and *tôrâ* (vs. 10), but it would be precarious to base an argument on this text. As noted above, the pertinent part of the passage, vss. 8-10, may well be a late interpolation.[23] Further, it is not at all clear that the reference to *tôrâ* in vs. 10 is necessarily connected with the urim and thummim in vs. 8; they may be intended as separate statements about those things that pertain to the priesthood—signs of the office on the one hand, functions of the office on the other.[24] If *tôrâ* were the normal word for oracular responses from urim and thummim, it ought to be the first word used; instead, it is *mišpāṭîm* that comes first, while *tôrâ* enters to complete the parallelism. And it may be asked why *tôrâ* is not plural, as *mišpāṭîm* is.[25] If *tôrâ* is understood here to mean the whole law in the deuteronomic sense (see below), it is easy to see why it is singular and how it can stand parallel to *mišpāṭîm*; but then it doesn't mean oracular response.[26]

[21]The use of the qal of *yrh* in Jos 18:6 is of no special significance; as Murphy points out, *gôrāl* is used with many verbs, all of them connected with the idea of setting something in motion (*A Study . . .*, 1f.).

[22]See above, n. 20.

[23]See n. 18, above, and the discussion in the text.

[24]Commentators often do, in fact, treat these separated verses as dealing with two distinct realities. See Gerhard von Rad, *Old Testament Theology*, tr. D. M. G. Stalker (New York: Harper & Row, Publishers, 1962), I, 244f. If one is willing to admit a date of composition for vss. 8-10 late enough for the fusion of D and P traditions, these elements of the priestly description are easily explicable; cf. Ex 28:30; Dt 17:8-13.

[25]Begrich, "Die priesterliche Tora," 64, is possibly dealing with this difficulty when, following Gressmann, he repoints the text to read *tôrōtᵉkā*. The best that can be said for this reading is that it is possible. The suspicion arises that Begrich wants to retain this as an ancient proof text, for he uses it to argue that *tôrâ* originally pertained to priests alone.

[26]Neither is priestly divination indicated by the use of *hôrâ* in Mic 3:11. It cannot be argued from what is said of the prophets that the priestly activity contained in *hôrâ* also implies divination. The parallelism of the verse is in the description of each class "doing its own thing," but doing it corruptly.

Priestly *tôrâ* as *Responsum*

That priestly *tôrâ* arises primarily as a response to a question is a frequent assertion,[27] perhaps too easily made. That *tôrâ* often comes by way of *responsum* is no doubt true, but it doesn't seem to be especially characteristic of *tôrâ*; a better case could be made out for *mišpāṭ*. Aside from the arguments that have to do with oracular techniques, appeal is most often made to Hag 2:11-14, where the priests are asked concerning the effects of contact with that which is holy and that which is unclean. One possible interpretation of the phrase *šeʾal-nāʾ ʾet hakkōhănîm tôrâ* (vs. 11) is that *tôrâ* here stands as a technical term for a decision given by priests in response to a query.[28] Even if that is the proper interpretation, the text gives direct witness only to post-exilic practice—which may or may not accord with earlier practice—and does not necessarily tell us anything about the primitive and original meaning of *tôrâ*. It is worth pointing out, too, that the "question-response" context given to the priestly pronouncements here serves a pedagogical purpose within the prophetic passage and that the same pronouncements of priestly teaching might well be called *tôrâ* outside such context. Finally, it is hard to see how the simple meaning "instruction" can be excluded here. Is the use of *tôrâ* here wholly different from that in Mal 2:7 (*kî śiptê kōhēn yišmerû daʿat wetôrâ yebaqšû mippîhû*), where the context clearly demands "instruction"?

Ritual Distinctions and Priestly *tôrâ*

The third assertion, that the distinction between sacred and profane, clean and unclean, is basic to the concept of priestly *tôrâ*, is insisted upon by Begrich and others.[29] There are many biblical passages to which one may refer for confirmation,[30] but the striking thing to note is that they are all late.

[27]Bentzen, *Introduction to the Old Testament*, I, 188f., seems to see priestly lore as the accumulation of centuries of oracular decisions. For Lindars' view, see n. 13.

[28]Reference is often made also to Zech 7:1-3 and 8:18f. (which apparently were originally a connected unity) as a further confirmation of *tôrâ* as *responsum*. Yet the term *tôrâ* does not appear here at all; and it is to be noted that the query is addressed not only to priests but also to prophets (7:3).

[29]See Begrich, p. 69: "Die priesterliche Tora ist beherrscht von den Begriffen 'heilig' und 'profan,' 'unrein' und 'rein.'" Cf. also his p. 66 and Östborn, *Tōrā in the Old Testament*, pp. 98f.

[30]Zeph 3:4; Ezek 22:26; 44:23; Hag 2:11; Lev 11:46f.; 14:2.32.54.57; 15:32; and elsewhere in P. It is to be noted that *tôrâ* is not used in this sense in Dt, not even with regard to the list of clean and unclean animals in Dt 14:3-20.

The authors who cite them are aware of this, but are willing to assume that they reflect an early usage.[31] This may well be the case, but in the absence of specific arguments it remains an assumption; ritualism seems to occupy a privileged sanctuary, for such a distribution of texts ordinarily would be sufficient grounds for a conviction that the usage in question was late. It is worth remembering that at one time P was considered the earliest of the pentateuchal sources.

Priestly *tôrâ* in Hosea

In any attempt to study priestly *tôrâ* it would seem that certain texts from Hosea should be given prominent place, for they are at least datable and relatively clear as to import, unlike many of the texts already referred to. Although Hosea's eighth century date is not "early," absolutely speaking, in a development which undoubtedly begins far earlier, his texts are the earliest that give clear indication of the nature of priestly *tôrâ*. And since he argues that the practice in his day did not live up to the ideal, he undoubtedly presents a more ancient concept.

The pertinent texts are Hos 4:6 and 8:1. The first of these, especially, reveals a very positive attitude on the part of Hosea towards priestly *tôrâ*; his complaint is that its absence is the root of grave evils. The *'ĕmet* and *ḥesed* of 4:1 are qualities of covenant loyalty, while the crimes of vs. 2 may well allude to transgressions of covenant law; even if vss. 1-3 are considered a separate composition, they help reveal what is in Hosea's mind when in 4:6 he says "the people perish."[32] In any case, it is the exclamation that explains the twin accusations leveled against the priests: "you have rejected knowledge" and "you have ignored the *tôrâ* of your God." The obvious inference is that the priests have failed to provide the people with the instruction it is their duty to give. It is probable that one of the chief functions of the priests was to provide instruction in covenant obligations within the context of liturgical ceremonies,[33] and it is in this they have failed.[34]

[31]Begrich, "Die priesterliche Tora," 66; Eissfeldt, *The Old Testament*, 74.

[32]It is assumed that vss. 4ff., on the priests, are closely related to vv. 1-3, on the sins of the people; the opening of v. 4 supposes some such discourse as that of vv. 1-3.

[33]See, e.g., G. von Rad, *Old Testament Theology*, I, 190-94; Bruce Vawter, "Introduction to Prophetic Literature," *JBC* 12:13; Artur Weiser, *Introduction to the Old Testament*, tr. D. A. Barton (London: Darton, Longman & Todd, 1961), 81-99; R. B. Y. Scott, "Priesthood, Prophecy, Wisdom, and the Knowledge of God," *JBL* 80 (1961) 6f.

[34]R. E. Clements, *Prophecy and Covenant* (*SBT* 1/43; London: SCM Press Ltd., 1965), 96 f.

Although *tôrâ* in this passage is often translated "law," it should probably be given a more general sense, namely, priestly instruction with reference to commandments and observances;[35] *tôrâ* (in the singular) seems to have been used to designate the law as a whole only at a later period (see below). The *tôrâ* that Hosea so esteems is clearly not a decision arrived at through divination, nor does it regard merely ritual or ceremonial matters, but would seem to be related to matters with which Hosea is concerned, namely, covenant loyalty to Yahweh. Even the terminology is different from that which is regularly used by P for *tôrâ* which relates to cultic observances. While Hosea speaks of "the *tôrâ* of your God" (*tôrat 'ĕlōhèkā*), the almost invariable phrase in P is "This is the *tôrâ* of the holocaust (or: cereal offering, sin offering, child birth, etc.)" (*zō't tôrat hā'ōlâ*—or: *hamminḥâ, haḥaṭṭā't,* etc.).[36]

The other text, Hos 8:1, appears to be similar in meaning, though priests are not mentioned in the passage. It is again God's *tôrâ* ("my *tôrâ*"—*tôrātî*) and here, too, it is closely related to knowledge of God; this is seen in the parallel intended between Israel's rebellion against *tôrâ* and the false claim in vs. 2, "O God of Israel, we know you!" Here the fault is not laid to the priests but to Israel itself. The temptation to translate *tôrâ* by "law" is stronger here than in 4:6, but should be resisted, if Lindars' thesis is correct;[37] "to rebel against instruction (in covenant obligations)" gives as good a parallel to "to violate covenant" and "not to know God" as "to rebel against law" does; so due weight should be given to the evidence Lindars gives that *tôrâ* does not become a term that can be applied to the whole of the law before Deuteronomy. The case is somewhat different in Hos 8:12, where the plural *tôrōtay* should be read.[38] This is probably still priestly *tôrâ*, but the

[35]Lindars, "Torah in Deuteronomy," 123: "When *twrh* is applied to the law, we should expect it in the first instance to refer to the explicitation of law, and authoritative ruling on the manner in which a law is to be kept, or on the scope of its operation. If the ceremony of covenant renewal included recitation of the law, as most scholars think, it is to be expected that the priests or other covenant officials, would give *twrh* in explanation of it . . ." See also R. B. Y. Scott, "Priesthood, Prophecy, Wisdom, and the Knowledge of God," pp. 6-8.

[36]Lev 6:2.7.18; 7:1.11.37; 11:46; 12:7; 13:59; etc. The variant usage in Num 19:2 ("the regulation which the *tôrâ* of the Lord prescribes") and 31:21 ("*tôrâ*, as prescribed by the Lord to Moses") is probably not to be attributed to P; see Martin Noth, *Numbers: A Commentary*, tr. J. D. Martin (Philadelphia: The Westminster Press, 1968), 139f. and 229.

[37]See below. On Hos 8:1 Lindars says: "Here we should give due weight to the fact that *bryt* and *twrh* are strictly parallel. Yahweh's covenant can also be referred to as his 'instruction,' because it embodies his directive to the people" ("Torah in Deuteronomy," 132).

[38]This verse, as so many passages in Hos, appears to be corrupt and to need emendation in both the consonantal text and the pointing; that of the *NAB* is assumed here. The plural, *tôrōtay*, seems to be required by the plural verb at the end of the line.

plural suggests it has to do with individual regulations, possibly cultic ones (cf. vss. 11 and 13a) which would have prevented the paganizing of Israel's shrines and worship if they had been observed. The text is too uncertain to be a basis for firm conclusions, but Hosea's esteem even for these *tôrôt* (which he identifies as God's) is evident.

Thesis of Begrich

A few words should be said about the article by Begrich which has already been cited, especially because his views on passages in Isaiah directly concern this study. After asserting that in the earliest traditions *tôrâ* pertained to priests alone, Begrich goes on to assert: "Für die Quellenverwertung bedeutet diese Beobachtung, dass alle Züge, in welchen nichtpriesterliche Tora mit priesterlicher übereinstimmt, als Nachwirkungen der priesterliche Tora aufzufassen sind und zu deren Kennzeichnung herangezogen werden dürfen."[39] The suggestion is a reasonable one in the abstract, but putting it into practice supposes that we know enough about priestly *tôrâ* to be able to recognize with precision its traits even when seen in non-priestly compositions. In fact, we do not have such exact knowledge of priestly *tora*, and Begrich makes some illogical steps in trying to apply the method.

Begrich is convinced that the content of early priestly *tôrâ* had to do with discernment of sacred and profane, clean and unclean (see above, n. 31). Further, he admits that to ascertain the significance of what the priests intended to teach by their *tôrâ* we can turn only to allusions contained in prophetic passages (in a footnote he lists Isa 2:3; Mic 4:2; Isa 1:10ff.) and to more recent texts (p. 66). He insists on the inner connection between content and form and then tells us that the form can be ascertained through certain prophetic imitations of priestly *tôrâ* and from the Hexateuch tradition (p. 73). The prophetic texts he lists this time are: Am 4:4f.; 5:4f.21-24; Hos 6:6; Isa 1:10-17; 66:2b-3; Mal 1:10. The prophetic examples are naturally older than those from the Hexateuch. There is no danger of misunderstanding, he says, since the prophetic touch, which consists in a reversal (*Umkehrung*) of the priestly judgment and the introduction of specifically prophetic demands, can easily be recognized, as well as that of the priests (from the Hexateuch examples). Later we are told that the *best* illustrations are the prophetic imitations of priestly *tôrâ*, once the prophetic *Einschlag* (which is now said to include the poetic form) has been removed.[40]

[39]Begrich, "Die priesterliche Tora," 64.

[40]"Die beste Veranschaulichung bieten die prophetischen Nachahmungen priesterlicher Tora, bei denen man nur den prophetischen Einschlag abziehen möge," which is clarified in the footnote: "Zu ihm scheint ausser der Umkehrung des priesterlichen Urteils und der Einfuhrung der prophetischen Forderungen auch die poetische Form zu gehören" (p. 77). One is tempted to ask, "What's left?"

There is here a methodological weakness that comes very close to arguing in a circle: the clearest evidence for the form of priestly *tôrâ* is found in prophetic imitations of the form; but how can we recognize them as imitations of priestly *tôrâ* unless we have already clearly established the elements of the latter? Begrich is aware that the content of the prophetic passages he calls imitations diverges widely from priestly teaching and often amounts to a condemnation of priestly practices (cf., e.g., pp. 65f.), but he insists that it is the *form* which matters;[41] yet the evidence of what *is* priestly form is taken largely from prophetic texts. The difficulty becomes very clear when he isolates four forms of priestly *tôrâ*. The first of these is couched in the imperative, second person plural, is directed to the people, and claims to be the word of Yahweh; but the only examples he gives for the final assertion come from prophetic texts (pp. 73f.), and there is nothing to identify the priestly imperatives as the word of God except the editorial "And Yahweh said to Moses."[42] For the second form, consisting of statements in which Yahweh declares what He demands and what He rejects, *only* examples from prophetic texts are given (p. 75). And criticisms can be made of the manner of identifying the other forms, too.

These observations suggest that some prophetic texts may have been labeled "priestly *tôrâ*" without sufficient grounds. Of the prophetic texts that Begrich so labels, Hag 2:10-14 is rather a *description* of a priestly *tôrâ* rite which serves as the basis for a prophetic pronouncement; it has value as a witness to sixth century (and possibly earlier) practice. Of the other texts, Mic 6:6-8 probably has the best claim to be called "priestly *tôrâ*," but even here there is danger of asserting too much. We can group together Mic 6:6-8; Isa 33:14-16; Ps 15; and Ps 24:3-6 (all texts utilized by Begrich) and see a similar pattern: someone inquires about the prerequisites for coming before God; another voice lists the ethical qualities demanded. It is quite reasonable to suppose that the second speaker is a priest,[43] and this, along with the question and response in a cultic setting, gives the form a resemblance to Hag 2:10-14, where the term *tôrâ* occurs. The resemblance is superficial, however, for there is a great difference between a question concerning the effects of touching sacrificial meat or a corpse and one concerning the dispositions for entering the sanctuary. Further, the OT does not use *tôrâ* in these passages and we have no guarantee that the men of Israel would have used it for this

[41]"Die Nachahmungen entfernen sich zwar vom ursprünglichen priesterlichen Stoff, zeigen aber in der Form, dass die priesterliche Folgerung ausgesprochen wird: man vergleiche z. B. den Satz: 'wer solches tut, wird ewig nicht wanken' mit der Form und der Stellung der entsprechenden vorhin behandelten priesterlichen Sätze"; the "corresponding" priestly texts cited in the footnote (Lev 7:25.27) do not appear very similar (p. 80).

[42]In some of his examples references to Yahweh in the third person positively exclude his contention that they present themselves as His word; cf. Lev 19:5; and on Lev 7:23, cf. vs. 25.

[43]This is not conceded by all, for many scholars think of a cult prophet (see following note).

rite. Some scholars use, rather, the designation "entrance liturgy," and this is perhaps more accurate.[44]

The other passages cited by Begrich do not seem to conform to any pattern and it is far from clear that they imitate priestly *tôrâ*; this is certainly not the necessary explanation when a prophet proclaims that God desires *ḥesed* rather than sacrifice (Hos 6:6). The teaching of Amos is very similar, and the fact that he consigns it in a series of sarcastic imperatives (4:4f.) or earnest imperatives (5:4f.) does not prove he is imitating a priestly form, much less when he simply portrays God's loathing at sacrifice without justice (5:21-24); a prophet should be permitted to rail at insincere cult without being thought to imitate priestly speech. Amos can make the same call for justice through imperatives with no reference at all to cultic matters (5:14f.). The passage Begrich classifies as priestly *tôrâ* that most concerns this study, Isa 1:10-17, will be dealt with in detail in a later chapter.

tôrâ as a "Legal" Term

The designation of *tôrâ* as a legal term is found in two different contexts, though in neither case is the adjective truly applicable in its proper sense. Collections of priestly regulations (*tôrôt*) are found among the legislative sections of the Pentateuch that are sometimes referred to as "law codes." It has become increasingly apparent that such ancient codes played a somewhat different role than law does in modern societies. Collections of priestly *tôrôt* are another step removed in that they were, generally speaking, a body of technical lore of a particular group. It is undoubtedly more accurate to leave such regulations in the category of priestly *tôrâ* than to classify them as laws.

The other "legal" reference of *tôrâ* is that which comes up in phrases like "the law of Moses." Our concern here is not to criticize the use of "law" as a translation, but to ask questions about this usage by which one term is employed to sum up the whole collection of Israel's customary and religious law. The time at which this came to pass is of some importance, for there is all too general a tendency to translate *tôrâ* as "law" wherever it occurs and to understand this as a reference to the whole body of Israel's legislation. If *tôrâ* acquired this meaning during the period in which Dt began to assume its present form, as many hold,[45] then there is a certain presumption that occurrences in texts of an earlier period ought to be understood in some other sense.

[44]The description of this form in E. Sellin-G. Fohrer, *Einleitung in das Alte Testament* (10th ed., rev.; Heidelberg: Quelle & Meyer, 1965), 292, is interesting for its inclusion of all the possibilities; Hans-Joachim Kraus, *Psalmen* (*BKAT* XV/1; Neukirchen: Neukirchener Verlag, 1960), pp. 111 and 194, also uses more than one designation.

[45]L. P. Smith, "*twrh* in Isaiah," 17-20; Gutbrod, "The Meaning of *tôrâ*," 1045f.; and especially Lindars, "Torah in Deuteronomy," *in toto.*

Lindars presents a very compelling case for this position, maintaining "that the cardinal point in this development is not the Priestly Code as such, but the Book of Deuteronomy."[46] The reasons Lindars gives for this development are relevant to the present study. He points out that Dt uses a number of synonyms for the laws contained in it (*mišpāṭîm*, *ḥuqqîm*, *'ēdôt*, and *miṣwôt*), and the question thus arises of why *tôrâ* came to acquire such unique importance.[47] Noting Dt's consistent and fervent attempt to persuade the hearers to obey, he says:

> The approach is didactic in a manner reminiscent of the Wisdom tradition. Östborn has drawn attention to the parenetic use of the theme of the 'Way' in the introductory historical retrospect. He is surely right also in connecting the use of *twrh* with the didactic character of the editorial work. This means that the generalized notion of 'instruction,' as found in the Wisdom literature, is closer to the Deuteronomic meaning than the priestly 'regulations in answer to a question,' in spite of the fact that Deuteronomy is a product of priestly reformers.[48]

Lindars asserts that *tôrâ* is never used in this generalized sense within the laws of Dt (17:11 he takes for a late expansion) but is restricted to the editorial parts. [49] His understanding is that these passages function to make the book as a whole a substitute for the Decalogue or at least to put it on the same level, and that the term *tôrâ* is therefore employed "to convey their concept of the code as a complete expression of the will of God, having the same binding force as the Decalogue . . . to be learnt and pondered by them" (p. 131). In summary, then, it can be said:

> The choice of *twrh* to designate the whole corpus is thus dictated by the fact that the code is regarded as a single and complete entity, given by God through the mediation of Moses for men to ponder and lay to heart. . . . This can even be expressed in specifically Wisdom terminology, as if the code is the instruction of a father to his sons (4:5-8).[50]

[46]P. 117. Lindars points out that in Lev and Num *tôrâ* always means "rule" or "regulation," never the law as a whole, even though they are compiled in post-deuteronomic times, and that therefore the use of *tôrâ* in this comprehensive sense in Chr, Ezra, Neh, and Dan 9 is to be traced to the influence of deuteronomic literature rather than to P (pp. 120f.).

[47]With reference to specific codes, he notes that the Decalogue is not called *tôrâ* but *d^{e}bārîm*, while the Covenant Code is called *mišpāṭîm* (pp. 123-25).

[48]Pp. 129f.

[49]He lists 1:5 and 4:44 in the early part of the book (both probably later insertions); then, leaving aside ch. 27, lists 28:58.61; 29:20.28 (which von Rad thinks is modeled on a wisdom saying); 30:10; 31:9-13; 31:24-29 (pp. 130f.).

[50]P. 130. Lindars does not explain the final assertion; presumably he would see its justification in Moses' assertion that he had taught (*limmadtî*) the prescriptions as commanded him by God, that keeping them will give evidence of the Israelites' wisdom and intelligence (*ḥokmâ ûbînâ*) in the eyes of their pagan neighbors, who will conclude that this is a wise and intelligent people (*'am ḥākām w^{e}nābôn*); cf. also 8:5.

One consequence is that "the term retains its didactic overtones, and to say 'the book of divine instruction' might represent the real meaning better than the usual translation 'the book of the law' " (p. 131). As Israel's sacred literature evolved, the term eventually came to be applied to the completed Pentateuch (p. 135).

Lindars dates the work of the deuteronomic editors "most probably in the early part of the exile" (p. 135). However, he does not suppose the development came this late, but points to the use of *tôrâ* in the Hezekiah collection of Prov in the sense of "instruction" (pp. 134f.), and even asserts that many occurrences in Jer "can be taken as a parallel usage in the time of the prophet himelf, instead of being assigned to the later editing . . . for it was in that time that the Deuteronomic usage was evolved" (pp. 131f.).

Much of what Lindars presents is significant for the present study. It follows from his argument that: 1) the thesis of those who hold that the wisdom use of *tôrâ* developed from its meaning of "law" in the post-exilic period is highly improbable, at the very least; rather, it was because the word already had wisdom connotations that it was an apt term for the deuteronomists to use to designate the aggregate of Israel's rules of life; 2) it is likely that *tôrâ* already has the generalized meaning of "instruction" in the days of Jeremiah; 3) it is unlikely that *tôrâ* is to be understood to refer to law in a general or aggregate sense before the deuteronomic period. But it is not clear that Lindars is correct in the development he has worked out for the term. He takes its early meaning to be "instruction" with a quite specific reference, from which it passes to a more general reference.[51] He sees the development that enables *tôrâ* to be used as it is in Dt as "a result of growth in the range of meaning of the term itself, which now becomes the appropriate word for an idea which has previously been expressed in other ways" (p. 118). It is much more likely that the new usage is a result of a different concept of Israel's laws, namely, the attempt to visualize the aggregate as a unity which gave direction for a way of life.[52]

Furthermore, it is possible, in terms of Lindars' thesis, to suggest that *tôrâ* must already have had the overtones that made it apt for the deuteronomists' purpose before the days of Jeremiah. Lindars follows the school of literary criticism that dates the principal editorial work on Dt and the deuteronomic history during the Exile; but many hold that the deuteronomic activity was a close adjunct of the reform of Josiah, that much of the material outside the core legislation of Dt and the basic form of the deuteronomic history (Jos, Jgs, Sam, Kgs) took shape during the reign of Josiah, and that only certain additions are to be attributed to editorial activity during the Exile.[53] Thus it

[51]See n. 13, above.

[52]Lindars admits *also* a change in the concept of law (p. 118).

[53]W. Nowack, "Deuteronomium und Regum," *BZAW* 41 (1925) 221-31; Eissfeldt, *The Old Testament*, 232f., 285; A. Weiser, *Introduction to the Old Testament*, 172f.; Bentzen, *Introduction to the Old Testament*, II, 99f.; John Gray, *I & II Kings* (Philadelphia: The Westminster Press, 1963), 13f.; G. W. Anderson, *A Critical Introduction to the Old Testament* (London: Gerald Duckworth & Co. Ltd., 1959), 90; B. W. Anderson, *Understanding the Old Testament* (2nd ed.; Englewood Cliffs, N.J.: Prentice-Hall, Inc., 1966), 379.

can be argued that much of the deuteronomic writing is to be dated to the period between 621 and 609, including some of the *tôrâ* passages.[54] On this dating it would be necessary to suppose that the deuteronomists found their term, *tôrâ*, already having a range of meaning that included "instruction" in

[54]The verses in Dt where *tôrâ* occurs are the following: 1:5; 4:8.44; 17:11.18.19; 27:3.8.26; 28:58.61; 29:20.28; 30:10; 31:9.11.12.24.26; 32:46; 33:4.10. Of these occurrences, 17:11 is the only one within the core legislation (on 17:18.19 see below), and here it means "judicial decision." The second occurrence of *tôrâ* in Dt 33 (vs. 10) has already been discussed at length (n. 18 and text); the earlier one (vs. 4) occurs within a section generally considered to be originally a separate composition (vss. 2-5.26-29) from the Blessing, and Lindars, "Torah in Deuteronomy," 133, demonstrates that the phrase "Moses commanded us a law" is a gloss. Cross and Freedman, "The Blessing of Moses," 202f., omit vss. 3f. from their reconstruction of the Blessing.

The remaining references may all be attributed to the deuteronomists; whether they will be dated to the Exile or the time of the monarchy will depend in large part on the theory of the genesis of the complete Dt one adopts; but aside from preconceptions, it is difficult to exclude a fairly early date for some of them. Eissfeldt, *The Old Testament*, 233, seems willing to grant an early date to 4:1-40, and this would include the *tôrâ* reference in 4:8 (see also Joseph Blenkinsopp, "Deuteronomy," *JBC* 6:17); many authors believe the "core" Dt included the address of Moses in 4:44-11:32, and this opens with *wᵉzō't hattôrâ* (though it is also easy to argue, in the light of the following verse, that this introduction is secondary). R. E. Clements, "Deuteronomy and the Jerusalem Cult Tradition," *VT* 15 (1965) 300-312, provides a basis for arguing that 17:18f. goes back to the time of the monarchy; he points out that Dt reinterprets a number of ancient traditions relevant to Yahweh's abode in Jerusalem and to the Davidic monarchy in a polemical vein; within this context the election of David's line becomes conditional on observation of the law (cf. concluding words of vs. 20). Needless to say, all aspects of this polemic make better sense during the monarchy than during the Exile. Since G. Minette de Tillesse, "Sections 'tu' et sections 'vous' dans le Deutéronome," *VT* 12 (1962) 29-87, considers the use of the plural form a major criterion for distinguishing the work of the deuteronomic historian from the earlier composition he worked with, it is worth noting that *tôrâ* occurs in the following passages in which the second person singular is employed: 27:3.8; 28:58.61; 30:10; 31:9.11.12. It is easy to argue that 28:58.61 are from monarchic times since the section they belong to (vss. 58-62) threatens every kind of calamity, without reference to an exile, while the following section (vss. 63-68) has all the ear-marks of a supplement to remedy the defect. The prescriptions for the reading of the law in Dt 31 seem to be a description of contemporary practice rather than an exilic invention (and note vs. 13, which regards the land as being in secure possession). Norbert Lohfink, *Das Hauptgebot: Eine Untersuchung literarischer Einleitungsfragen zu Dtn 5-11* (*AnBib* 20; Rome: Pontifical Biblical Institute, 1963), 58, considers *tôrâ* in Dt to pertain to a late stratum, but this stands in some tension with the treatment of Dt 31:11 in his unpublished notes, *Lectures in Deuteronomy* (Norbert Lohfink - Rome, 1968), 59. Louis Derousseaux, *La crainte de Dieu dans l'Ancien Testament* (Paris: Les Éditions du Cerf, 1970), 305n., holds that *tôrâ* to designate the deuteronomic law is found only in the second edition of Dt, but he offers no new arguments.

The verses in the deuteronomic history where *tôrâ* occurs are the following: Jos 1:7.8; 8:31.32.34 (twice); 22:5; 23:6; 24:26; 1 Kgs 2:3; 2 Kgs 10:31; 14:6; 17:13.34.37; 21:8; 22:8.11; 23:24.25; although *tôrâ* stands in the MT at 2 Sam 7:19, this seems to be a corruption. Some of these verses can be judged exilic with reasonable assurance; e.g., the three occurrences of *tôrâ* in 2 Kgs 17. But for some of the remaining texts it is possible to argue for an origin during the monarchy; this is especially the case for the four occurrences in 2 Kgs 22-23, which describe the finding of the law book and Josiah's reform. In 2 Kgs 10:31 the *tôrâ* reference pertains to the "framework" that judges Jehu's reign, an essential part of the original edition (though the matter is complicated by the possibility of a double conclusion). 2 Kgs 14:6, too, may well be early.

a broad sense, and with wisdom overtones, and this made it apt for their purpose.[55]

Prophetic *tôrâ*

It is widely held that one of the standard uses of *tôrâ* was as a designation for prophetic utterances, or at least for certain types of prophetic utterances. This is obviously the thesis of those who distinguish three types of *tôrâ*, priestly, prophetic, and wisdom.[56] The position here maintained is that it is very doubtful that *tôrâ* was used in the OT to designate prophetic utterances. The approach will be to show first that no eighth century prophetic texts (leaving those of Isaiah aside for now) use *tôrâ* with this meaning; that alone could suffice for this study, for if the usage appears in subsequent centuries, it could well be a later development. However, it is also possible to argue that few, if any, of the later *tôrâ* texts should be understood in this sense. Finally,

[55]The presence of wisdom traits in Dt on almost every level has been recognized by many, but the nature of the relationship of Dt—or the circle from which it comes—to the wisdom tradition remains obscure. Among the works which treat the subject or at least touch on it, the following may be noted: J. L'Hour, "Les interdits *to'eba* dans le Deutéronome," *RB* 71 (1964) 481-503; J. Malfroy, "Sagesse et loi dans le Deutéronome," *VT* 15 (1965) 49-65; J. R. Boston, "The Wisdom Influence Upon the Song of Moses," *JBL* 87 (1968) 196-202; F. Horst, "Deuteronomium," *RGG*³ II, 102; M. Weinfeld, "The Dependence of Deuteronomy upon the Wisdom Literature" (Hebr.), *Kaufmann Jubilee Volume* (Jerusalem: Magnes Press, 1960), 89-108; "The Origin of Humanism in Deuteronomy," *JBL* 80 (1961) 241-47; and "Deuteronomy—The Present State of Inquiry," *JBL* 86 (1967) 249-62; his most recent contribution is the major study, *Deuteronomy and the Deuteronomic School* (Oxford: Clarendon Press, 1972). He argues that law and wisdom were separate disciplines until fused in Dt in the seventh century (pp. 151n., 255f.) and that Dt was influenced by wisdom literature, not the other way around (pp. 260, 274, 296); he does not seem to attempt to explain how *tôrâ* came to be used to designate the laws of Dt. Wolfgang Richter, *Recht und Ethos. Versuch einer Ortung des weisheitlichen Mahnspruches* (*StANT* 15; Munich: Kosel-Verlag, 1966), has touched upon wisdom influence in Dt (and in other law codes), especially in Dt 23-25. His starting point is the isolation of series of "prohibitives" (*lō'* with the imperfect), in which he sees the ethos of a particular group (the ruling class). The grouping of prohibitives he takes to be evidence for a *Schule*, in which, in addition, were developed "vetitives" (*'al* with the jussive) and the *Mahnspruch* (vetitive plus *Begründung*); the *Mahnspruch* is found most frequently in wisdom literature, the prohibitive in law codes, but the identity of content in many cases shows that the same school was at work in both. Many prohibitives are also provided with motivations (secondarily) and in them often betray wisdom influence, especially when they are based on creation, God's role as guaranteer and rewarder, length of days, and (possibly) the "strangers in Egypt" theme.

[56]See n. 14. See also Östborn, *Tōrā in the Old Testament*, p. 128; Gutbrod, "The Meaning of *tôrâ*," 1045; R. B. Y. Scott, "Priesthood, Prophecy, Wisdom, and the Knowledge of God," 3; H. W. Robinson, *Inspiration and Revelation*, 204; Haldar, *Associations of Cult Prophets among the Ancient Semites*, 124; Johannes Lindblom, *Prophecy in Ancient Israel* (London: Basil Blackwell, 1962), 156f.; Johannes Pedersen, *Israel, Its Life and Culture*, III-IV (London: Oxford University Press, 1940), 162.

the question of prophetic *tôrâ* as a literary form (where the term is not used) will be taken up.

Eighth Century Prophets: Amos, Hosea, Micah

Our term occurs only once in Amos (2:4), in a verse which virtually all admit to be a later, probably deuteronomic, interpolation. The use of *miš-pāṭîm* as a parallel expression for *tôrâ*[57] is good deuteronomic usage, as is *šmr* to mean observance of precepts (though this is also frequent in P); *m's*, the verb used with *tôrâ*, does not appear to be deuteronomic usage, at least not in the manner it is employed here,[58] but arguments are also drawn from the third line of the verse. In any event, this is not a case of prophetic *tôrâ*.

We have already discussed the *tôrâ* passages in Hosea (4:6; 8:1.12), and it is clear that they do not refer to the word of the prophet.

Our term occurs once in Micah (4:2) in a passage that is found also in Isaiah; in Ch. 4 I will argue that the oracle in which it occurs should be attributed to Isaiah (Isa 2:2-4) and will deal with it there. Micah uses the verb *hôrâ* once (3:11), but the subject is explicitly given as the priests.

Seventh Century Prophets: Zephaniah, Habakkuk, Jeremiah, Nahum

There is no occurrence of *tôrâ* in Nahum, and it comes but once each in Zephaniah (3:4) and Habakkuk (1:4). The Zephaniah passage clearly refers to priestly *tôrâ* of the cultic type. In the Habakkuk passage, the term stands

[57]On the other hand, *tôrat yhwh*, as in this verse, does not seem to be a typical deuteronomic expression. Georg Braulik, "Die Ausdrücke für 'Gesetz' im Buch Deuteronomium," *Bib* 51 (1970) 65, notes that in Dt *tôrâ* is never referred back to Yahweh by means of the construct, suffix, or *Promulgationssatz*. Within the other books of the deuteronomic corpus *tôrâ* sometimes occurs in the construct, but usually as *tôrat mōšeh* (Jos 8:31.32; 23:6; 1 Kgs 2:3; 2 Kgs 14:6; 23:25); *tôrat 'ĕlōhîm* occurs only once (Jos 24:26) and *tôrat yhwh* likewise only once (2 Kgs 10:31).

[58]The verb *m's* does not occur at all in Dt. It occurs thirteen times in the deuteronomic history (not always in passages that can be considered deuteronomic compositions), never with *tôrâ*, and only once with a legal term (*ḥuqqîm*, in 2 Kgs 17:15, part of a passage that Gray argues is late), almost always with a personal object (Yahweh, Saul, the people, and—once—"the city"). Twice it is used with *d^ebar yhwh* (1 Sam 15:23.26), a prophetic command issued by Samuel; but it is easy to argue that other considerations have determined the verb here. The verb is used four times to tell of the rejection of Saul (1 Sam 15:23.26; 16:1.7), and it can be assumed that this theme is the operative factor which occasions the use of the verb with *d^ebar yhwh* (so that it can then be repeated with Saul): "because you have rejected the command of Yahweh, he has rejected you from being king" (1 Sam 15:23.26). More will be said of the use of *m's* in the discussion of Isa 5:24 in Ch. 4.

for judicial decision, whether priestly or civil.[59] Habakkuk uses *hôrâ* in 2:19, where the reference is to idolatrous divination.

Jeremiah presents more serious difficulties, both because of the number of times *tôrâ* occurs[60] and because of the complicated question of deuteronomic influence in the compilation of his oracles. In not a few of them the sense of *tôrâ* is disputed. It will be sufficient for our purpose to determine whether or not the term refers to the prophetic word.

Three of the passages can be eliminated from consideration at once. In 18:18 *tôrâ* is clearly presented as the prerogative of the priest. In 2:8 the reference is not quite so transparent, but "those who dealt with (*tōp śê*) the *tôrâ* are clearly not prophets.[61] The import of 8:8 is also disputed, but the charge that the scribes' pen has falsified the *tôrâ* in question is enough to show it isn't the prophetic word.

The authenticity of a number of the remaining passages has been called into question by the majority of scholars, usually on the grounds of their being the work of deuteronomic editors of Jeremiah's oracles.[62] The position adopted on the composition of the book in general will have a bearing on the judgment made on these "deuteronomic" passages. John Bright, who adopts a very moderate position on the question, recognizes that the prose discourses do not provide the *ipsissima verba* of the prophet quite the way the poetic oracles do.[63] He believes these discourses represent Jeremiah's preaching, but as remembered, preserved, and repeated in the circle of his followers, including no doubt, men sympathetic to the deuteronomic reform. But even if we were to assign all the doubtful passages to the deuteronomists, they would not thereby become irrelevant to our investigation, for they could still stand as witnesses to "prophetic *tôrâ*" in the OT; on the other hand, in passages

[59]Lindars, "Torah in Deuteronomy," 133; R. T. Murphy, "Zephaniah, Nahum, Habakkuk," *JBC* 18:36.

[60]Jer contains eleven occurrences of *tôrâ*: 2:8, 6:19; 8:8; 9:12; 16:11; 18:18; 26:4; 31:33; 32:23; 44:10.23.

[61]Gutbrod, "The Meaning of *tôrâ*," 1045. J. Philip Hyatt, "Torah in the Book of Jeremiah," *JBL* 60 (1941) 386; G. W. Ahlström, "Oral and Written Transmission: Some Considerations," *HTR* 59 (1966) 74.

[62]Lindars, "Torah in Deuteronomy," 131; Hyatt, "Torah in the Book of Jeremiah," 392; Smith, "The Use of the Word *twrh* in Isaiah," 18f. For a thorough discussion of the relationship between Jeremiah and Dt, see H. H. Rowley, "The Prophet Jeremiah and the Book of Deuteronomy," *Studies in Old Testament Prophecy*, ed. H. H. Rowley (Edinburgh: T. & T. Clark, 1946), 157-74.

[63]John Bright, *Jeremiah* (*AB* 21; Garden City, N. Y.: Doubleday & Company, Inc., 1965), LXX-LXXIII; a fuller presentation is given by Bright in "The Date of the Prose Sermons of Jeremiah," *JBL* 70 (1951) 15-35.

which display a pronounced deuteronomic diction, there is an antecedent likelihood that *tôrâ* will have its deuteronomic sense of "law."

We can eliminate 31:33 from consideration at once, for *tôrâ* here clearly means "law" in the deuteronomic sense; this is strongly suggested by its relation to *b^e^rît* and imposed by the statement that it is to be written (on the heart). Yet one can insist that the term retains strong overtones of "wise instruction," especially in that it is to be rooted in the heart and will dispense with the need for teaching from others (vs. 34).

Four of the remaining passages, all in prose, can conveniently be treated together, namely, 16:11; 32:23; 44:10; and 44:23. In none of them is there any basis for thinking *tôrâ* refers to the prophetic word and in all of them it seems to mean "law" in the deuteronomic sense. The clearest case is 44:23, where the accusation that the people have not obeyed (*šm'*) the voice of Yahweh is continued with "you have not walked (*hlk*) according to his *tôrâ*, his *ḥuqqôt*, and his *'edôt*." Similarly, in 44:10 it is a question of not walking (*hlk*) in the *tôrâ* and the *ḥuqqôt* "which I set before (*ntn lipnê*) you and your fathers." In 32:23 there is no additional legal term to specify *tôrâ*, but otherwise similar expressions appear; prophetic word is hardly a possible interpretation. In 16:11 the pertinent phrase is "but me they have forsaken (*'zb*), and my *tôrâ* they have not observed (*šmr*)." Nothing suggests the prophetic word and the use of *šmr* virtually imposes the legal sense.[64]

In 9:12 the only possible basis for thinking of the prophetic word is that "they have abandoned (*'zb*) my *tôrâ*, which I set before them (*nātattî lipnêhem*)" is followed by "and have not listened to (*šm'*) my voice"; but this phrase is at once continued by "and they have not walked in it (*hāl^e^kû bāh*)," which indicates that we are dealing with the same expressions and thoughts as in the preceding passages. Almost every term in this verse finds its parallels in those verses where the sense is clearly legal. Bright assigns an exilic date to this passage.

The two remaining passages (6:19; 26:4) present a little more difficulty. In 26:4f., part of a prose composition, "if you do not obey me" is carried forward by two infinitive expressions: "to walk (*hlk*) in my *tôrâ* which I set before you (*natattî lipnêkem*)" and (in vs. 5) "to listen to the words of my servants the prophets whom I send to you . . ." If the two infinitive expressions are intended to say the same thing, *tôrâ* here is the prophetic word. In fact, however, the expressions used with *tôrâ* indicate that it means "law." Thus *hlk b^e^tôrâ* occurs in 32:23; 44:10 (and cf. 9:12); *ntn lipnê* is

[64]It is also worth mentioning that none of the six uses of *šmr* in Jer resembles the sense it has in this passage except for 35:18, where it is a question of the *miṣwôt* imposed by Jonadab on his sons. In Dt, on the other hand, *šmr* is used almost fifty times with one or more of the legal terms it employs.

found in 9:12 and 44:10. The two infinitive expressions, therefore, are complementary rather than parallel; there are two ways in which the people can know the will of God, the *tôrâ* and the words of the prophets.[65]

In 6:19 *tôrâ* comes in sequence after, and in some sense parallel to, *d^e^bāray*; if *d^e^bāray* refers to the prophetic word and if the two terms are strictly parallel, this would be the one text in Jer that speaks of prophetic *tôrâ*. It seems likely, in the light of the rest of the passage (which begins at vs. 16), that *d^e^bāray* does refer to the prophetic word: the watchmen God raised up to say to the people, "Attend (*haqšîb*) to the sound of the trumpet" (vs. 17) are surely the prophets; in vs. 19 the same verb, now in the indicative, is used to say that "they have not attended (*hiqšîb*) to my words." But the passage includes reference to another demand which is anterior to the cry of the prophets, to which, in fact, the cry of the prophets was intended to recall the people: in vs. 16 there is word about "the pathways of old," "the way to good," in which the people were to walk (*derek haṭṭôb ûl^e^kû bāh*); it is when they have refused to do this that the prophets raise their warning. Thus vs. 19 refers back chiastically to the two obligations already raised and rejected: "they did not attend to my words" in vs. 19 refers back to "we will not attend" in vs. 17, while "they despised my *tôrâ*" in vs. 19 refers back to "we will not walk" in vs. 16.[66] Therefore, *tôrâ* does not refer here or anywhere in Jeremiah's collection to the prophetic word. As in some of the other passages in Jer that we have discussed, *tôrâ* here seems to have wisdom overtones; while Jeremiah may be thinking of laws or a lawcode, even Dt, the ancient pathways he commends as the good road and the way to rest may well be Israel's holy instruction in a broader sense.

Exilic Prophets: Ezekiel and Deutero-Isaiah

The term *tôrâ* occurs seven times in Ezekiel,[67] but all of the texts refer so clearly to priestly *tôrâ* that no further comment is needed; some of them have already been referred to.

[65]This conjunction of *tôrâ* and the prophetic word is found also in the late deuteronomic passage (see n. 58) of 2 Kgs 17:13, with the curious difference that the prophets are presented as sent by God to preach the *tôrâ*. The meaning of "the law" is imposed because *tôrâ* is a third term along with *miṣwôt* and *ḥuqqôt*. The presentation may be influenced by the description of Moses as prophet and lawgiver in Dt. The same conception seems to lie behind the reference to "the *tôrâ* you gave us through your servants, the prophets" in Dan 9:10 (part of a late interpolation—vss. 4-20—in the prayer of Daniel; see L. F. Hartman, "Daniel," *JBC* 26:30). But those who allege this text in favor of prophetic *tôrâ* ignore the fact that the context explicitly relates *tôrâ* here to the Mosaic law.

[66]This accords with Bright's interpretation; in the "Notes" he identifies the watchmen as prophets and the "law" as probably a reference to the Deuteronomic code. Hyatt, "Torah in the Book of Jeremiah," 391, rejects "words" and *tôrâ* as equivalent expressions in this verse. So also John Skinner, *Prophecy and Religion: Studies in the Life of Jeremiah* (Cambridge: Cambridge University Press, 1922), 116.

[67]The texts are 7:26; 22:26; 43:11 (*Q^e^re* reads plural); 43:12 (*bis*); 44:5 (*Q^e^re* reads plural).24. The type of expression in 43:12 (*zō't tôrat habbāyit*) is identical with that found so often in P.

Deutero-Isaiah uses *tôrâ* five times: 42:4.21.24; 51:4.7. It is not easy to determine an exact significance for the term in any of these passages; it seems to have the broadest possible sense of "instruction" or "revelation," and is employed with other terms that would not usually be considered synonymous or even similar in meaning.

The interpretation of 42:4 is complicated by the fact that the activity described in this section (vss. 1-4) is attributed to the Servant of Yahweh, this being the first of the "Servant Songs"; our understanding of the *tôrâ* he is to provide will depend to some extent on what sort of a figure we conceive the Servant to be. Some believe he is depicted as a prophet; others, perhaps with equal evidence (or lack of it), see a kingly figure.[68] At any rate, *tôrâ* occurs here in parallel with *mišpāṭ*, both attributed to the Servant's work and mission. In the context of Deutero-Isaiah, *mišpāṭ* (which is the leading concept in this section—see vs. 1: "he shall bring forth *mišpāṭ* to the nations") suggests the broader concept of the Kingdom of God, the universal establishment of the order willed by God; *tôrâ* is the instruction or revelation which accompanies it as an inevitable corollary or even an indispensable condition.[69]

Commentators disagree on the import of *tôrâ* in 42:21. Lindars, [70] e.g., follows Volz in considering the verse a later addition and *tôrâ* legal in sense, while McKenzie[71] takes the verse as an integral part of a poem comprising vss. 18-25 and translates *tôrâ* by "teaching"; in neither case would the term refer to the prophetic word. The final assertion holds good also for 42:24, though here it is not a case of Yahweh making His *tôrâ* great and glorious, but of a refusal on the part of the people to hear or to obey (*šmʻ*). Deutero-Isaiah does not seem to use *tôrâ* in a legal sense, so it could well be a wisdom term here; the parallel expression (*bidᵉrākāyw hālôk*) is compatible with either interpretation.

In 51:4 *tôrâ* is parallel to *mišpāṭ*, as it was in 42:4, and the sense seems to be the same as in that verse. The meaning is not essentially different in the final text, 51:7, though the perspective seems to have passed to a "realized eschatology," as the gifts promised in vss. 4-5 appear to be already present in vss. 6-8. Whether the author has Jeremiah's "new covenant" text in mind or not, he has given a profound meaning to *tôrâ*. Here it is something that can be possessed interiorly, undoubtedly is a well-spring for conduct, and stands

[68]For a discussion of such theories, see H. H. Rowley, "The Suffering Servant and the Davidic Messiah," *OTS* 8 (1950) 100-136, reprinted in *The Servant of the Lord and Other Essays on the Old Testament* (2nd ed., rev.; Oxford: Basil Blackwell, 1965), 61-93.

[69]H. H. Rowley, "The Servant of the Lord in the Light of Three Decades of Criticism," *The Servant of the Lord*, 15; John L. McKenzie, *Second Isaiah* (*AB* 20; Garden City, N.Y.: Doubleday & Company, Inc., 1968), 36-38.

[70]Lindars, "Torah in Deuteronomy," 134.

[71]McKenzie, *Second Isaiah*, 46.

in close conjunction with the gift of God's enduring salvation. But neither here nor in the other texts is it the prophetic word.

Post-Exilic Prophets: Haggai, Zechariah, Malachi[72]

The single occurrence of *tôrâ* in Haggai (2:11) is clearly priestly and has already been discussed (p. 13). It is found in four successive verses in Malachi (2:6-9) and is clearly identified as priestly doctrine; also in 3:22, in a reference to the law of Moses (*tôrat mōšeh*).

Finally, *tôrâ* is found once in Zechariah (7:12), from which the best case for prophetic *tôrâ* can be made. The verse reads: "And they made their hearts diamond-hard so as not to hear the *tôrâ* and message (*w^{e}'et hadd^{e}bārîm*) that Yahweh of Hosts had sent by his spirit through (*b^{e}yad*) the former prophets." Those who see this text as a witness for prophetic *tôrâ* would be taking "words sent through the prophets" as the basic expression, with *tôrâ* functioning as a strictly synonymous term, saying no more and no less. However, this is not the only possible interpretation, nor is it even the most probable. While the whole chapter (vss. 1-14) forms the general context for this verse, the most instructive part begins with vs. 7, where the expression "the words which God spoke through the former prophets" is introduced; vss. 9-10 (vs. 8 is an interpolation) summarize the prophetic teaching, and vs. 11 describes the disobedience of the people. Even as vs. 12 now stands, it is quite possible to understand *tôrâ* as "teaching" or "instruction" in a very general sense; although it has been delivered through the prophets, it is the underlying conception of "instruction" from Yahweh that determines the choice of *tôrâ*, not that the term is a technical expression for the prophetic word.

This suggestion is presented first because tampering with a text in the interest of a theory is always suspect. However, there is good reason to suppose that vs. 12 has suffered interpolation. Thus Mitchell, e.g., takes *w^{e}'et hadd^{e}bārîm* to be a gloss and translates: "Not to hear the instruction that Yahweh of Hosts had sent them."[73] In this or in the previously suggested interpretation, *tôrâ* might possibly have been selected under the influence of the usage of Isaiah, especially of Isa 1:10-17;[74] the summary of prophetic teaching in Zech 7:9-10 recalls Isa 1:17.23, and God's refusal to "hear" in Zech 7:13 recalls Isa 1:15.

[72]The term *tôrâ* is not found in Obadiah, Joel, or Jonah. On Dan 9:10.11.13, see n. 65.

[73]H. G. Mitchell *et al.*, *A Critical and Exegetical Commentary on Haggai, Zechariah, Malachi and Jonah* (New York: Charles Scribner's Sons, 1912), 205.

[74]Smith, "The Meaning of the Word *twrh* in Isaiah," 21, suggests that in this text Zechariah has consciously imitated Isaiah. C. Stuhlmueller, "Zechariah," *JBC* 23:33, says on vss. 8-14: "These final words echo many biblical texts. We hear again the prophetic preaching of . . . Isaiah (1:17, 23)."

If one is to think of interpolation, however (and the awkwardness of vs. 12 invites it), it is perhaps more likely that the term *tôrâ* itself has been added. Vs. 7 had already introduced the expression "words of the former prophets," so its presence in vs. 12 is not surprising. If *tôrâ* were later added, it could only have the meaning "the law" and would betray a rabbinical zeal to point to the *primary* source of Israel's knowledge of God's will.

Prophetic *tôrâ* as a Literary (Liturgical) Form

Even though the OT does not use *tôrâ* to designate the prophetic word, it may be argued that some prophetic passages ought to be considered "prophetic *tôrâ*" on the basis of literary form or other criteria. In fact, there are those who do call any number of passages "prophetic *tôrâ*" even where the term does not appear. Some scholars are willing to identify the cultic official who answers in the "entrance liturgies" (frequently called "*tôrâ*-liturgies") as a prophet.[75] And while Begrich spoke of prophetic imitations of priestly *tôrâ*, there are others who call the same passages "prophetic *tôrâ*." For example, Bentzen raises the topic of *tôrâ*-liturgies (which he had discussed earlier), says that it is also found among the prophets, and adds: "In pure form we find it e.g. Is. 1,10-17, cf. also Micah 6,6-8; Is. 56,1-8; Zech.7,1-7."[76]

Here it seems legitimate to raise again an objection raised earlier when discussing priestly *tôrâ*: "entrance liturgies" such as Ps 15; 24; Isa 33:14-16 are nowhere in the OT called "*tôrâ*"; and if it is legitimate to question whether just *any* question and answer pattern deserves to be called priestly *tôrâ*, with much better right can it be raised when we have left the priestly sphere. Furthermore, in many of the texts that are classified as "prophetic *tôrâ*," a question-answer pattern is not even found. And if we should turn to the four prime texts cited by Bentzen, we may ask what they have in common that justifies their being lumped under one term. That Isa 1:10-17 is consistently placed in this category is no doubt occasioned by the presence of the term *tôrâ* in vs. 10, but it has nothing in common with Zech 7:1-7; the only

[75]Some scholars tend to regard the prophets in general, or at least a great number of them, as cult officials, often leaving but slight distinction between prophet and priest; cf. Haldar, *Associations of Cult Prophets among the Ancient Semites*, 109-114; Sigmund Mowinckel, *The Psalms in Israel's Worship*, tr. D. R. Ap-Thomas (New York: Abingdon Press, 1962), II, 54f. Gerhard von Rad, *Old Testament Theology*, II, tr. D. M. G. Stalker (New York: Harper & Row, Publishers, 1965), 189, on the other hand, states that "Nahum is the only prophet who may possibly have had a function within the framework of the cult." For a balanced discussion and further literature, see H. H. Rowley, "The Nature of Old Testament Prophecy in the Light of Recent Study," *The Servant of the Lord*, 109-113; more recently and at greater length in *Worship in Ancient Israel: Its Forms and Meaning* (Philadelphia: Fortress Press, 1967), 144-75.

[76]A. Bentzen, *Introduction to the Old Testament*, I, 201; see also Mowinckel, *The Psalms in Israel's Worship*, II, 58; Lindblom, *Prophecy in Ancient Israel*, 157.

link between the two, apparently, is that *tôrâ* appears in Isa 1:10 and the Zechariah passage includes the sort of question-answer pattern that might have been called *tôrâ*, and that each in its own way says something about the pointlessness of observance without justice—a very common theme of prophetic teaching.

Again, Isa 1:10-17 and Mic 6:6-8 are quite different in respect to form. The Micah piece is part of a longer passage (vss. 1-8), usually classified as a covenant lawsuit (*rîb*).[77] The imperative call to hear is directed to witnesses, not to those accused; there follows a catalogue of God's *ṣid^{e}qôt* on behalf of Israel; only in this context does the question of sacrifice arise, as Israel's repentant voice asks what can be offered as atonement. "With what shall I come before the Lord?" is a question that may well come from the cult, but that alone does not justify the term *tôrâ* for the piece. In all these particulars it diverges in form from the Isaiah passage.[78]

The fourth of these texts, Isa 56:1-8, does not contain the word *tôrâ* and does not exhibit a question-answer pattern; it is essentially an announcement of salvation which is introduced with the exhortation to "Observe what is right, do what is just." Aside from some use of the imperative,[79] it has little formal similarity with any of the other passages.

Conclusions

Two conclusions that are of particular significance for this study may be singled out. The first is that there is no compelling evidence for the use of *tôrâ* as a term to designate the prophetic word.

The second conclusion is that, at least phenomenologically speaking, the basic meaning of *tôrâ* is "instruction," as many excellent scholars have

[77]See especially H. B. Huffmon, "The Covenant Lawsuit in the Prophets," *JBL* 78 (1959) 285-95; J. Harvey, "Le 'Rîb-Pattern', réquisitoire prophétique sur la rupture de l'alliance," *Bib* 43 (1962) 172-96.

[78]This catalogue of differences isn't weakened by the fact that some authors, e.g., Harvey, "Le 'Rîb-Pattern'," 177-79, join vss. 18-20 to Isa 1:10-17 and classify them as an indictment or disputation saying (cf. Eissfeldt, *The Old Testament*, 80, 309); in any case, no number of *rîb*s can add up to a single *tôrâ*.

[79]It should be noted that Erhard Gerstenberger, *Wesen und Herkunft des "apodiktischen Rechts"* (Neukirchen-Vluyn: Neukirchener Verlag, 1965) has shown that the imperatives of Israel's apodictic laws are not rooted in the priestly proclamation of the covenant festivals, but in the more ancient clan ethic; the same conclusions are reached by Richter, *Recht und Ethos*, though he broadens the point of origin to include types of groups other than the clan; the imperatives found in some priestly proclamations or instructions (whether or not these deserve to be called *tôrôt*) are derivative from a broader background of proclamation of ethic, and there is nothing to suggest the prophets depend on the priests for this form.

always maintained.[80] Whatever is to be said on the question of etymology, the attempt to begin with one particularized meaning for the term (e.g., oracular response, response to question, instruction concerning clean and unclean) and to derive all the others from it leads to insoluble difficulties, at least if the probable chronology of the texts and developments is taken into account. On the other hand, if one begins with the assumption that *tôrâ* is basically "instruction" in a fairly generalized sense, the derivation of the more specific meanings is not difficult to understand. Thus, in a culture where priests were custodians of covenant law, its interpretation, and its application, it is intelligible that *tôrâ* is primarily sought from the priest, whether this be by way of instruction in ethical obligations under the covenant (as we must suppose Hosea to have in mind), or by way of judicial decision (as in Ex 18; Dt 17:11), or by way of response to a question on a cultic matter (as in Hag 2:11), or whether it is simply a body of instruction that is passed down within priestly circles (as in P). And if we take *hôrâ* as a denominative meaning "to impart instruction," even the obtaining of oracles by technical means of divination is not excluded (as possibly indicated in Gen 12:6; Hab 2:19). This explanation makes intelligible the development by which Israel's body of laws, conceived as divine instruction in the right way of life, could be called *tôrâ*—a development that Lindars conceives as taking place simultaneously, in parallel fashion, in more than one circle. The explanation would also make clear why we find *tôrâ* used as the term that designates the instruction dispensed by the teacher; no elaborate development is needed, for the term is simply reflecting, within a specialized context, the basic meaning it carries.

[80]George B. Gray, *A Critical and Exegetical Commentary on the Book of Isaiah, I-XXXIX* (New York: Charles Scribner's Sons, 1912), 18; de Vaux, *Ancient Israel*, 354; H.Duesberg and I. Fransen, *Les scribes inspirés* (Rev. ed.; Maredsous: Éditions de Maredsous, 1966), 231. See also R. B. Y. Scott, "Priesthood, Prophecy, Wisdom, and the Knowledge of God," 7n.; Östborn, *Tōrā in the Old Testament*, 5f.; and John Skinner, *Prophecy and Religion*, 3.

2

ANTIQUITY OF *tôrâ* AS WISDOM TERMINOLOGY

That *tôrâ* eventually came to function as a technical term within the wisdom tradition, standing for the "wise instruction" imparted by the sage to his pupil, is not a matter of dispute. But it is crucial to the position being argued in this study to determine whether this comes only as a late (i.e., post-exilic) usage, as many hold, or whether it is possible to establish a strong case, at least, for a much earlier date.

The assertion that *tôrâ* as a wisdom term is late is sometimes made as a statement that needs no justification.[1] When the assertion is explained, the argument is usually that in the post-exilic period *tôrâ*, in the sense of "law," became the concern of the sages; this is the development as set forth by, e.g., de Vaux[2] and Lindblom.[3] Östborn is less clear in his presentation, choosing to speak of the "dual meaning" inherent in *tôrâ* (i.e., both law and instruction); he doesn't clearly date the development, but does attribute it to the role "the law" had in the curriculum of the wisdom school.[4]

Some possible reasons for the view of de Vaux, Lindblom, and others of like persuasion come easily to mind. Aside from the quite understandable desire to find a development which explains one meaning of the term from another (earlier and more basic?) meaning, one must reckon with the after-effects of the now generally rejected view that the wisdom movement is a late development in Israel. Again, there is the fact that most of the clear examples of *tôrâ* in the wisdom sense are in Prov, a post-exilic compilation, most especially in Prov 1-9, a post-exilic composition. Finally, one encounters other terms in Prov (*mišpāṭ*, *miṣwâ*) that might seem to fit well into a theory which sees a legal tradition become the basis for more general instruction.

[1]Thus Hans Wildberger, *Jesaja: I. Teilband, Jesaja 1-12* (*BKAT* X; Neukirchen: Neukirchener Verlag, 1965-72), shows himself very much aware of the wisdom overtones in Isa 1:10-17, and in discussing the use of *tôrâ* in vs. 10 says "auch der Weisheit *twrh* erteilen kann," but then adds, "aber offensichtlich doch erst in ihrer jüngeren Ausgestaltung, in welcher die Bereiche von Weisheit und Kult nicht mehr scharf getrennt sind" (p. 36).

[2]R. de Vaux, *Ancient Israel*, 355. A preliminary objection which can be raised is that de Vaux seems to identify priestly *tôrâ* and "law" in the deuteronomic sense and makes the same group the bearer of both; neither P (on Num 19:2 and 31:21, see above, Ch. 1, n. 36) nor Ezekiel uses *tôrâ* as a term for the aggregate of the law, this usage being the work of the deuteronomists and those who shared their traditions.

[3]Johannes Lindblom, "Wisdom in the Old Testament Prophets," *VTSup* 3 (1955) 196. See also, Gutbrod, "The Meaning of the word *tôrâ*," 1045.

[4]G. Östborn, *Tōrā in the Old Testament*, 122.

Yet whatever logic the explanation might appear to have in the abstract, it stands in contradiction to the findings of Lindars and others, as presented in Ch. 1. The term did not mean "law" first and then acquire a broader meaning; rather, it was precisely because *tôrâ* already had the meaning "instruction," with wisdom overtones, that it was an apt term under which to gather a whole code of rules and regulations which are now conceived of in a unified fashion as a way of life given to man by God.[5] There is every reason to hold that *tôrâ* already meant "law" in *this* sense (which is not the meaning it had in priestly circles) in the days of the monarchy, perhaps even in the original Dt. Furthermore, there are other passages, such as those in Deutero-Isaiah, in which *tôrâ* clearly has a far broader sense than "law" before post-exilic times.

As for the other "legal" terms found in Prov, it must be said that though *mišpāṭ* and *miṣwâ* do figure in the legal tradition, their basic reference is far broader; the former can refer to any sort of judgment or decision, the latter to anything imposed by a person in authority.[6] Some of the other terms from Israel's legal tradition occur in Prov either quite rarely or not at all; thus *ḥōq* occurs only three times and never in a legal sense,[7] while *ḥuqqâ* and *ʿēdût* are not found.

It is not surprising, therefore, that there are some authors who date the wisdom use of *tôrâ* early.[8] The case for an early dating of this usage will be made by arguing from the antiquity and ubiquity of "wise instruction" in the Near Eastern wisdom tradition, by arguing directly from *tôrâ* passages in Prov which have claim to being ancient, and by arguing indirectly from *tôrâ* passages in Prov 1-9, which, on the whole, is a recent composition.

"Instruction" in Ancient Near Eastern Wisdom Tradition

Although it is common to speak of the "wisdom tradition" of the ancient Near East, the category is of modern making and is a term of convenience. W. G. Lambert goes so far as to say that " 'Wisdom' is strictly a misnomer applied to Babylonian literature," for the Babylonian terms that actually mean "wise," "wisdom," etc. refer primarily to skill in cult and magic; but he concedes: "Though this term is thus foreign to ancient Mesopotamia, it

[5]This comes across most clearly in a passage like Dt 5:32f., whose diction would fit well into the wisdom tradition. Even its theme of "possession of the land" is at home in wisdom texts; see Ps 25:13; 37:3.9.11.22.29.34; cf. Prov 2:21; 10:30.

[6]This is seen most clearly in Jer 35:14.16.18, where *miṣwâ* refers to the command of the clan father.

[7]Prov 8:29; 30:8; 31:15.

[8]William McKane, *Prophets and Wise Men* (*STB* 1/44; London: SCM Press Ltd., 1965), 106; E. W. Heaton, *The Hebrew Kingdoms. New Clarendon Bible*, Vol. III (London: Oxford University Press, 1968), 304f.

has been used for a group of texts which correspond in subject-matter with the Hebrew Wisdom books, and may be retained as a convenient short description."[9] Applying our terms to Egyptian compositions can also be misleading; Cazelles, discussing Hebrew terms and their equivalents in other ancient Near Eastern languages, does not seem to find an Egyptian equivalent for *ḥokmâ*.[10] With reference to both Egypt and Mesopotamia, then, it is mainly a question of gathering the types of composition that seem to fit under the rubric "wisdom."[11] The salient characteristics of compositions so classified would seem to be didactic intent, concern for matters of human conduct, and the attempt to discover the order and meaning of things, especially as they touch man's existence.[12] It is now generally recognized that earlier characterizations of wisdom as "profane" in its interests and concerns were false; the will of the gods and the part they play in man's life are often prominent even in the early period.[13]

The term "instruction" in the title of this section of our study is not intended to restrict consideration to those compositions which are classified as "instructions," but extends to the concept of the communication of learning from teacher to student, whether the teacher be presented as a god, a king, a father, or a professional member of a school. The point to be made here is that this concept and the practice it rests upon was very widely spread and goes back to the very beginnings of the wisdom tradition. This concept is found in Israel, too, and its presence there is in unbroken continuity with the broader development of the wisdom tradition; sometimes the literary expressions which embody this concept in the OT strikingly resemble compositions from Egypt or Mesopotamia. The literary form of the proverb is

[9]W. G. Lambert, *Babylonian Wisdom Literature* (Oxford: Clarendon Press, 1960), 1, where he also lists the pertinent terms.

[10]Henri Cazelles, "Les débuts de la sagesse en Israël," *Les Sagesses du Proche-Orient ancien*: Colloque de Strasbourg 17-19 mai 1962 (Bibliothèque des Centres d'Études supérieures spécialisés; Paris: Presses Universitaires de France, 1963), 27-40, especially 36f. For further discussion of some Egyptian terminology, see Jean Leclant, "Documents nouveaux et points de vue récents sur les sagesses de l'Égypte ancienne," *ibid.*, 5-26, who says there is no Egyptian term for wisdom, properly speaking (p. 14).

[11]Scholars do not always agree on the types of compositions to be classified as wisdom; see, e.g., the diverse listings for Mesopotamia given by Hans H. Schmid, *Wesen und Geschichte der Weisheit: Ein Untersuchung zur altorientalischen und israelitischen Weisheitsliteratur* (*BZAW* 101; Berlin: Verlag Alfred Töpelmann, 1966), 88-94, and Edward I. Gordon, "A New Look at the Wisdom of Sumer and Akkad," *BO* 17 (1960) 124.

[12]Samuel N. Kramer, "Sumerian Wisdom Literature: A Preliminary Survey," *BASOR* 122 (Apr. 1951) 28-31, lists five categories of Sumerian wisdom literature: proverbs, miniature essays, instructions and precepts, essays concerned with school and scribe, and disputes and debates.

[13]See especially Schmid, *Wesen und Geschichte der Weisheit*, 1-7 and *passim*; Aksel Volten, "Der Begriff der Maat in den Ägyptischen Weisheitstexten," *Les Sagesses du Proche-Orient ancien*, 73-101; Jean Nougayrol, "Les sagesses babyloniennes: Études récentes et textes inédits," *ibid.*, 41-51.

relevant here, for those who formulated proverbs or collected and transmitted proverbs formulated by others were knowingly engaging in the work of instruction.

The procedure of introducing a series of proverbs under the title of "instruction," precisely that of a father to his son, is very ancient. A fragmentary Akkadian composition, "The Instruction of Shuruppak," begins as follows:

> Shuruppak [son of Uburtutu gave instructions],
> To Utnapushtu [his son he gave instructions, saying],
> "My son, [I will give you instructions, take my instructions];
> Utnapushtu, [I will give you instructions],
> [Do not neglect] my instructions.
> [Do not disobey] the words [I have spoken to you].[14]

And then there follows a series of proverbs. This text is not original in the Akkadian, but goes back to a still more ancient Sumerian composition, on the basis of which the very fragmentary Akkadian text can be reconstructed. The Sumerian text is attested before 2500 B.C. and so ranks as "one of the oldest known pieces of Mesopotamian literature."[15] The corresponding lines are as follows:

> [Šuruppa]k offered instructions to his son,
> [Šuruppa]k, the son of Ubartutu,
> Offered instructions to his son Ziusudra,
> "O my [son], instruction I offer thee, take my instruction,
> O Ziusudra, a word I would speak to thee, give ear to my word,
> My instruction do not neglect,
> My spoken word do not transgress.[16]

The content of such instruction from father to son might be of a much more practical nature. Again from Sumer comes a text that tells of the professional techniques passed on by a farmer; the text begins: "In days of yore a farmer gave (these) instructions to his son: when you are about to irrigate your field . . ."[17] This text will be of special interest to us later because it ends with the statement that the rules laid down by the farmer came from the god Ninurta.[18]

But it was especially in Egypt that the genre of "instruction" flourished, as well as other quite diverse types of compositions which apply the same term,

[14] *ANESTP*, 594.

[15] *Ibid.*

[16] Given by S. N. Kramer, "Gilgamesh and the Land of the Living," *JCS* 1 (1947) 33, n. 208.

[17] S. N. Kramer, *History Begins at Sumer* (Garden City, N.Y.: Doubleday & Company, Inc., 1959 [c1956]), 68.

[18] *Ibid.*, 67.

sebayit, the common Egyptian word for "instruction," to themselves.[19] Schmid lists some twelve texts or fragments that can be classified as "instructions," plus one other that is cited in Egyptian literature but has never been recovered.[20] Although these stretch in time from the 28th to the first century, B.C., they often display a great similarity in procedure and content; as Schmid explains the genre: "Ein Vater (resp. Lehrer) erteilt seinem Sohn (resp. Schüler) auf Grund eigener Erfahrung und überlieferter Erkenntnis Anweisungen zu rechtem Leben" (p. 9).

The opening lines of several of these provide information on most of these points. For example, "The Instruction of Ptah-hotep" begins: "The instruction of the Mayor and Vizier Ptah-hotep, under the majesty of the King of Upper and Lower Egypt . . ." The conclusion of the introductory section contains reference to instruction and rules "as of advantage to him who will hearken and of disadvantage to him who may neglect them." Toward the end, there is a long admonition about the importance of hearing:

> To hear is of advantage for a son who hearkens. . . . To hear is better than anything that is, (and thus) comes the goodly love (of a man). How good it is when a son accepts what his father says! Thereby *maturity* comes to him. He whom God loves is a hearkener, (but) he whom God hates cannot hear.[21]

Though fuller and more detailed, the resemblance of this piece on many points with the passage cited above from "The Instruction of Shuruppak," from distant Mesopotamia, is clear. In each case it is a question of a man addressing his son; in each case there is insistence upon the importance of giving ear and of the danger of neglecting to do so. The same points are found in most of the other Egyptian "instructions."

The admonition to harken in "The Instruction of King Amen-em-het" appears at the beginning, in the imperative, and again refers to the advantage to be gained: ". . . hearken to what I have to say to thee, . . . that thou mayest achieve an overabundance of good."[22]

The introduction to "The Instruction of Amen-em-Opet" opens with these words: "The beginning of the teaching of life, the testimony for prosperity, . . . in order to direct him to the ways of life, to make him prosper upon earth, let his heart go down into its shrine, steer him away from evil . . ." The connection made here between wise instruction and life and well-being is one we

[19]Leclant, "Documents nouveaux," 11f., discusses the term and notes that the *Onomasticon* of Amen-em-Opet, a sort of encyclopedia, is also called *sebayit*; see also Albrecht Alt, "Die Weisheit Salomos," *TLZ* 76 (1951) 141. J. A. Wilson says: "The word *sebayit* 'teaching,' came to be used by the Egyptians for 'wisdom,' because of their orientation towards the models of the past" (*ANET*, 412).

[20]Schmid, *Wesen und Geschichte der Weisheit*, 9-13. See also B. Gemser, "The Instructions of 'Onchsheshonqy and Biblical Wisdom Literature," *VTSup* 7 (1959) 102-128.

[21]*ANET*, 412-14.

[22]*ANET*, 418.

will encounter again. The first chapter begins:

Give thy ears, hear what is said,
Give thy heart to understand them.
To put them in thy heart is worth while
(But) it is damaging to him who neglects them.[23]

This is very similar to the Mesopotamian piece, especially in the direct imperative address, the call to give ear, the negative as well as positive part of the exhortation.

It is clear that Israel's own wisdom movement, and specifically her concept of "instruction," is in continuity with what is found in Egypt and Mesopotamia and is to some extent dependent upon them.[24] The best known example, of course, is the use made of "The Instruction of Amen-em-Opet" in Prov 22:17-24:22,[25] but this is simply an unusually clear instance of a much broader phenomenon. It is now generally admitted that although Israel's wisdom literature (i.e., the books as we have them now) is recent, the wisdom movement itself goes back at least to the time of the early monarchy.[26] Wisdom techniques (e.g., literary forms) and terminology must have become established quite early; although study is required for specific cases, the supposition is valid that Israel's wisdom compositions attest to early procedures and terminology. The supposition is justified both by the evidence for the wide distribution, in time and in space, for such procedures and by the basically conservative nature of the movement itself. This conservatism is explicable, in part at least, by the fact that the content of the wisdom tradition consisted largely of the accumulated experience and insight of earlier generations (the father-son pattern is relevant here),[27] but also the type of

[23]*ANET*, 421.

[24]Paul Humbert, *Recherches sur les sources égyptiennes de la littérature sapientiale d'Israël* (Mémoires de l'Université de Neuchâtel: Secrétariat de l'Université, 1929); O. S. Rankin, *Israel's Wisdom Literature: Its Bearing on Theology and the History of Religion* (New York: Schocken Books, 1969 [c1936]), 7f., 14; H. P. Couroyer, "Le chemin de vie en Égypte et en Israël," *RB* 56 (1949) 412-32; *idem.*, "Idéal sapiential en Égypte et en Israël," *RB* 57 (1950) 174-79; W. S. Smith, "The Relationship between Egyptian Ideas and Old Testament Thought," *JBR* 19 (1951) 12-15; G. von Rad, "Job XXXVIII and Ancient Egyptian Wisdom," *The Problem of the Hexateuch and Other Essays*, tr. E. W. T. Dicken (New York: McGraw-Hill Book Company, 1966), 281-91 (originally published in German in *VTSup* 3 [1955]); H. Gunkel, "Aegyptische Parallelen zum alten Testament," *ZDMG* 63 (1909) 531-39; Schmid, *Wesen und Geschichte der Weisheit*, 144.

[25]See A. Alt, "Zur literarischen Analyses der Weisheit des Amenemope," *VTSup* 3 (1955) 16-25; Gerstenberger, *Wesen und Herkunft*, 136-40; Richter, *Recht und Ethos*, pp. 21f.

[26]A. Alt, "Die Weisheit Salomos," argues for the existence in the early monarchy of a wisdom form, the *onomasticon*, that is not directly witnessed to in the OT, but is widely known from the ancient Near East; W. Baumgartner, "The Wisdom Literature," *The Old Testament and Modern Study*, ed. H. H. Rowley (London: Oxford University Press, 1961 [c1951]), 211; Heaton, *The Hebrew Kingdoms*, 167-74.

[27]Schmid, *Wesen und Geschichte der Weisheit*, 27f.: according to Egyptian teaching, no one is born wise; he is a wise man who listens to what the ancestors of earlier times have said.

drill used in the schools where writing was taught, namely, the copying out of standard texts.[28] Whatever the reason, the fact is demonstrable in any number of areas; in addition to those already discussed, we might mention the theme of the praise of the wise man or scribe, to the disadvantage of every other kind of calling, found in such widely separated compositions as the Egyptian "Satire on the Trades" (*ANET*, 432-34) and Sir 38:24-39:11.

This general argumentation is intended, of course, for specific application to the term *tôrâ*: the fact that in Israel's wisdom literature it has the meaning "wise instruction" already suggests it had that meaning at a much earlier period; Israel must have had a well established wisdom terminology at an early date. When one encounters a passage such as Prov 1:8, the resemblance to some of the Mesopotamian and Egyptian pieces we have already discussed is obvious.

> Hear, my son, your father's instruction (*mûsār*),
> and reject not your mother's teaching (*tôrâ*).

Whatever the age of the document in which it is found, the form is early and gives good grounds for supposing the terminology is early, too.

It would be tempting to argue that *tôrâ* is the Hebrew equivalent of the Egyptian *sebayit*. Albright appears to say this,[29] and a good case could be made out from the non-wisdom compositions of the OT, where *tôrâ* often functions in the broad sense of "instruction" in a way that no other term (including *mûsār*) can be said to do; the fact that the deuteronomists chose *tôrâ* for the meaning they wanted to convey should carry some little weight. However, scholars more generally hold that *mûsār* is the Hebrew equivalent of *sebayit*,[30] and a comparison of the manner in which the two terms are employed in Prov does not favor giving pride of place to *tôrâ*.[31] It will be sufficient for the purpose of this study to establish, to whatever extent pos-

[28]Baudoin van de Walle, "Problèmes relatifs aux méthodes d'enseignement dans l'Égypte ancien," *Les Sagesses du Proche-Orient ancien*, 203.

[29]W. F. Albright, *From the Stone Age to Christianity* (2nd ed.; Garden City, N.Y.: Doubleday & Company, Inc., 1957), 220f., 269f.

[30]Cf. Leclant, "Documents nouveaux," 13n., following R. Weill; Roger N. Whybray, *Wisdom in Proverbs: The Concept of Wisdom in Proverbs 1-9* (*SBT* 1/45; London: SCM Press Ltd., 1965), 67. Duesberg and Fransen, *Les scribes inspirés*, 229.

[31]This is not primarily because *mûsār* is used much more frequently than *tôrâ* (30 times as compared with 12 times). Of the six texts in which *tôrâ* stands in parallel with a comparable term (1:8; 3:1; 4:2; 6:20.23; 7:2; 31:26), in only one (3:1) does it stand as the first term; in the single text (1:8) where it stands parallel to *mûsār*, it is *mûsār* that stands first. Furthermore, *tôrâ* does not occur at all in the programmatic seven opening verses, while *mûsār* is found there three times; these facts would indeed be surprising, even inexplicable, if it were supposed that *tôrâ* stood for "the law" in the sense it had in post-exilic times. As for *mûsār*, it is the first term in the father's (teacher's) address in 1:8 and 4:1; it is that by which one is set on "a path of life" in 10:17, and is parallel to "words of knowledge" in 19:27 and 23:12. On the other hand, it most frequently means "reproof" or "punishment" (most clearly in 16:22 and 23:13), sometimes the lot of fools, in a way that is not obvious for *sebayit* in the Egyptian "instructions," while *tôrâ* seems always to mean "instruction."

sible, that *tôrâ* could function as a term for "wise instruction" at a fairly early period. This will be done by investigating the *tôrâ* texts in those parts of Prov that have a claim to being early, and then in the Prologue, which is conceded by virtually all to be late.

tôrâ in the Collections of Proverbs

The materials in Prov are notoriously difficult to date, and no attempt will be made here to do so. There is a series of titles that would assign two of the collections (10:1-22:16 and 25:1-29:27) to Solomon, the second of them through the activity of "the men of Hezekiah," but Skehan has demonstrated that the names in the titles have numerological rather than historical value,[32] so no argument is to be based on them. His argumentation does not directly impugn any claim to antiquity that may be made for these collections, and, as a matter of fact, those who hold that they are ancient usually argue from grounds other than the titles. See, e.g., Gemser, Heaton, McKane, von Rad, and Albright.[33] Murphy argues that the Egyptian works are instructions on a *modus vivendi* at the royal court and that the same or similar life-setting for Israelite wisdom literature would be a reasonable assumption, pointing in particular to Prov 16 and 25 and the broad characterization of a careerist they contain.[34]

Though it is impossible to prove with any certainty the antiquity of the material in the two "Solomonic" collections (it is mainly with these that we are concerned), there are strong reasons for holding that much of it comes from the period of the monarchy. Simply *a priori* one must assume that some sort of scribal school was established in Jerusalem early in the monarchy and that it conformed, more or less, to the pattern found in Egypt and Mesopotamia; many authors do, in fact, assume or argue for these points.[35]

[32]Patrick W. Skehan, "A Single Editor for the Whole Book of Proverbs," *CBQ* 10 (1948) 115-30 (revised in *CBQMS* 1, *Studies in Israelite Poetry and Wisdom* [Washington, D.C.: The Catholic Biblical Association of America, 1971], 15-26).

[33]Schmid, *Wesen und Geschichte der Weisheit*, 145; Berend Gemser, *Sprüche Salomos* (*HAT* 16; Tübingen: J. C. B. Mohr, 1963), 4. Of the sayings in this collection, Heaton, *The Hebrew Kingdoms*, 185f., says that they "are certainly pre-exilic and probably the oldest material in the book." William McKane, *Proverbs: A New Approach* (Philadelphia: The Westminster Press, 1970), 262; G. von Rad, *Old Testament Theology*, I, 430; see also his *Wisdom in Israel*, tr. J. D. Martin (Nashville: Abingdon Press, 1972), 11; W. F. Albright, "Some Canaanite-Phoenician Sources of Hebrew Wisdom," *VTSup* 3 (1955) 13.

[34]Roland Murphy, "The Concept of Wisdom Literature," *The Bible in Current Catholic Thought*, ed. J. L. McKenzie (New York: Herder and Herder, 1962), 47f. See also Udo Skladny, *Die ältesten Spruchsammlungen in Israel* (Göttingen: Vandenhoeck & Ruprecht, 1962), 80-82; A. M. Dubarle, *Les sages d'Israël* (*Lectio Divina* 1; Paris: Les Éditions du Cerf, 1946), 25f.

[35]Eissfeldt, *Introduction to the Old Testament*, 86; R. B. Y. Scott, "Solomon and the Beginnings of Wisdom in Israel," *VTSup* 3 (1955), 273; Richter, *Recht und Ethos*, *passim* (see Ch. 1, n. 55, above); Heaton, *The Hebrew Kingdoms*, 168-76; Brevard S. Childs, *Isaiah and the Assyrian Crisis* (*SBT* 2/3; London: SCM Press Ltd., 1967), 136; von Rad, *Wisdom in Israel*, 17; Hans-Jürgen Hermisson, *Studien zur israelitschen Spruchweisheit* (*WMANT* 28; Neukirchen: Neukirchener Verlag, 1968), 97-136.

R. B. Y. Scott points to the "secretaries" and "recorder" among the high officers of state in Solomon's court (1 Kgs 4:3—"scribes," "chancellor" in *NAB*) as evidence that "the scribal art and the literature associated with training in it were thus established at the royal court."[36] From a somewhat different direction one could argue from the circles of royal advisers mentioned in the historical narratives,[37] from the reference to "the wise" in the prophetic books,[38] and from evidence of wisdom concerns in compositions from the time of the early monarchy.[39] Again, the legends about the wisdom of Solomon (1 Kgs 3:4-12.16-28; 5:9-14; 10:1-13) and the attribution of the later wisdom books to him probably has at least this historical basis, that he became patron of wisdom in Israel through establishing a scribal school.[40]

Thus it seems almost certain that there was a professional wisdom school in Israel and that, like the schools in Egypt and Mesopotamia, after which it was no doubt patterned, it developed its own body of traditional wisdom, cast largely in the form of proverbs and instructions. No circle was better equipped to preserve its traditional lore, nor was any circle (with the possible exception of the priestly) more likely to do so. If we are to find that material anywhere, it is certainly in the collections of Prov. It is clear that the final editor of Prov was working with collections already formed;[41] it is likely that the collections were formed over a long period of time and that, in addition to more recent materials, they contained much that was ancient. Thus a usage attested in the collections enjoys a certain presumption in favor of its antiquity; at the very least, it cannot be dismissed as recent without solid arguments.

[36]R. B. Y. Scott, *Proverbs, Ecclesiastes* (*AB* 18; Garden City, N.Y.: Doubleday & Company, Inc., 1965), 12.

[37]E.g., the account of the "wisdom duel" between Hushai and Ahitophel in David's court (2 Sam 15:32-37; 16:23-17:14) and that of Rehoboam's tragic choice of counsel (1 Kgs 12:6-15).

[38]E.g., Isa 5:21; 29:14; Jer 8:9; 18:18.

[39]Gerhard von Rad, "The Joseph Narrative and Ancient Wisdom," *The Problem of the Hexateuch*, 292-300 (translated from "Josephgeschichte und ältere Chokma," *VTSup* 1 [1953] 120-127); R. N. Whybray, *The Succession Narrative: A Study of II Sam. 9-20 and I Kings 1 and 2* (*SBT* 2/9; London: SCM Press Ltd., 1968), 56-95. Whybray's contention that the author of the Succession Narrative was himself a wisdom teacher does not appear to be sustainable, for "wisdom" and professional counseling is regularly put in a bad, or at least ambiguous, light; nevertheless, acquaintance with professional wisdom is there. J. L. Crenshaw, "Method in Determining Wisdom Influence upon 'Historical' Literature," *JBL* 88 (1969) 129-42, is critical of the presentations of both von Rad and Whybray, but von Rad's basic thesis does not appear to have been demolished.

[40]Authors in general argue for some factual basis for the stories of Solomon's relationship to wisdom. So Scott, *Proverbs, Ecclesiastes*, 12f.; Gemser, *Sprüche Salomos*, 2; McKane, *Proverbs*, 262; Alt, "Die Weisheit Salomos," 139-44.

[41]Skehan, "A Single Editor," pp. 117f. (*CBQMS* 1, 17f.). And, in general, authors discuss the characteristics which differentiate one collection from another, in terms of type of proverb, terminology, interests, religious character, etc.

There are six passages in the Prov collections in which *tôrâ* is used: 13:14; 28:4.7.9; 29:18; and 31:26; all but the last of these are found in the two "Solomonic" collections, four of them in the second "Solomonic" collection, considered by some the most primitive of the collections in Prov. Because *tôrâ* in these passages is sometimes taken to mean "law" by translators and commentators, it will be necessary to look at each of them to determine, where possible, the precise meaning.[42]

Proverbs 13:14

tôrat ḥākām m^eqôr ḥayyîm lasûr mimmōq^ešê māwet

The teaching of the wise is a fountain of life,
that a man may avoid the snares of death.

Neither text nor translation presents any difficulty. The wisdom meaning for *tôrâ* is imposed by its conjunction with *ḥākām*, and the reference to life and death set it firmly within a wisdom theme which can be traced back to Egyptian tradition.[43]

Proverbs 28:4

'ōz^ebê tôrâ y^ehal^elû rāšā' w^ešōm^erê tôrâ yitgārû bām[44]

Those who abandon *tôrâ* praise the wicked man,
but those who keep *tôrâ* war against him.

It is difficult to decide in this text whether *tôrâ* means "instruction" or "law." Perhaps the greatest obstacle to understanding the verse in a typical wisdom sense is the use of *grh* in a favorable sense; elsewhere in Prov (15:18; 28:25; 29:22) the root is used of the greedy or hot-tempered man. But this difficulty remains no matter what meaning is assigned to *tôrâ*, given the wisdom context. The use of *šmr*, frequent in the legal tradition, is equally at home in the wisdom tradition,[45] and the other terms suit a wisdom interpretation better than the legal. Though *'zb* can occur with legal terms,[46] it is

[42] In addition to the general remarks already directed against assuming a legal sense for *tôrâ* in Prov, see the detailed argument of Johannes Fichtner, *Die altorientalische Weisheit in ihrer israelitisch-jüdischen Ausprägung* (*BZAW* 62; Giessen: Verlag Alfred Töpelmann, 1933), 82f. See also Duesberg and Fransen, *Les scribes inspirés*, 280; von Rad, *Wisdom in Israel*, 87f., n. 21, says with reference to *tôrâ*: "The word which is to be translated by 'instruction' always means, in the book of Proverbs, and thus in the later passages, too . . ., 'wise teaching' and not the 'law'."

[43] See especially the two articles by Couroyer cited in n. 24.

[44] So MT. *NAB* rightly emends to *bô*.

[45] Prov 2:20 (*'or^eḥôt*); 4:4 (*miṣwôtay*).21 (*d^ebāray*—vs. 20); 7:1 (*'ămāray*).2 (*miṣwôtay*); 8:32 (*d^erākay*); 10:17 (*mûsār*); 13:18 (*tôkaḥat*); 15:5 (*tôkaḥat*); 19:8 (*t^ebûnâ*).16 (*miṣwâ*); 22:18 (see vs. 17); 29:18 (*tôrâ*).

[46] A total of nine times, scattered throughout the OT: 1 Kgs 18:18; 2 Kgs 17:16; Jer 9:12; Ps 89:31; 119:53.87; Ezra 9:10; 2 Chr 7:19; 12:1.

also used with wisdom terms, most especially within Prov, but also in the historical books;[47] its use within Prov would seem to deserve first place in explaining its sense here. Further, although *rāšā'* is widely distributed in the OT, it occurs but seldom in a legal context[48] and never in a way that would satisfactorily explain the present verse. On the other hand, it is employed most freely in Prov (about 77 times) to designate the "heavy," the person criticized or disapproved of, often functioning as a synonym for one of the terms used to designate "the fool." Thus "to praise the *rāšā'*" would indeed be folly, the sort of behavior to be expected from one who has forsaken the wise instruction delivered to him by his father-teacher, and directly contrary to the behavior of the one who adheres to his wise teaching.[49] It is perhaps along this line that the uncharacteristic use of *grh* is to be explained: the primary statement has to do with praising the *rāšā'*, while *grh* is brought in, somewhat secondarily, as an appropriate antithesis. With reason, therefore, many commentators take *tôrâ* in this verse to mean "wise instruction."[50]

Proverbs 28:7

nôṣēr tôrâ bēn mēbîn w^erō'eh zôl^elîm yaklîm 'ābîw
He who pays attention to instruction is a wise son,
but the gluttons' companion disgraces his father.

Here the wisdom background of the expression, especially that of the parallel second member, argues against translating *tôrâ* by "the law." Within the wisdom tradition one becomes a wise son by hearing, remembering, and observing the instruction of the father-teacher.[51]

The verb *nṣr* does occur with various legal terms (including *tôrâ)* as the object,[52] but it is also at home in wisdom diction. It is used of the care with which God or some form of wisdom or instruction guards the wise and faithful[53] and of the prudent guard to be kept over the heart or mouth,[54] but it is also used frequently of the father's instructions or admonitions to the son.[55]

[47] Prov 2:13, 4:2.6; 10:17; 15:10; see also 1 Kgs 12:8.13; 2 Chr 10:13.14; Prov 9:6.

[48] Ex 23:1.7; Num 35:31; Dt 25:1f.

[49] To condone the *rāšā'* is an abomination to the Lord (17:15); a wise king crushes the *rāšā'* (20:26); the wise man appraises the house of the *rāšā'* and knows it is set for ruin (21:12); the *rāšā'* is to be removed from the presence of the king (25:5).

[50] Crawford H. Toy, *A Critical and Exegetical Commentary on the Book of Proverbs* (New York: Charles Scribner's Sons, 1899), 496f.; Gemser, *Sprüche Salomos*, 98; Fichtner, *Die altorientalische Weisheit*, 85.

[51] See especially Prov 2:1-8; 4:1-4.10-13; 5:1f.; 19:27; 23:19f.; also 4:20-22; 6:20-24; 7:1-5; 23:15; 27:11.

[52] Ps 25:10; 78:7; 105:45; and frequently in Ps 119.

[53] Prov 2:8.11; 4:6; 5:2; 13:6; 20:28.

[54] Prov 4:23; 13:3.

[55] Prov 3:1.21; 4:13; 6:20; 23:26.

However, it is especially the second member that imposes a wisdom sense for ***nôṣēr tôrâ***: the antithesis to the son who pays attention to instruction is the consort of gluttons (*zôlᵉlîm*).[56] Israel's legislation does not impose the obligation of avoiding bad company, but this is a favorite wisdom theme.[57] The other Prov text in which *zôlēl* occurs, 23:20f., provides the best commentary on the present verse:[58]

Hear, my son, and be wise,
  and guide your heart in the right way.
Consort not with winebibbers,
  nor with those who eat meat to excess (*zōlălê bāśār lāmô*);
For the drunkard and the glutton (*zôlēl*) come to poverty,
  and torpor clothes a man in rags.

Proverbs 28:9

mēsîr 'oznô miššᵉma' tôrâ gam tᵉpillātô tô'ēbâ
When one turns his ear away from hearing *tôrâ*,
  even his prayer is an abomination.

The expression *šm' tôrâ* fits with the legal meaning of *tôrâ* when *šm'* has the transferred sense "to obey," but here the presence of *mēsîr 'oznô* strongly suggests the literal meaning "to hear."[59] And given the context of Prov, where there is repeated emphasis on the son's obligation to accept instruction,[60] the most likely interpretation is "to hear instruction." The fact that the consequence of failure to hear is that "even his prayer is an abomination" presents no difficulty; the positive refusal suggested in "turning the ear away" implies a stubborn disobedience that would displease God as well as men, especially when the instruction in question is the reproof which conduces to right living (13:1; 15:31.32; 23:19). The case is strengthened by other *tô'ēbâ* passages in Prov; the perverse man is an abomination to Yahweh (3:32) as are the

[56]The general sense of *zôlēl* appears to be "base, low, vile" (see Lam 1:11; Jer 15:19), though the contexts in Prov 23:20f. and Dt 21:20 suggest that it easily takes on the meaning "debauched through excess."

[57]Prov 1:10-19; 13:20; 23:20f.; 29:3; Instruction of Amen-em-Opet, Ch. 21 (*ANET*, 424); Sayings of Ahikar I and III, tr. A. E. Goodman in *Documents from Old Testament Times*, ed. D. W. Thomas (New York and Evanston: Harper & Row, Publishers, 1961 [c1958]), 271.

[58]See also Toy, *Proverbs*, 498; Gemser, *Sprüche Salomos*, 98; Scott, *Proverbs, Ecclesiastes*, 164; McKane, *Proverbs*, 623f. (the shift in meaning he suggests is doubtful but can be left out of consideration here; our concern is with the earliest meaning this verse would have had, not one it may have acquired through a later context).

[59]This conclusion would be further strengthened if one follows the Targum and Peshitta in reading *masgîr* for *mēsîr*.

[60]Prov 1:8; 4:1.10; 5:7.13; 7:24; 8:6.32.33; 12:15; 13:1; 15:31.32; 19:20.27; 22:17; 23:19.22.

depraved in heart (11:20) and lying lips (12:22). In 15:8 the sacrifice of the *rāšā'* is said to be an abomination to Yahweh and is contrasted with the prayer (*t^e^pillâ*) of the upright (cf. also 21:27). The way of the *rāšā'* is an abomination to Yahweh (15:9) as is every proud man (16:5). The dispositions condemned in such expressions are those which are constantly opposed in wisdom instruction and from which the hearer of right teaching will be safeguarded; they don't suggest the prescriptions of Israel's legislation.[61]

Proverbs 29:18

b^e^'ên ḥāzôn yippāra' 'ām w^e^šōmēr tôrâ 'ašrēhû

Without prophecy the people become demoralized;
but happy is he who keeps *tôrâ*.

It would be equally difficult to exclude or impose the legal sense of *tôrâ* in this obscure verse. Certain things are clear: there is reference to two types of guidance, to dire results when one (prophetic) is lacking, to the happy state of those who observe the other (*tôrâ*). Other points are less clear: are the two members abstract statements that are related only through similarity of subject matter, or is it said that although the first situation does (or may) exist, the disadvantage of it can be nullified (or mitigated) by the second? A related question is whether there is a contrast between *šōmēr* and *'am*, in that the individual can always preserve himself in spite of the fate of the people, or whether *šōmēr* is a collective and minimizes such contrast. The commentators, probably rightly, understand the first member to refer to a time when prophecy has ceased and take *šōmēr* in the second member as individual. Rather than favoring a legal interpretation, as McKane contends (p. 640), such a shift from nation to individual would seem to favor a wisdom meaning for *tôrâ*: far more than the law, wisdom instruction was delivered to the individual, and the keeping of it was far more removed from any sort of community sanctions than was that of the law.

The *'ašrê* formula which is pronounced over the *šōmēr tôrâ* might provide a clue. It is used of the keeper of the law in a few texts, namely, in Ps 1:1; 119:1.2.[62] But preference ought rather to be given to parallels within Prov and in other wisdom texts. In Prov 8:32, Wisdom says *w^e^'ašrê d^e^rākay yišmōrû*; this is a very good parallel to our text. In Prov 3:18 the man who finds wisdom is pronounced happy, and in Job 5:17, the one whom God reproves. In Ps 128:1 the *'ašrê* is pronounced on the one who fears Yahweh

[61] See also Scott, *Proverbs, Ecclesiastes*, 164; Gemser, *Sprüche Salomos*, 98f.; Toy, *Proverbs*, 499; Fichtner, *Die altorientalische Weisheit*, 84.

[62] There *may* be a connection with law in Ps 94:12; 112:1, but this is questionable.

and the further specification is *hahōlēk bidᵉrākāyw*; this is a Wisdom Psalm and the diction is that of the wisdom tradition. Finally, reference can be made to Ps 106:3. The *mišpāṭ* in this somewhat intrusive verse (*'ašrê šōmᵉrê mišpāṭ/'ōsēh ṣᵉdāqâ bᵉkol-'ēt*) probably is not legal, but more likely wisdom diction. The *ṣᵉdāqâ* of the second member is used frequently in Prov and other wisdom compositions; see especially Prov 21:3. In any case, the text (supposing the usual interpretation of the absence of vision to be correct) is probably late and does not bear direct witness to early usage.[63]

Proverbs 31:26

pîhā pātᵉḥâ bᵉḥokmâ wᵉtôrat ḥesed 'al lᵉšônāh

She opens her mouth in wisdom,
and on her tongue is kindly counsel.

The meaning of *tôrâ* in this text is not in doubt. The mother, too, imparted wise instruction to her children (1:8; 6:20; 31:1); no doubt its gentler quality merits here the phrase *tôrat-ḥesed*. It is likely that this acrostic poem is a late composition, though the usage accords with that attested throughout Prov.

Thus it is possible to defend the wisdom sense for *tôrâ* in every occurrence in the Prov collections. There is every reason to believe that the usage is an early one.

tôrâ in Proverbs 1-9

There can be no doubt that Israel's wisdom tradition was influenced by other streams of piety, and there can be no reason to reject *a priori* the possibility, even likelihood, that influences from other traditions and even late piety will be found in Prov 1-9. But it would seem to be a good methodological rule *not* to postulate such influence when the word, procedure, concept, etc., under consideration is fully at home in the wisdom tradition; conversely, such influence should be admitted only when reason can be given for saying that it comes from outside, not within, the wisdom tradition.[64]

An earlier section of this chapter discussed the wisdom "instruction" in the ancient Near East in order to relate the contents of Prov in general to the broader wisdom stream; here it will be useful to return to that genre, for it is very prominent in Prov 1-9, and it is precisely within such context that the remaining occurrences of *tôrâ* are found. A number of recent books on Prov

[63] See also Toy, *Proverbs*, 512; Gemser, *Sprüche Salomos*, 101; Fichtner, *Die altorientalische Weisheit*, 84f.

[64] Considerations of this sort were largely neglected in the influential article of A. Robert, "Les attaches littéraires bibliques de Prov. I-IX," *RB* 43 (1934) 42-68, 172-204, 374-84; 44 (1935) 344-65, 502-525.

have stressed its connection with the Egyptian "instructions." In 1966 Kayatz[65] argued strongly for an early date for many of the procedures in Prov 1-9 on the basis of similarity with Egyptian literature. She argues against those who have postulated a development from one-line proverbs to longer compositions; longer compositions are found in Egypt at an early date and are not developed from one-line proverbs, but are a different literary form. By form-critical analysis she lists certain procedures in the Egyptian instructions—combinations of conditional clauses, imperatives, and motive clauses —and finds the same procedures in Prov 1-9: "Die überwiegende Mehrzahl der in Proverbien 1-9 vorkommenden Formtypen hat ihr Vorbild in den ägyptischen Weisheitslehren" (p. 135).

A work by Whybray, published in 1965 (see n. 30, above), also stresses the connection between Egyptian wisdom and Prov 1-9. As others have done, Whybray distinguishes two types of passages in Prov 1-9: those in which a wisdom teacher addresses his pupils and those in which a personified wisdom speaks (p. 31). The passages in which the teacher speaks consist of the preface and ten originally independent discourses. The original form can be seen most clearly in 1:8f., while three other examples of it (3:1-4; 4:20-22; 5:1f.) have been preserved virtually in their original form; the other six, recovered by removing interpolations and additions, are listed as: 2:1.9; 3:21-24; 4:1f.; 4:10-12; 6:20-22; and 7:1-3 (pp. 33f.). The original ten discourses he compares with the Egyptian instructions and finds a greater similarity here than to anything in the OT; his conclusion on this point is that "there can be no doubt that the discourses in Proverbs 1-9 stand firmly in the tradition of international wisdom and are not derived from, though they may have been to some extent influenced by, the Yahwistic tradition" (p. 37). One can object that Whybray's separation of primary and secondary material is not supported by solid arguments, but he is correct in asserting that the discourses reflect ancient Egyptian models and that the usage is old in Israel.

The recent commentary on Prov by McKane (see n. 33, above) gives much attention to ancient Near Eastern instructions and arrives at conclusions that are in substantial agreement with those of Kayatz, though his investigation was completed independently of hers. He makes a firm distinction between "instruction" and "sentence literature." The latter is composed of the sort of statements found in the proverb collections, which are usually indicative, third person, and often relate the effects of good or bad acts in a detached sort of way; the individual statement can be said, in general, to "have no context." The "instruction," on the other hand, is a longer development and

[65]Christa Kayatz, *Studien zu Proverbien 1-9: eine form- und motivgeschichtliche Untersuchung unter Einbeziehung ägyptischen Vergleichsmaterials* (*WMANT* 22; Neukirchen-Vluyn: Neukirchener Verlag, 1966).

is characterized by direct address, fervent exhortation, use of the imperative, and concern for motivation. These characteristics are found both in the other Near Eastern "instructions" and in Prov 1-9 (and in 22:17-24:22 and 31:1-9). He points out that the attempt to date Prov 1-9 could only show when it first existed as a literary unit, but would not touch the tradition-historical questions about form and contents. He suggests that the "instruction" form was appropriated by Israel as early as the time of Solomon and that a traditio-historical account of the genre should begin there (pp. 8f.).

This long discussion of the "instruction" genre is not introduced to argue that our present Prov 1-9 is ancient, but rather that it represents an ancient genre, whose procedures (e.g., "my son" type of address, imperative, exhortation, motivation—even specific motivations) are found in Prov much as they are in the earlier pieces. One may assume the same for much of its vocabulary. The regularity with which wisdom terminology and themes cut across the various parts of Prov is striking; cf. notes 45, 47, 51, 53, 54, 55, 57, and 60. If *tôrâ* is found in Prov in the sense of "wise instruction" both in the "collections" and in the "instructions" of 1-9, as in fact it is, there is every reason to affirm that this usage is ancient and constant rather than a late development.

The term *tôrâ* occurs in the "instructions" of Prov 1-9 in six places: 1:8; 3:1; 4:2; 6:20.23; and 7:2. Nothing in any of these passages suggests the meaning or even the influence of the concept of "the law of Yahweh (or of Moses)." On the contrary, in each case it is identified as the instruction of the parent-teacher,[66] parallel to other terms for parental or scholastic instruction or discipline; this is especially clear where the parallel term is *mûsār* (1:8) or *leqaḥ*[67] (4:2). The fact that *tôrâ* can stand parallel to *mûsār* is significant, especially if *mûsār* is to be considered the Hebrew equivalent of *sebayit*, as many believe. Parallelism in the opening lines of an "instruction" is found in ancient Mesopotamian examples and in Amen-em-Opet, and the OT materials give every reason to believe it was characteristic in Israel from early times; *mûsār* was probably one of the terms used from the beginning, and there is nothing to suggest that *tôrâ* here is a late substitute for some other term.

[66] 1:8 and 6:20, *tôrat 'immekā*; 3:1; 4:2; and 7:2, *tôrātî*; in 6:23 *tôrâ* is used absolutely, but here it is resuming the *tôrat 'immekā* of 6:20. These indications alone should be sufficient to refute the assertion of Derousseaux, *Crainte de Dieu*, 327, that the use of *tôrâ* and *miṣwâ* in 3:1 is an explicit allusion to Dt.

[67] *leqaḥ* is found only in wisdom or otherwise didactic contexts: Dt 32:2; Is 29:24; Job 11:4; Prov 1:5; 4:2; 7:21; 9:9; 16:21.23. *tôrâ* is parallel to *miṣwôt* in 3:1; 6:20.23; and 7:2, but it has already been argued that the use of *miṣwôt* in Prov reflects wisdom, not legal, usage; see Fichtner, *Die altorientalische Weisheit*, 82f.

It is also worth noting that the themes appearing in the "instruction" passages of Prov 1-9 are often those which are constants within the wisdom tradition. Thus, taking 1:8-19 as a unity,[68] we have basically a standard-type address to the son (vss. 8-9) for a beginning, then a developed exhortation to avoid evil companions (vss. 10-18), and a summary-appraisal (vs. 19) for a conclusion. The central section is introduced by a conditional formulation (*'im*—vss. 10-14), reaches its climax with an imperative statement (vs. 15), and is followed[69] by asyndetic motivations; these formal elements are characteristic of the Egyptian "instructions," as the analyses of Kayatz and McKane show. In this passage there is no personification of wisdom, no abstract reflection on its value, but only an argument to urge that "wise instruction" in one particular area be received and put into practice. Even the reference to the "diadem" and "torque" (vs. 9) does not allude to the binding of the law to the person, but is simply a symbolic way of describing the great value of the *mûsār-tôrâ* that one can acquire as his own adornment; this, too, goes back to ancient Egyptian prototypes.[70] The same may be said of other themes that appear in these passages, especially that of life (3:2; 7:2), [71] which occurs elsewhere in Prov[72] and in the broad stream of international wisdom.[73]

Therefore, while there is much in Prov 1-9 that represents the development of later thought, the author has clearly utilized ancient wisdom themes, literary forms and procedures, and terminology. The sense of *tôrâ* here is "wise instruction," precisely that sense which can be defended for every occurrence of the term in Prov 10-31. The point in the wisdom tradition at which there is a significant change in the meaning of *tôrâ* is when ben Sira identifies wisdom with the Law of Moses (Sir 24:22; see also Bar 4:1).[74]

[68]P. W. Skehan, "The Seven Columns of Wisdom's House in Proverbs 1-9," *CBQ* 9 (1947) 195 (*CBQMS* 1, 12).

[69]Prov 1:16 is a gloss from Is 59:7; see Skehan, *ibid.*

[70]Kayatz, *Studien zu Proverbien 1-9*, 108-112. The reference to binding on the fingers in 7:3, on the other hand is much closer to passages like Dt 6:8; 11:18; and Ex 13:16 and may possibly reflect their influence.

[71]The words "that you may live" in 4:4 are a gloss from 7:2; see Skehan, "Seven Columns," 193f. (*CBQMS* 1, 11).

[72]Prov 3:16; 9:11; 10:11.27; 11:30; 15:4; 28:16.

[73]McKane, *Proverbs*, on 3:2; Gemser, *Sprüche Salomos*, on 3:2; Kayatz, *Studien zu Proverbien 1-9*, 102-107. See the two articles by Couroyer cited in n. 24.

[74]See the remarks of Fichtner, *Die altorientalische Weisheit*, 81, on this development.

3

YAHWEH AND WISDOM IN ISAIAH

The real test of what Isaiah meant by *tôrâ* can come only with the investigation of the pertinent texts themselves. Before approaching that task, however, it will be useful to bring forward evidence to show that Isaiah's conception of Yahweh and the particular circumstances in which he set forth his teaching already suggest that he viewed Him as one who imparts "wise instruction." To this end we will review some of the evidence of wisdom influence in the career and teachings of Isaiah, then speak more explicitly of Isaiah's conflict with wisdom circles, and finally relate this to his presentation of Yahweh.

Wisdom Influence in Isaiah

The truly seminal study on the matter of wisdom influence in the career and teaching of Isaiah was that of Fichtner in 1949.[1] Fichtner found in Isaiah "ein ganz eigenartiges Verhältnis zur Weisheit." On the one hand, Isaiah turned sharply against that human wisdom which overvalued itself and went the way of its own political choices without (and therefore against) God. But on the other hand, Isaiah himself stood to some extent in the wisdom tradition and "weist mancherlei Beziehungen (veilleicht sogar literarische Abhängigkeit!) zur Weisheitsliteratur und zu ihren Gattungen auf und gestaltet auch sein Zukunftsbild chokmatisch" (col. 77). Fichtner points to Isaiah's love for *Gleichnisreden* (5:1ff.; 28:23ff.) and wordplays and to his use of a host of wisdom terms (*ḥākām*, *byn*, *y'ṣ*, *yd'*, *da'at*, *tûšîyâ*, etc.) and coining of proverbs; many of Isaiah's sayings he relates directly to passages in Prov. Attempting to explain this love-hate relationship to the wisdom tradition, Fichtner postulates that Isaiah himself had been a sage before his prophetic vocation; after his call, he finds himself the bearer of a message that men in their (human) wisdom will not grasp (6:9ff.).

While the "converted sage" hypothesis has generally been received rather coolly,[2] the broader assertion of wisdom influence in Isaiah can be said to be firmly established.[3] The more recent commentaries on Isaiah give ample at-

[1]Johannes Fichtner, "Jesaja unter den Weisen," *TLZ* 74 (1949) 75-80.

[2]The reserve has not been universal. See Robert Martin-Achard, "Sagesse de Dieu et sagesse humaine chez Ésaie," *maqqēl shâqēdh, La branche d'amandier: Hommage à Wilhelm Vischer* (Montpellier: Causse, Graille, Castelnau, 1960), 137-144. R. T. Anderson, "Was Isaiah a Scribe?" *JBL* 79 (1960) 57f. See L. Rost's revision of Ernst Sellin, *Einleitung in das Alte Testament* (9th ed.; Heidelberg: Quelle & Meyer, 1959), 100. The 10th edition (revision by G. Fohrer, 1965), p. 398, is more cautious.

[3]See Johannes Lindblom, "Wisdom in the Old Testament Prophets," *VTSup* 3 (1955) 192-204; R. B. Y. Scott, "Solomon and the Beginnings of Wisdom in Israel," *ibid.*, 262-79.

tention to wisdom influence on the prophet,[4] and some studies make it a major concern,[5] while others give it considerable or at least passing attention.[6] This approach to Isaiah has spilled over into the study of other prophets, most especially that of Amos.[7]

Recently a full-scale study of the relationship of Isaiah to the wisdom tradition has been done by J. William Whedbee.[8] This is a competent, systematic, and thorough work, one which reveals the author's familiarity with the pertinent literature and with form critical techniques. In his first chapter, Whedbee takes up the matter of criteria for determining "whether or not the language in question is wisdom in origin"; he considers that "the strongest line of argument is when one can show that a given prophetic speech has clear-cut parallels in distinctively wisdom texts." In the two following chapters, Whedbee discusses specific literary forms: parables, proverbs, and related didactic *Gattungen*,[9] and woe oracles.[10] While exception may be

[4]See, in particular, the commentaries of Otto Kaiser, *Isaiah 1-12*, tr. R. A. Wilson (Philadelphia: The Westminster Press, 1972—from 2d ed. of *ATD* 17, 1963); Georg Fohrer, *Das Buch Jesaja*, 2 vols. (*Zürcher Bibelkommentare*; Zurich: Zwingli Verlag, 1960); Hans Wildberger, *Jesaja*.

[5]For example, Ilse von Loewenclau, "Zur Auslegung von Jesaja 1, 2-3," *EvT* 26 (1966) 294-308; Oliver Blanchette, "The Wisdom of God in Isaia," *AER* 145 (1961) 413-23.

[6]Schmid, *Wesen und Geschichte der Weisheit*, 199; Joachim Becker, *Gottesfurcht im Alten Testament* (Rome: Pontifical Biblical Institute, 1965), *passim*; Cazelles, "Les débuts de la sagesse en Israël," 32; Scott, "Priesthood, Prophecy, Wisdom, and the Knowledge of God," 4; Heaton, *The Hebrew Kingdoms, passim*; McKane, *Prophets and Wise Men, passim*; Whybray, *Wisdom in Proverbs*, 22f.; Richter, *Recht und Ethos*, 166; Childs, *Isaiah and the Assyrian Crisis*, 128-36.

[7]See Samuel Terrien, "Amos and Wisdom," *Israel's Prophetic Heritage. Essays in Honor of James Muilenburg*, ed. B. W. Anderson and W. Harrelson (New York: Harper & Row, Publishers, 1962), 108-115, and especially Hans Walter Wolff, *Amos' geistige Heimat* (Neukirchen-Vluyn: Neukirchener Verlag, 1964). Wolff refutes the contention of R. Fey, *Amos und Jesaja* (*WMANT* 12; Neukirchen-Vluyn: Neukirchener Verlag, 1963), that many of Isaiah's sayings depend directly on Amos, by showing that the resemblances are to be traced, rather, to common dependence on the wisdom tradition. Not all of Wolff's conclusions have gone unchallenged; see James L. Crenshaw, "The Influence of the Wise upon Amos: The 'Doxologies of Amos' and Job 5:9-16; 9:5-10," *ZAW* 79 (1967) 42-51, which includes a critique also of the methodology of Fichtner and of others.

[8]J. William Whedbee, *Isaiah and Wisdom* (Nashville: Abingdon Press, 1971). This is a slightly revised form of his Yale Ph.D. dissertation of 1968.

[9]The passages treated under "parables" are 1:2-3; 5:1-7; and 28:23-29. Under "proverbial speech" come 10:15 and 29:15f. The third class of sayings treated in his Ch. 2 is the "summary-appraisal form," following Childs, *Isaiah and the Assyrian Crisis*, 128-36. He repeats the examples of summary-appraisals in wisdom texts given by Childs, though in fact two of them (Ps 49:14; Job 27:13) are not conclusions of sections (I owe this suggestion to Patrick Skehan), and adds two others (Sir 16:23; 39:27—the second of these, again, does not appear to conclude a section). See further my review in *CBQ* 34 (1972) on p. 128.

[10]Following E. Gerstenberger, "The Woe-Oracles of the Prophets," *JBL* 81 (1962) 249-63, Whedbee argues that the "woe" is basically a wisdom form, though it is to be noted that only certain woe-passages in Isaiah are thought significant enough for detailed study in this chapter (5:8-10.11-13.20.21.22f.; 10:1f.), and this is mainly in terms of their *content*. It will be necessary to return to the thorny question of the woe-form in our next chapter.

taken to some of the details of his treatment, it is a most useful discussion and places earlier conclusions concerning wisdom influence in Isaiah on a firmer basis; it would certainly be superfluous to undertake a similar study here.

In his Ch. 4, "Counsel/Counsellor and Jerusalem Court Wisdom," Whedbee is concerned especially with the reason for and the significance of Isaiah's employment of wisdom forms and vocabulary. He takes issue with the strongly contrasted, even contradictory, roles of the sage and of the prophet in McKane's presentation in *Prophets and Wise Men*; McKane insisted too much on the secular nature of wisdom, not recognizing the extent to which the wisdom tradition acknowledged the supreme power of God over human affairs.[11] Whedbee complains that McKane doesn't advert to the fact that the wise man dealt with the concept of the order in this world, something which was, in fact, crucial to the wisdom approach to reality; the wise man worked from experience, but he also sought through his experience to find an underlying order. At the same time, he realized that the world order was not at his disposal, but only at God's; thus the wise man always reckoned with God as a limiting factor. Whedbee insists, on the basis of the Joseph Story and the Succession Narrative, that these ideas were current precisely in the circles of royal wisdom in Jerusalem. From the references to God's control of events in these texts (Gen 50:20; 2 Sam 17:14) and from texts like Prov 19:21, he argues that "the wise men in the Jerusalem court possessed in their *own* traditions the recognition of a divine counsel which took priority over any human plans or counsels" (p. 124). Von Rad had said that Isaiah's references to Yahweh's *'ēṣâ* had been the prophet's own innovation, the taking over of a secular term for his own purposes; but Whedbee argues that it was a datum of the wisdom tradition which Isaiah "reactualized," using it now to condemn the wise for forgetting the limits of their own wisdom.

Much of this is quite acceptable: the wisdom tradition certainly did recognize that God's will is a limiting factor on man's activity and that no human

[11] This criticism is quite valid. McKane, *Prophets and Wise Men*, 48-50, took issue with von Rad's view (as set forth in "The Joseph Narrative and Ancient Wisdom") that "fear of the Lord" and the "man proposes but God disposes" theme (as, e.g., in Prov 16:9; 19:21; 20:24; 21:30f.) were part of ancient wisdom; passages like those just listed McKane takes to be rejoinders to the claims of old wisdom rather than an original ingredient. But no solid proof is offered for these assertions, and they are contradicted by non-israelite sources in which there is no dating problem. The "God disposes" theme is common in ancient Egyptian texts: see Volten, "Der Begriff der Maat in der Ägyptischen Weisheitstexten," 76, 85; Schmid, *Wesen und Geschichte der Weisheit*, 24, 59; Hellmut Brunner, "Der freie Wille Gottes in der ägyptischen Weisheit," *Les Sagesses du Proche-Orient ancien*, 107f.; Joseph Vergote, "La notion de Dieu dans les livres de sagesse égyptiennes," *ibid.*, 178. Since these authors take illustrations from Ptah-hotep, Amen-em-Opet, and Papyrus Insinger, it is clear that the conception was ancient and persistent. On "fear of the Lord," see R. H. Pfeiffer, "The Fear of God," *IEJ* 5 (1955) 42; H. A. Brongers, "La crainte du Seigneur (*Jir'at YHWH, Jir'at 'Elohim*)," *OTS* 5 (1948) 171-73; Derousseaux, *Crainte de Dieu*, 21-66.

'ēṣâ can prevail against that of God. Yet Whedbee seems to utilize, in an unacceptable way, the ambiguity inherent in *'ēṣâ* and its English equivalents.[12] It is one thing to affirm with Prov 19:21 that it is the *'ēṣâ* of Yahweh, not the *măḥašābôt* of men, that will be established, and to see this illustrated in the Joseph Story and the Succession Narrative;[13] it is quite another to affirm, on the basis of this, as Whedbee does, that the wisdom tradition recognized that Yahweh has a plan in history. Thus, for Whedbee, when Isaiah uses *'ēṣâ* to speak of a purpose of Yahweh that will be worked out in history, he is simply affirming a datum of the wisdom tradition, something the wise men already knew and accepted; furthermore, it was something they should always have been taking into account as a limiting factor in their own plans. In fact they did not, and this constituted the crisis of the wisdom movement in Isaiah's day (pp. 130f.). Here, it seems to me, Whedbee obscures the fact that Isaiah gives a much more specific content to Yahweh's *'ēṣâ* than do Prov or other wisdom compositions.[14]

Whedbee never suggests, as far as I can discover, that there is any dispute over what Yahweh's plan entails; the conflict consisted in the wise opposing their own plan to Yahweh's and forgetting that no plan can avail against Yahweh's.[15] Against this it must be stated again that the sources, properly weighed, do not suggest that the wisdom tradition knew of a plan of Yahweh in history, much less that it could identify the content of it in such a way as to oppose human counsel to it; only the prophet who claims knowledge of God's future act could speak in such terms.

Whedbee's estimate of the point of conflict between Isaiah and the wise men also leads him to assert that another disagreement lay in the question of whether or not Yahweh was wise and acted with wisdom; in this debate Isaiah took the affirmative, the sages the negative. Thus he asserts "that Yahweh's wisdom was a point of contention in Isaiah's confrontation with

[12]The use of "counsel" in the quotation from p. 124 given in the preceding paragraph is unexceptionable except that its meaning seems to blend with that of "plan" in the subsequent discussion—a meaning he had earlier (p. 115n.) found to have drawbacks.

[13]It is not at all clear that one ought to assert that the Succession Narrative represents "the theological understanding of the *royal* wise men," as Whedbee does (p. 125). The author of the Succession Narrative certainly takes an interest in courtly wisdom, but it seems to be for the purpose of waging a subtle polemic against it. The "wisdom duel" between Hushai and Ahitophel, in particular, is replete with bitter irony.

[14]Although Whedbee does occasionally advert to this difference in content (e.g., p. 138), it does not seem to influence his argumentation; he supposes that the wise men knew the content of Yahweh's *'ēṣâ*: "They had disregarded the divine limits and attempted to go on alone with no consideration of Yahweh's purpose" (p. 142). This is quite a different matter from the realization that Yahweh's (hidden!) purpose might overturn the deliberations of men acting according to their lights.

[15]See, e.g., pp. 142, 144, 148, 151.

the people is attested by his oracles."[16] In defending the authenticity of 31:2 he says: "But Yahweh's wisdom and power were not assumed as a matter of course in Isaiah's situation; rather they were held in doubt in the ruling circles of the Jerusalem court, especially by the royal wise men" (p. 134). I find this assessment of the situation frankly incredible. One aspect of the peculiar genius of Israel's religious tradition was its ability to absorb the valid elements of the religions of her neighbors and to reject—either directly or through gradual purification—their distortions of the divine image. That Yahweh's claim to be wise should have been considered and then rejected—in wisdom circles, of all places— would have been an utter reversal of this process. That God is preeminently wise and the source of wisdom was widely held in the ancient Near East,[17] and Israel would have yielded to none on this point, once the consideration had been raised. Their near neighbors at Ugarit claimed as much for El.[18] Israel may have been somewhat slow to make the claim explicitly,[19] though this is not conceded by all,[20] but this is a matter quite different from doubting or contesting Yahweh's wisdom.

So that this part of the discussion will not consist merely of a review of literature on the subject, brief reference will be made to the two passages in Isaiah that have attracted the greatest attention for their points of contact with the wisdom tradition: 1:2f. and 28:23-29. The first of these, 1:2f., is a complaint of Yahweh, presented as a father grieving over the behavior of his rebellious children. This text was first given a thorough and competent treatment for its wisdom form and content by Loewenclau.[21] The opening call

[16]P. 62. The oracles he discusses at this point (5:19.21; 7:5.7; 14:24-27; 28:29b; 29:14f.; 30:1; 31:2) do not sustain the assertion.

[17]For examples, see the following note and the last section of this chapter.

[18]The following passages from Ugaritic texts are relevant: Keret II, iv, 2f.: ". . . he who sees thee does perceive (that) thou art wise as El, as the bull Lutpan"; Baal II, iv, 41f.: "Thy bidding, El, is wise, thy wisdom everlasting; a life of good luck (is) thy bidding!"; the passage is found again in Baal V, v, 30f.; Baal II, v, 3f.: "Thou art great, El; surely the hoar hairs of thy beard are united to wisdom . . ." Translation by G. R. Driver, *Canaanite Myths and Legends* (Edinburgh: T. & T. Clark, 1956), 43, 91, 97.

[19]Martin Noth, "Die Bewährung von Salomos 'Göttlicher Weisheit'," *VTSup* 3 (1955) 232f., suggests the term "wise" was not readily applied to Yahweh because "mit ihm [das Prädikat "weise"] allzu sehr der Gedanke an menschliche Klugheit verbunden war"; G. von Rad, *Old Testament Theology*, I, 442n.; R. E. Murphy, "Assumptions and Problems in Old Testament Wisdom Research," *CBQ* 29 (1967) 411.

[20]Paul van Imschoot, "Sagesse et esprit dans l'Ancien Testament," *RB* 47 (1938) 29; Th. C. Vriezen, "Ruach Yahweh (Elohim) in the Old Testament," *Biblical Essays 1966. Proceedings of the Ninth Meeting of "Die Ou-Testamentiese Werkgemeenskap in Suid-Afrika"* (Potchefstroom: Pro Rege-Pers Besperk, 1967), 56.

[21]Loewenclau, "Zur Auslegung von Jesaja 1, 2-3," 294-308. See also Whedbee, *Isaiah and Wisdom*, 26-43; Heaton, *The Hebrew Kingdoms*, 323; Wildberger, *Jesaja*, 12-14, sees the "sonship" referred to here as that which is at home in the sphere of education and wisdom, with the lack of insight and understanding of which Isaiah accuses the people pointing in the same direction: "Damit können wir präzisieren Jahwe als Vater ist hier der wohlmeinende, guten Rat erteilende, Weisheit zur Bewältigung des Lebens vermittelnde, alle Gefahren abwehrende Erzieher."

to attention (*šim'û . . . w^eha'ăzînî*) should not be considered a *Lehreröffnungsformel*, however, as Loewenclau thinks, for the address is to the heavens and the earth, which cannot be considered apt subjects for instruction. Rather, by analogy with other texts, for the form is not fully developed here, they are probably called upon as witnesses, as in the *rîb*-pattern. The piece is not developed in that pattern, however, and Fohrer is precise in remarking, "Das Wort ist dem Beginn einer Gerichtsverhandlung nachgebildet";[22] though some authors do classify it as a *rîb* (e.g., Wildberger), Loewenclau seems more correct in calling it a "complaint" (*Klage*). Whedbee calls it an accusation, but in doing so supposes a legal basis for it in Dt 21:18-21 (p. 29). In fact, there is nothing concrete to tie the two texts together; one could as well, perhaps even better, think of the theme of obedience and respect for parents that is so widely spread in the wisdom tradition, both in Israel and elsewhere.[23]

In vs. 3 Isaiah employs an animal proverb, probably of his own fashioning, to illustrate the stupidity and stubbornness of Israel. This sort of comparison of one realm of activity with another for purposes of instruction is, of course, a characteristic of the wisdom tradition. Animal proverbs were frequently used,[24] with the ox sometimes an example of stupidity (Prov 7:22), the ass of stubbornness;[25] Israel, Isaiah implies, is even worse, for here these animals are said to have a perception and docility that is lacking in God's children. The verbs used in this verse to designate Israel's lack of perception, *lō' yāda' . . . lō' hitbônān*, also have strong wisdom overtones; the latter form especially (the hithpolel of *byn*) is found most frequently in wisdom contexts. Both of the verbs are used absolutely, and no object is to be supplied from the context: Israel does not know, has not understood.

The other passage worthy of special note is the "Parable of the Farmer," Isa 28:23-29, a composition whose authenticity is virtually unchallenged and whose wisdom traits are acknowledged by all.[26] It opens with the invitation to

[22]G. Fohrer, *Das Buch Jesaja*, I, 31.

[23]See Ch. 2, n. 51; see also Prov 19:26; 23:22.26; Richter, *Recht und Ethos*, 171; O. Eissfeldt, "Sohnespflichten im alten Orient," *Syria* 43 (1966) 39-47.

[24]Prov 6:6-8; 7:22; 14:4; 26:3.11.17; 27:8; 28:1; 30:18f.24-31.

[25]Prov 26:3. Edmund I. Gordon, "Sumerian Animal Proverbs and Fables: 'Collection Five'," *JCS* 12 (1958), pp. 11 and 44. See also Schmid, *Wesen und Geschichte der Weisheit*, 75.

[26]Cazelles, "Les débuts de la sagesse en Israël," 32, refers to the piece as a wisdom composition whose ancestor is the agricultural advice of the god Ninurta transmitted through a farmer to his son (see above, Ch. 2, n. 17); Johannes Fichtner, "Jahves Plan in der Botschaft des Jesaja," *ZAW* 63 (1951) 33n.; *idem*, "Jesaja unter den Weisen," 75; Lindblom, "Wisdom in the Old Testament Prophets," 198; McKane, *Prophets and Wise Men*, 80f.; Scott, "Solomon and the Beginnings of Wisdom," 278; Fohrer, *Jesaja*, II, 64; Wildberger, *Jesaja*, 188f.; Whedbee, *Isaiah and Wisdom*, 51-68, 143f.

give ear and listen (*ha'ăzînû w^{e}šim'û*) so often found in wisdom compositions,[27] employs the rhetorical question, traces the farmer's wisdom back to the instruction received from "his God," and draws from the observable order a lesson to be applied in another area. Above all, it employs the wisdom word *tûšîyâ*[28] and praises the *'ēṣâ* of Yahweh. Fohrer's judgment is apposite: "Das Wort klingt nicht wie ein Prophetenspruch, sondern wie ein Weisheitsgedicht" (see n. 26). The piece is, nevertheless, profoundly prophetic in its teaching (as is also 1:2f.) and operates in a sphere largely foreign to the wisdom tradition—Yahweh's activity in history. Although the precise meaning is disputed, it seems to say that there can be a wise and consistent purpose behind a series of diverse and apparently inconsistent acts of God; this is illustrated from the example of the farmer's manner of dealing with his various crops, the reasonableness of which was apparent and whose wisdom in so behaving was believed to have originated in God.

Why did Isaiah choose this manner of speech? In all likelihood it was because he was addressing primarily a group for which such diction would be particularly relevant. These would be "the wise," against whom Isaiah carried on a particular polemic. It is to this matter that we must now turn our attention.

Isaiah's Polemic Against "The Wise"

An indication of the negative side of Isaiah's attitude towards the wisdom circles of his day is seen in his use of some basic terms. In two of his uses of *ḥokmâ* (10:13; 29:14) the contexts give the term an unfavorable nuance; in the third (11:2) it has a good sense but looks to a future time when true wisdom will be present as God's gift. Two of Isaiah's uses of *ḥākām* have an unfavorable sense,[29] while the third (3:3) is difficult to evaluate.[30] As for the

[27]See Ps 49:2; Prov 5:1; 22:17; etc.; this type of formula will be discussed in more detail in Ch. 4, on Isa 1:10.

[28]The term *tûšîyâ* occurs twelve times in MT: six times in Job, four times in Prov, in the present text, and in Mic 6:9, where it is rightly considered a wisdom gloss.

[29]These are 5:21 and 29:14. The term occurs also in 19:11 (*bis*) .12, but the passage is generally taken to be late; see, e.g., Georg Fohrer, "Entstehung, Komposition und Überlieferung von Jesaja 1-39," *Studien zur alttestamentlichen Prophetie [1949-1965]* (*BZAW* 99; Berlin: Verlag Alfred Töpelmann, 1967), 132. (This article is reprinted from the *Annual of Leeds University Oriental Society* 3 [1961/62] 3-38.) On 31:2, see text and the following notes.

[30]As the MT stands, *ḥākām* is construct with *ḥărāšîm* in 3:3 and would mean something like "skilled magician" (*NAB*), a good parallel to the *n^{e}bôn lāḥaš* that follows. The problem is complicated, however, for these two terms do not fit well with the preceding *yô'ēṣ* and the three together break the pattern of pairs otherwise found in this passage (vss. 1-3), in which, moreover, the descriptions generally are susceptible of a favorable interpretation and the lot designated as "support and prop" of Judah and Jerusalem. Little is gained by deleting *ḥărāšîm*, as Fichtner does ("Jesaja unter den Weisen," 77), on the belief that Isaiah foretold the deportation of the wise men, unless the parallel *ûn^{e}bôn lāḥaš* is also deleted; but there appears to be no justification in the textual tradition for either change.

verse in which Yahweh is said to be *ḥākām* (31:2), Childs' arguments against its authenticity appear to be conclusive.[31] Whedbee leans heavily on this verse to prove that Isaiah was compelled to defend Yahweh's wisdom, but his arguments in defense of its authenticity do not adequately counter those of Childs and are to some extent based on the theory he is attempting to prove.[32]

If we ask who were the *ḥăkāmîm*, the practitioners of *ḥokmâ*, against whom Isaiah polemicizes, the answer will involve some uncertainties. The group surely includes the circle of royal advisers (princes, nobles, and professional counselors), but may be more extensive. If we accept the opinion of those who hold for a wisdom school in Jerusalem in which sons of the upper, ruling, class would have been trained, the term might well have been applied to a whole host of other officials, including, e.g., those who in fact exercised the office of judge.[33] The latter alternative has much to commend it and might help explain some of Isaiah's polemic, especially as contained in the "woes" he pronounces in Ch. 5 and in 10:1-4. The prophet's complaints against "the wise" were not necessarily restricted to matters of foreign policy.

It would be rather misleading to speak of Isaiah having a "foreign policy"; he was a prophet whose vocation was to proclaim the word of Yahweh. However, this "word" did have implications for Judah's foreign policy, frequently came into conflict with the plans hatched out in the ruling circles, and implied (and ultimately sprang from) a purpose or policy on the part of Yahweh. It seems clear that Isaiah opposed the decision of Ahaz to turn to Assyria for help at the time of the Syro-Ephraimitic invasion (7:1-9.10-20; 8:1-4.5-8), warned against joining the Philistines in revolt in 711 (20:1-6), and

[31]Childs, *Isaiah and the Assyrian Crisis*, 34f. Herbert Donner, *Israel unter den Völkern. Die Stellung der klassischen Propheten des 8. Jahrhunderts v. Chr. zur Aussenpolitik der Könige von Israel und Juda* (*VTSup* 11; Leiden: E. J. Brill, 1964), 135, had already taken the verse as a secondary interpretation because of the change in subject and because the meter fluctuates ("schwankt"). M. Noth, "Die Bewährung von Salomos," 232f., accepts the passage as authentic but sees it intended in an ironical sense that would demand the translation "klug" or even "schlau" rather than "weise" for *ḥākām*.

[32]Whedbee, *Isaiah and Wisdom*, 133-35.

[33]See references in Ch. 2, n. 35. See especially Richter, *Recht und Ethos*, 122f.: discussing the *Richtersspiegel* in Ex 23, he says that the address is not primarily to those of the judicial profession, but holds, rather, that the judicial function is one of the tasks of those addressed—obviously the upper, ruling, class; see also pp. 186, 188. On the elders and princes as counselors, see C. U. Wolf, "Traces of Primitive Democracy in Ancient Israel," *JNES* 6 (1947) 98-108; J. L. McKenzie, "The Elders in the Old Testament," *BibOr* 1 (*AnBib* 10; Rome: Pontifical Biblical Institute, 1959) 388-406; Abraham Malamat, "Kingship and Council in Israel and Sumer: A Parallel," *JNES* 22 (1963) 247-53; and, by way of rejoinder, D. Geoffrey Evans, "Rehoboam's Advisers at Shechem and Political Institutions in Israel and Sumer," *JNES* 25 (1966) 273-79. On the function of the counselor, see P. A. H. de Boer, "The Counsellor," *VTSup* 3 (1955) 42-71; Heaton, *The Hebrew Kingdoms*, 166f., 177. See Scott, "Priesthood, Prophecy, Wisdom, and the Knowledge of God," 10; Lindblom, "Wisdom in the Old Testament Prophets," 192-95.

opposed the anti-Assyrian uprising of 705-701 (28:14-22; 29:15f.; 30:1-17; 31:1-3). On what basis did Isaiah take the positions he did on these occasions? To some extent, no doubt, his convictions sprang from Israel's sacred traditions; we might think of the traditions of the Holy War, by which victory came from Yahweh and did not depend on human might,[34] of the perpetuity of the Davidic dynasty,[35] and possibly, though doubtfully, of the inviolability of Zion.[36] But beyond these, Isaiah's convictions would have rested on properly prophetic knowledge, most especially on what he believed Yahweh had revealed to him about His imminent judgment (cf. 2:6-21; 5:9; 6:11f.; 28:22).

And it is precisely at this point that Isaiah's conflict with "the wise" would have arisen. It is necessary to insist on this, for Whedbee's argumentation tends to obscure the role that properly prophetic knowledge, as distinct from the knowledge which is drawn from experience and observation, plays in the teaching of Isaiah. Whedbee argues that to Isaiah "there is no dichotomy between his insight into Yahweh's character and activity gained by empirical observation of phenomena (e.g., Isa. 28:23ff.), and that derived in a vision (Isa.6)" (p. 79). One can agree that there is "no dichotomy" and yet feel compelled to insist that it wasn't empirical observation that determined the content of Isaiah's message; the most that can be said is that he uses wisdom procedures to illustrate and defend the content of his message. But Whedbee goes beyond this, even to the point of rejecting a contrast between insight gained by empirical observation and that given in visionary form (pp. 152f.). It is quite impossible, however, to explain the content of Isaiah's message and the conviction with which he delivered it, in terms of empirical observation. By what stretch of the imagination can one conclude that passages like "For the Lord of hosts will have his day against all that is proud and arrogant . . ." (2:12), "In my hearing the Lord of hosts has sworn: Many houses shall be in ruins . . ." (5:9), "This shall not stand, it shall not be!" (7:7), "The Lord of hosts has sworn: As I have resolved, so shall it be; As I have proposed, so shall it stand: I will break the Assyrian in my land . . ." (14:24) reflect knowledge arrived at by empirical observation or by any other approach to reality normally employed by the wise man? If prophet and wise man come

[34]Gerhard von Rad, *Der Heilige Krieg im alten Israel* (Zurich: Zwingli-Verlag, 1951), 57f.; H. W. Wolff, *Frieden ohne Ende: Jesaja 7, 1-17 und 9, 1-6 ausgelegt* (Neukirchen: Neukirchener Verlag, 1962), 18; Ernst Würthwein, "Jesaja 7,1-9. Ein Beitrag zur Thema 'Prophetie und Politik'," *Theologie als Glaubenswagnis. Festschrift für Karl Heim* (Hamburg: Furche-Verlag, 1954) 47-52.

[35]Donner, *Israel unter den Völkern*, 13f.

[36]G. von Rad, *Old Testament Theology*, II, 155-69, makes the belief a basic item in his treatment of Isaiah's theology; John H. Hayes, "The Tradition of Zion's Inviolability," *JBL* 82 (1963) 419-26, holds a similar position. But Childs, *Isaiah and the Assyrian Crisis*, finds most of the passages on which such claims are made to be secondary. See Heaton, *The Hebrew Kingdoms*, 354f.

into conflict, it isn't because, as Whedbee supposes, they agree that Yahweh has a plan, but disagree as to whether His plan is wise or whether human plans can avail against it. Rather, it is a question of knowledge or insight into God's will that the prophet has, or claims to have, that comes to him in a manner over which the calculations of the wise have no control.

We receive a very detailed picture of the procedure of taking counsel in the royal court from the account of Absalom's seeking advice from Hushai and Ahitophel (2 Sam 17:1-14); the discussion involved matters such as the number of troops likely to be needed, the physical and emotional state of the enemy, the propitious moment to act, the probable psychological effect of an initial reverse on one's followers, etc. This is precisely as we would expect it to be; it is difficult to see how else royal advisers could proceed. Their traditional lore may well have admitted that Yahweh might have an *'ēṣâ* that would stand against their own and that it would surely prevail. But how does one know beforehand? How does one take such a thing into account? One can only lay wise plans and then shrug philosophically if they go astray, sadly murmuring Prov 19:21:

> Many are the plans in a man's heart,
> but it is the *'ēṣâ* of Yahweh that will be established.

But if, during such deliberations, a prophet should stand up to claim that he knows what Yahweh's *'ēṣâ* is, a completely new situation is born for the wise man. His choices are very limited: he can either accept the word of the prophet and be put out of business as a counselor, or he can doubt the word of the prophet and try by every means to discredit his message. The temptation to the latter course would be very strong, especially for those convinced that their counsel was wise and would be effective, and the wise men of Isaiah's day seem to have succumbed to it.

Much of this process can be traced in Isaiah's oracles concerning Yahweh's work (*mă'aśeh*) and purpose (*'ēṣâ/y'ṣ*).[37] In 5:19 Isaiah pronounces a "woe" against those who show contempt for his prophetic message by taunting him with its nonfulfillment.[38] Their words obviously echo the terminology of his own oracles as they gleefully urge that Yahweh "speed his work" (*mă'aśēhû*) and say, "On with the plan of the Holy One of Israel" (*'ăṣat qᵉdôš yiśrā'ēl*). The phrases "that we may see it," "that we may know it," may suggest that Isaiah's prophetic word would be worth taking into account in forming plans if it were true, for the scoffers are most probably the

[37]See especially Fichtner, "Jahves Plan in der Botschaft des Jesaja," 16-33, who, however, proposes a more sweeping and comprehensive "plan" on the part of Isaiah's Yahweh than the terminology he discusses supports; for a criticism of Fichtner's firm distinction between "advice" and "plan" in the term *'ēṣâ*, see McKane, *Prophets and Wise Men*, 66, and Wildberger, *Jesaja*, "Excursus," 188f.

[38]Jer 17:15 is remarkably similar, though the term corresponding to *'ēṣâ* is *dābār*; a similar reproach is found in Ezek 12:22.

circle of royal advisers.[39] Within the extant oracles of Isaiah these two terms occur together to refer to Yahweh's activity in 14:24-27, a passage in which *y'ṣ* also occurs three times. The oracle speaks of judgment, primarily upon Assyria, but also upon all nations. There is a particular insistence upon the firmness and certainty of execution of what has been determined, from the opening reference to Yahweh's oath (vs. 24a), through his assertion that what He has purposed (*yā'aṣtî*) shall be accomplished (*hî' tāqûm*—vs. 24b), to the statement and rhetorical question near the end, "Yahweh of hosts has planned (*yā'āṣ*); who can thwart (him)?" (vs. 27). The emphasis here is on irresistible power rather than on wisdom.

It would seem to be on this point of firmness and power that Isaiah contrasts human *'ēṣâ* with that of Yahweh; this appears very clearly if the passage just discussed is compared with 8:10, in which peoples and distant lands are advised:

> Form a plan (*'uṣû 'ēṣâ*), and it shall be thwarted;
> make a resolve, and it shall not be carried out (*lō' yāqûm*) . . .

The same theme is present when Isaiah, referring to what Aram has plotted (*yā'aṣ*) against Ahaz (7:5), tells him that it will not come to pass: *lō' tāqûm wᵉlō' tihyeh* (vs. 7).

Such passages suggest that Isaiah connects this terminology with a conception of Yahweh's lordship of the world and of history, and the possibility easily comes to mind that, for Isaiah, the only legitimate *'ēṣâ* was that of Yahweh. The suggestion receives confirmation from a passage like 30:1, where the men of Judah are called "rebellious children" because they "carry out an *'ēṣâ* which is not mine." The idea emerges even more strongly in 29:15f., where the leaders of Judah are accused of attempting to renounce their status as creatures when they initiate *'ēṣâ* and *ma'ăśîm* on their own.

From all of this it appears that Isaiah claimed to have a knowledge of Yahweh's *'ēṣâ*, a knowledge not derivable from empirical observation or the wisdom tradition, that should have been of vital concern to the policy-makers of Judah, but that they refused to admit this foreign, incalculable element into their deliberations, probably questioning the authenticity of his message[40] and certainly taunting him over its non-fulfillment. Isaiah, on his part, condemns the royal counselors, saying that they are wise only in their own eyes (5:21) and promising that on the day that Yahweh deals with His people "the wisdom of its wise men shall perish" (29:14). Such criticism is readily intelligible, but it is especially so if we suppose that Isaiah was led to adopt his *'ēṣâ* terminology at least partly as a strategem for bringing his

[39] McKane, *Prophets and Wise Men*, 65.

[40] This is all the more likely if, as seems probable, the prophets that Isaiah condemns (28:7) contradicted his message, thus giving the royal counselors a choice even within the realm of prophecy; Micah, Jeremiah, and Ezekiel all seem to have experienced the embarrassment of having their message contradicted by other prophets.

message into the royal council where vital decisions were to be made;[41] much of its content could have been expressed in the phrase that was more usually employed by the prophets, *d^{e}bar yhwh* (and see n. 38, above).

If Isaiah's extant oracles leave the content of Yahweh's *'ēṣâ* rather vague, the matter was undoubtedly far clearer to the prophet's contemporaries. They had knowledge of Yahweh's "purpose" and "work" sufficiently detailed to enable them to taunt the prophet concerning the non-fulfillment of his words (5:19), and he could reproach them for not seeing the "work" Yahweh has already performed. The "Parable of the Farmer," too, which is a defense of Yahweh's *'ēṣâ* rather than of His wisdom, seems to indicate the sort of knowledge on the part of Isaiah's enemies that permitted them to see inconsistencies or turn-abouts in Yahweh's purpose. In reply, Isaiah shows by the example of the farmer that seemingly diverse and unrelated actions can fit into a purposeful pattern of behavior. Yet for all that, the closing expression ("wonderful is his *'ēṣâ* and great his *tûšîyâ*"[42]—vs. 29) notes not the logical, rational, intelligible, or wise nature of Yahweh's *'ēṣâ*, but precisely its wonderful" (*hiplî'*), i.e., its marvelous, incomprehensible nature.[43] Elsewhere Isaiah insists upon this aspect of Yahweh's action: "Therefore I will again deal with this people in surprising and wondrous fashion" (*l^{e}haplî' . . . haplē' wāpele'*—29:14), and this same verse says that the wisdom of the wise is to be destroyed. In spite of all his wisdom terminology, it was a prophet's message that he presented, and "the wise" refused to accept it or give it a place in their council.

This exposition of the nature of Isaiah's conflict with "the wise" illumines and draws support from two other passages in particular: the reference to his mission of hardening and blinding in his vocation narrative (6:10) and his demand that Ahaz ask for a sign (7:11). Recent authors have asserted that the primary purpose of a prophet's vocation narrative is to justify the

[41]The word *'ēṣâ* is a technical term to designate advice or counsel given or decision arrived at in council, always with a view to action. Von Rad, *Old Testament Theology*, II, 162, says that Isaiah adopted this secular term to express his teaching about Yahweh's action in history, and there can be no doubt that the prophet gave the term a new content; it is very possible, however, that Isaiah chose precisely *this* term because of the impact it could have in the circle of policy makers. Whedbee, *Isaiah and Wisdom*, 112f., thinks von Rad's suggestion is "deficient" in that it overlooks important evidence in the wisdom tradition explaining Isaiah's use of this term. It must be asserted again, however, that there is a vast distance between the proverbial sayings about Yahweh's *'ēṣâ* being an incalculable factor in human affairs and the function and content the term has as Isaiah employs it.

[42]McKane, *Prophets and Wise Men*, 80f., looking at evidence for the true meaning of *tûšîyâ*, including its coupling with *'ēṣâ* and the paralleling of this pair by *bînâ* and *g^{e}bûrâ* in Prov 8:14, concludes that *tûšîyâ* suggests the idea of effective and successful action, that the pair *'ēṣâ* and *tûšîyâ* in Isa 28:29 is comparable to *'ēṣâ* and *g^{e}bûrâ* in Isa 36:5.

[43]In the seventeen pages Whedbee dedicates to discussion of this parable, he does not allude to the term *hiplî'* or its implications.

message, frequently unpopular and sometimes considered even sacrilegious and seditious, that he preaches.[44] If Isaiah's ministry was characterized by opposition to the policies adopted by the kings under whom he prophesied and by opposition to the counsel of the circle of the kings' royal advisers, those who were held in esteem by all for their wisdom, prudence, and insight, this could well call for some justification. In the light of this it is interesting to note that the message of destruction (6:11) is preceded by the command to deafen, blind, and harden (vss. 9f.). In vs. 9 it is said that they are to hear but not understand (*byn*), to see but not know (*yd'*); these are the same verbs used in the wisdom passage of Isa 1:2f. and, as there, they are used absolutely, without an object. The action affects the whole people ("say to this people"), but it is not surprising if it affected first and primarily those within the people who had the special office of understanding and knowing. However we answer the difficult question of what is really intended by the *command* to harden, there is every reason to think that these verses deal with the problem of the opposition Isaiah experienced from the wise on the question of policy. There is widespread conviction that the vocation narrative is intimately connected with the following two chapters and Isaiah's action during the Syro-Ephraimitic crisis.[45] If this is correct, then we see the opposition supposed in 6:9f. already apparent in Isaiah's encounter(s) with Ahaz and the counselors whose advice he is bent on following (7:1-17), whose reaction is then mirrored in that of the people when Isaiah turns to them. (8:1-8).

It is very likely that Isaiah's demand that Ahaz ask for a sign also fits into this picture. If Ahaz's council, having weighed all the pros and cons, came to the decision that the prudent thing to do was to call to Assyria for help in the face of the combined attack of Aram and Israel, and if Isaiah denounced such advice, declaring that the threat would come to nothing (7:4-9), then Ahaz was faced with a dilemma. In such circumstances the counselors could urge their advice upon the king, using as arguments all those considerations that had led them to choose this course in the first place. The prophet was not able, in like manner, to present rational arguments for the word of the Lord that he proclaimed; but he was able to challenge the king to ask for a sign (7:11) to prove whether or not he really spoke in the name of the Lord. Isaiah is obviously irritated when Ahaz refused to admit to the deliberations an element that would have restricted his freedom to chart a course on purely

[44]See Ernst Jenni, "Jesajas Berufung in der neueren Forschung," *TZ* 15 (1959) 328; Rolf Knierim, "The Vocation of Isaiah," *VT* 18 (1968) 62; N. Habel, "The Form and Significance of the Call Narrative," *ZAW* 77 (1965) 323.

[45]Fohrer, "Entstehung, Komposition und Überlieferung von Jesaja 1-39," 123-25; Martin Buber, *The Prophetic Faith*, tr. C. Witton-Davies (New York: Harper & Row, Publishers, 1960 [c1949]), 126; Wolff, *Frieden ohne Ende*, 11.

rational grounds.[46] It should be clear that Isaiah's challenge and Ahaz's refusal make sense only if, contrary to Whedbee's supposition, the royal circles did, in fact, recognize that their own *'ēṣâ* must yield to Yahweh's if the latter could be known; their fault lay in the voluntary blindness of refusing the light that was offered.

Yahweh as Imparter of *tôrâ*

Isaiah's disgust with the wisdom circles led him to repudiate the claim that these men had "wisdom" in any meaningful sense of the term. This does not mean he didn't hold the ideals of wisdom in high esteem; on the contrary, his reproaches show that something of great value was missing. Israel, the children Yahweh has brought up, *should* know and understand (1:2f.); one *ought* to hear and understand, *ought* to see and know, not be deafened and blinded (6:9). Of the wise behavior of the farmer Isaiah says: "This too comes from Yahweh of hosts" (28:29). The correlative of denying all wisdom to the wise men is attributing all wisdom to Yahweh.[47]

Fichtner had explained Isaiah's use of wisdom techniques by the theory that Isaiah was a converted sage. McKane, on the other hand, recognizes that Isaiah's use of wisdom techniques is itself a function of his polemic against the wise: the prophet is trying to wrest *'ēṣâ* from the sages and to exhibit it as an exclusive activity of Yahweh.[48] He points out that, in Isaiah's thought, the

[46]On the use of "sign" (*'ôt*) to confirm the reliability of a prophetic oracle, see Aubrey R. Johnson, *The Cultic Prophet in Ancient Israel* (2nd ed.; Cardiff: University of Wales Press, 1962), 52.

[47]Thus it may be stressed that 31:2 is wholly consonant with Isaiah's thought; if its authenticity is rejected, this is on grounds of form, style, and context, not of content. Strong arguments for Isaiah's relating wisdom and Yahweh can be drawn from 9:1-6 and 11:1-9, but they will be passed over for the present since their authenticity is disputed; but they will be discussed in Ch. 5.

[48]McKane, *Prophets and Wise Men*, 67. I believe his statement is quite true, but I would disagree with some points of McKane's understanding of this struggle over *'ēṣâ*. For McKane it is basically a question of power: "The test of *'ēṣā* is its effectiveness as policy and this presupposes that those who formulate it should have the energy and power . . . to effect its successful implementation" (p. 67; cf. p. 128). Yet there is certainly more to it than the question of power. It is when Isaiah speaks of the "wonderful" aspect of God's plan that he also speaks of the wisdom of the wise men perishing (29:14), and he even calls Yahweh's work strange and alien (28:21). God's is the kind of wisdom that looks upside-down to the wise of this world, a point that St. Paul would be insisting upon some centuries later (1 Cor 1:17-25). The amazing aspect of Yahweh's work does not detract from its wisdom, but is present because it springs from a wisdom too deep to fathom; this is something that the sages' own tradition should have led them to accept. But McKane strips early wisdom of all its religious values (it is "ethically neutral" and "fear of the Lord" and the "man proposes but God disposes" theme come only later—pp. 47f., 50, 65) and then says that the prophets do not merely claim that the sages are unworthy representatives of their tradition but that they call into question the basic presuppositions of the tradition itself (p. 128). On this point Whedbee is surely more in the right in insisting that Isaiah was challenging the wise to be true to their own tradition.

wise are not creative agents in history; words such as *'ēṣâ*, *t^ebûnâ*, and *kōaḥ* can only be correctly used with reference to Yahweh Himself.[49] This is a fair assessment, and Isaiah brings into the debate a good many other terms; for example, *ḥākām*, *ḥokmâ*, *yd'*, *byn*, *nābôn*, *tûšîyâ*, *hôrâ* (28:26), *'iqqēš* (30:12—emended), and *nālôz* (30:12).

Given these circumstances, it seems fair to ask whether Isaiah did not also attribute to Yahweh another prerogative of the sage, namely, that of giving wise instruction, and whether he did not use the technical wisdom term *tôrâ* to express this. It is clear that Isaiah made *'ēṣâ* Yahweh's prerogative, but even though he expanded its range of meaning greatly, it remained a term that was less than apt for some of the more positive elements of the wisdom tradition. As employed by Isaiah, *'ēṣâ* seems always to be oriented towards practical, effective action, never towards the broader concept of "the way," the moral demands, the ethics of behavior, which are such important elements of the wisdom tradition. This may be a peculiarity, possibly deliberately intended by the prophet, for the term is used both ways in Prov;[50] *'ēṣâ* can also have an unfavorable sense, both as employed by Isaiah and elsewhere,[51] and so would be less apt to express the "instruction" of the wisdom tradition in a positive sense. Supposing that Isaiah did want to express this broader, more positive concept, the choice of another term would be a desideratum, perhaps even a necessity.

All that we know of Isaiah's polemic against the wisdom circles of his day and of his conception of Yahweh suggests that he would have thought of Him and would have presented Him as the imparter of wise instruction. The "instruction" texts from Egypt and Mesopotamia are typically the address of a teacher who is at the same time a king and the father of the son and student who is being instructed, and the father-son, teacher-student relationship is well attested in Israelite wisdom texts, too. Furthermore, the conception of God as possessing the fulness of wisdom and imparting instruction to men was widely spread in the ancient Near East. Father, King, God—these are the three foremost elements of Isaiah's presentation of Yahweh, and in each case it is easy to find links with the wisdom tradition.

[49] McKane, *Prophets and Wise Men*, 70f.

[50] The term *'ēṣâ* occurs nine times in Prov (omitting the apparently corrupt 27:9): 1:25.30; 8:14; 12:15; 19:20.21; 20:5.18; 21:30. In six cases (1:25.30; 8:14; 12:15; 19:20; 21:30) it seems to refer to behavior or wisdom in a broad sense, being used with *tôkaḥat*, *bînâ*, *mûsār*, *ḥokmâ*, *derek*. In 20:18 the reference is to "advice" in a more specific sense, and Yahweh's *'ēṣâ* in 19:21 is also specific. The "intention of the human heart" in 20:5 is probably specific, though the precise sense is difficult to determine. In other compositions it frequently has the specific sense; e.g., 2 Sam 16:23; 17:14; 1 Kgs 12:14; 2 Kgs 18:20; Job 29:21.

[51] Thus, except in 16:3, it has an unfavorable sense when Isaiah predicates it of anyone but Yahweh (8:10; 29:15; 30:1). In Prov, the *'ēṣâ* of man's heart in 20:5 would appear to be devious; and cf. Ps 1:1; Job 5:13; 10:3. Thus the OT has no hesitation in speaking of the "*'ēṣâ* of the wicked," whereas "*tôrâ* of the wicked" is not found and probably would have been inconceivable.

Although Isaiah does not directly refer to Yahweh as father, he does refer to the people of Judah as Yahweh's childen.This is seen most clearly in 1:2. The people are referred to as "children" also in 1:4; 30:1.9. In each case the term is associated with rebelliousness or disobedience against Yahweh, so there is no doubt *whose* children are involved.We have already seen that 1:2f. is a passage that manifests strong wisdom influence, and it may be that the teacher-student relationship is reflected in all these passages;[52] later I will argue for the presence of wisdom motifs in 30:9. The chosen people are referred to as Yahweh's children in many OT contexts,[53] of course, quite apart from any wisdom influence; for present purposes it is sufficient to note that the father-son relationship is congenial to the conception of Yahweh as imparter of instruction and that at least one passage (1:2f.) is stamped with that character. The reference to raising and rearing sons in this text regards primarily their education, their moral and intellectual formation, not simply the provision of food and clothes, for the reproach in vs. 3 does not refer to ingratitude but to the fact that they do not know or understand. Thus Yahweh is here envisioned as a father who imparts instruction, the people as disobedient children who will not accept instruction.

An interesting possibility that might be raised in this connection is that Israel's custom of putting apodictic laws in the mouth of Yahweh may be explicable, at least in part, in terms of seeing Him as a father-figure. Gerstenberger and Richter have demonstrated convincingly that the primary *Sitz im Leben* of Israelite second person imperative "law" is not the covenant renewal ceremony, to which, rather, it has been attached secondarily.[54] Gerstenberger sees the origin of the form in the precepts given by the clan father to his children, spoken on his own authority and containing the rules by which they ought to live (cf. Jer 35:6-19). The characteristic personal address relates, in the first instance, says Gerstenberger, not to divine self-revelation, but to the use of the prohibition in clan instruction.[55] If this is

[52]Heaton, *The Hebrew Kingdoms*, 323, even remarks, with reference to Isa 1:2f., that "sons" here need not necessarily imply the father-son relationship, since teachers addressed their pupils as sons.

[53]One thinks most easily of the covenant context. When it comes to Isaiah, however, it is difficult to know how much influence the Sinai covenant ideology exercised upon him; there are no explicit references to the covenant, Moses, or Sinai in his extant oracles. Cf. Norman K. Gottwald, *All the Kingdoms of the Earth: Israelite Prophecy and International Relations in the Ancient Near East* (New York: Harper & Row, Publishers, 1964), 198; B. D. Napier, "Isaiah and the Isaian," *VTSup* 15 (1966) 249; Georg Fohrer, "Die Propheten des Alten Testaments im Blickfeld neuer Forschung," *Studien zur alttestamentlichen Prophetie*, 1-17; and "Bemerkungen zum neueren Verständnis der Propheten," *ibid.*, 18-31. On the other hand, Hans Wildberger, "Jesajas Verständnis der Geschichte," *VTSup* 9 (1963) 83-117, argues that Isaiah knew the covenant tradition; see especially pp. 104-108.

[54]See Ch. 1, n. 79, above.

[55]Gerstenberger, *Wesen und Herkunft*, 112f.

correct, the reason that Israel so easily adopted this form of address for the revelation of the divine will and transferred it into the context of the Sinai covenant may be found in their conception of Yahweh as father.[56]

It cannot be denied, however, that this change in context introduces an altered relationship: Yahweh imposing commands as senior covenant partner stands "over against" Israel in a manner that the clan father in relation to his sons does not.[57] There is no doubt that Isaiah and the other prophets often placed Yahweh "over against" Israel, but in many passages, especially where the people are referred to as sons, the image of the clan father is more appropriate than that of covenant Lord. This is suggested also by the norms of behavior supposed by the prophets, which are often closer to clan ethic and wisdom instructions than to covenant law.[58] With special reference to Isaiah's moral demands, Gerstenberger remarks: "Jesaja beruft sich etwa in seinen Weherufen auf volkstümliche, ethische Regeln, nicht auf göttliches, offenbartes Recht . . ."[59] But examples of this are found in many passages other than "woes," as we shall see later.

The king, most especially, was considered to be the recipient and source of wisdom in Israel and in the ancient Near East in general. The reasons for this are no doubt to be seen in his special relationship to God, to his patronage of the scribal circles of the court, and to his presiding over the royal council. In Egypt and in Mesopotamia the teacher of the "instructions" is most often the king, or some other high official, especially in the earlier compositions. Schmid speaks of the role the Egyptian king has in establishing Maat and suggests that, at least in earlier times, the king's proverbial wisdom was closely connected with this relationship (almost identity) with God;[60] similar conclusions can be drawn concerning kings, gods, and wisdom in Mesopotamia.[61]

[56]There is no intention here of ignoring the influence the treaty form with its apodictic stipulations may have had in this process, but it is not clear when this influence begins; it no longer seems likely that it stands at the beginning of Israel's covenant tradition—see especially Dennis J. McCarthy, *Treaty and Covenant* (*AnBib* 21; Rome: Pontifical Biblical Institute, 1963). At any period, the process would have been facilitated by the conception of Yahweh as a father-God.

[57]Cf. Gerstenberger, *Wesen und Herkunft*, 113. Richter, *Recht und Ethos*, takes a position comparable to that of Gerstenberger in many ways, but puts the precept in the broader context of group-ethic, thinking particularly of "die Schule"; for present purposes the difference is not great, for such circles seem readily to have adopted the father-son image for the teacher-student relationship.

[58]On Israel's use of these norms, see Gerstenberger, *Wesen und Herkunft*, 147f.

[59]*Ibid.*, 108n. See also Gerstenberger's "The Woe-Oracles of the Prophets," *JBL* 81 (1962) 249-63; see also Whedbee, *Isaiah and Wisdom*, 93-110.

[60]Schmid, *Wesen und Geschichte der Weisheit*, 37-42.

[61]See especially the wisdom attributes listed in parallel columns for "king" and "god" in Ivan Engnell, *Studies in Divine Kingship in the Ancient Near East* (Oxford: Basil Blackwell, 1967), 189-91.

In Israel, of course, there was a much greater reluctance to associate the king so closely with God, but even here there was a tendency to attribute remarkable wisdom to the king and to relate it to the divine sphere. Thus the "wise woman" from Tekoa says of David that he is "like an angel of God, evaluating[62] good and bad" (2 Sam 14:17), and Solomon's wisdom is said to have been given him by God (1 Kgs 3:4-14.28). He is said to have composed three thousand proverbs (1 Kgs 5:9-14) and to have astounded the Queen of Sheba by his wisdom (10:1-13).[63] Another eloquent witness to wisdom as a kingly ideal is seen in the qualities attributed to the messianic king to come (Isa 9:5; 11:2; Jer 23:5). The widespread tradition of the king as source of instruction finds its counterpart in Israel in the pseudonymous attribution of Prov, Eccl, and Wis to Solomon. And it is at least possible that Lam 2:9 sees the king as source of *tôrâ*.[64]

It is most likely that Isaiah's conception of Yahweh as king included the ideal of kingly wisdom so widely attested throughout the culture of the ancient Near East. It could hardly be accidental that the one passage in his prophecy that explicitly designates Yahweh as king (6:1.5) is set within the context of Yahweh's heavenly council (see below). On the supposition of the authenticity of 2:2-4, we would have, in these two texts taken together, the picture of the nations coming to the King throned on Zion for the instructions on the way of life that would be expected of the wise king sovereign over all.

That God is seen as the possessor and source of wisdom in the ancient Near East is already clear from what was said above of the origin of the king's wisdom. Schmid and others note that it is the creator-god who is most especially the God of wisdom.[65] That this conception is congenial to Isaiah and consonant with his view of Yahweh is suggested by at least two passages. In

[62]MT has *lišmōaʿ*, but the context makes the meaning clear.

[63]See Alt, "Die Weisheit Salomos," 139-44; Heaton, *The Hebrew Kingdoms*, 165; van Imschoot, "Sagesse et esprit dans l'Ancien Testament," 31f.; Lindblom, "Wisdom in the Old Testament Prophets," 198f.; Norman W. Porteous, "Royal Wisdom," *VTSup* 3 (1955) 247-61; Noth, "Die Bewährung von Salomos 'Göttlicher Weisheit'," 225-37.

[64]This is a difficult verse to construe, but the structure of the second and third lines would seem to favor associating the phrase *'ên tôrâ* in the latter half of the second line with the officials named in the first half; this would make that line parallel with the third, in which other personnel (the prophets) are named in the first half and that guidance which is proper to them (*ḥāzôn myhwh*) in the second half.

Östborn, *Tōrā in the Old Testament*, dedicates a chapter to "The King as Imparter of Tora" (pp. 54ff.), but does not make out a convincing case.

[65]Schmid, *Wesen und Geschichte der Weisheit*, 27; Rankin, *Israel's Wisdom Literature*, 10. However, Egypt also saw Thoth, the god of scribes, as having a special role in imparting wisdom; see Leclant, "Documents nouveaux," 12n.; see also Vergote, "La notion de Dieu dans les livres de sagesse égyptienne," 164.

10:5-15, in which judgment is pronounced upon Assyria, the proud nation is blamed for not realizing that it is only Yahweh's instrument, for vaunting its strength and claiming it has succeeded "by my wisdom, for I am shrewd" (vs. 13). Assyria's guilt is outlined in vs. 15, a proverb-like composition in which Yahweh is identified as the power which moves Assyria as though it were an axe, a saw, or a rod. In 29:15f., it is Judah which is blamed for its independence and the belief that it formulated and put into effect its own *'ēṣâ*; here the guilt is again described by means of a proverb in which Yahweh is now explicitly the "potter," the "maker," while Judah is the "clay," "what is made," and the "vessel."[66]

The composition that is of the greatest importance on this point is undoubtedly the "Parable of the Farmer" in 28:23-29, for it speaks explicitly of God giving instruction and precisely in the terminology we are concerned with. Vs. 26 should be translated, "And he teaches him (*yissᵉrô*) by rule, his God instructs him (*yôrennû*)." Since *hôrâ* is in all likelihood the denominative of *tôrâ*, one could legitimately translate the phrase: "his God imparts *tôrâ* to him." Furthermore, while there may be controversy as to the kind of *tôrâ* involved in those passages where Isaiah uses the noun, there can be no doubt here: it is not a question of priestly or prophetic *tôrâ*, but instruction that fits into the category of *ḥokmâ*. Furthermore, this passage must be seen within the broader context of the ancient Near Eastern tradition of the God as imparter of instruction; we have already spoken of the Sumerian piece which tells of the instructions on agriculture given by a farmer to his son; "The document closes with the statement that the agricultural rules laid down were not the farmer's own but those of the god Ninurta, the son and 'true farmer' of the leading Sumerian deity, Enlil."[67]

Finally, Isaiah's teaching on Yahweh's *'ēṣâ* is almost certainly related to the conception of Yahweh as divine king who presides over the heavenly council.[68] This is suggested most explicitly by Wildberger.[69]

The fullest description of Yahweh's heavenly council and its deliberation is, of course, that found in the story of Micaiah ben Imlah in 1 Kgs 22:19-23.[70] Several authors have noted the resemblance between this scene

[66]See Whedbee, *Isaiah and Wisdom*, 68-75, on these two passages.

[67]Kramer, *History Begins at Sumer*, 67. See further n. 26, above.

[68]See von Rad, *Old Testament Theology*, II, 162; Th. C. Vriezen, "Essentials of the Theology of Isaiah," *Israel's Prophetic Heritage*, 142; Edwin C. Kingsbury, "The Prophets and the Council of Yahweh," *JBL* 83 (1964) 279-86. The suggestion is treated with considerable reserve by Whedbee, *Isaiah and Wisdom*, 112f., 145f.

[69]Wildberger, *Jesaja*, 189.

[70]There seems little point in arguing, as Whedbee does, *Isaiah and Wisdom*, 145f., that "the term *'ēṣâ* and the heavenly council are nowhere explicitly linked"; if the procedure described in this scene is compared with that described in 2 Sam 17:1-14, where *'ēṣâ* does occur (vss. 7.14; cf. vs. 23), there can be no doubt what was involved.

and the inaugural vision of Isaiah[71] and with good reason, for there are a number of striking similarities: 1) the vision of Yahweh enthroned; 2) reference to the heavenly court (in Isa 6 this is found in the mention of the seraphim and in the plural in "who will go for us" of vs. 8); 3) a question is proposed; 4) a volunteer comes forth with a response; 5) the commission: "Go forth and do this!" "Go and say to this people . . ." In all probability it is significant that Isaiah does not depict Yahweh as asking and receiving advice; unlike the author of the Micaiah story, Isaiah was probably unwilling to see Yahweh formulating His *'ēṣâ* on the basis of any wisdom but His own.

By way of conclusion, then, it may be said that in Isaiah's teaching Yahweh is described as king and father as well as God. In the ancient Near East, all three of these figures hold an important place in the wisdom tradition as imparters of instruction. In Isaiah's presentation all three figures have links with wisdom; of God it is explicitly said that he "instructs," and of Yahweh as father it is clearly implied.

[71]H. W. Robinson, "The Council of Yahweh," *JTS* 45 (1944) 154; Kingsbury, "The Prophets and the Council of Yahweh," 282; Knierim, "The Vocation of Isaiah," 55.

4

tôrâ IN ISAIAH

Isaiah's use of the term *tôrâ* seems to have captured the interest of relatively few. Vriezen thinks that it plays an important role in the prophet's teaching, for he comments: "Just as there is in fact only one great sin for Isaiah, the contempt of the *tôrâ*, the Word of God (5:24; cf. 8:16,20), so there is only one message for the salvation of the world and that is the *tôrâ*, the Word of God (2:3), which radiates throughout the nations."[1] This judgment seems a bit extreme, especially since it is not easy to ascertain precisely what Isaiah means by the term. Some commentators suppose he is simply referring to "the law"; Begrich, as we have seen, argues for a prophetic imitation of priestly *tôrâ* in some of the pertinent passages. Smith, the one author to dedicate a study to Isaiah's use of this term, concludes that, of the six *tôrâ*-texts of Isaiah, three certainly and two others probably refer to the teaching of the prophets.[2] Some other authors, as we have seen, take several of the Isaiah usages of *tôrâ* to designate the prophetic word.[3]

Only an investigation of the individual texts can determine the precise meaning of the term, but some general comments on the suggestion that Isaiah uses *tôrâ* to designate "the law" are in order here. We have already pointed to indications that *tôrâ* comes to designate the aggregate of the law during the period of deuteronomic influence,[4] so that development is unlikely to be found in the oracles of Isaiah. There is even the question of what aggregate of laws it might designate in the Judah of the eighth century. Scholars generally see the Covenant Code as a northern collection; it could have been known in Judah, too, but there is little evidence for this, and serious and moderate scholars have doubted that the covenant tradition of the north was influential in Judah before the deuteronomic reform.[5] Certainly it was not the ritual prescriptions of the various collections in P that Isaiah had in mind when he spoke of Yahweh's *tôrâ*. The Decalogue, whose formation and history is so much disputed, cannot be ruled out, but there is little evidence that it was ever referred to simply as *tôrâ*. Furthermore, Isaiah can use the term "*tôrâ* of Yahweh" to include matters that have no counterpart in Israel's law codes.

[1]Vriezen, "Essentials of the Theology of Isaiah," 134.

[2]Smith, "The Use of the Word *twrh* in Isaiah," 20f. Her conclusions on the five passages referred to are based almost exclusively on a brief, rather superficial examination of the expressions used parallel to *tôrâ.*

[3]See above, Ch. 1, n. 56; other references will be given in the discussion of individual texts.

[4]See above, Ch. 1, notes 46-50, and text.

[5]See above, Ch. 3, n. 53: also von Rad, *Old Testament Theology*, I, 73; Georg Fohrer, "Prophetie und Geschichte," *TLZ* 89 (1964) 490f.

Isaiah clearly knew of demands for moral behavior that he believed the people should be familiar with and he castigated them for non-observance. It is likely, however, that we ought to think rather in terms of more general ethical and social norms than in terms of collected laws that could be called *tôrâ*; such norms would not remain simply those of the ancient world, for they had been given a place within the context of the national religion of Yahwism.[6] Gemser, commenting on the use of proverbial formulations as motive clauses in legal prescriptions (cf. Ex 23:8; Dt 16:19), points out that "here we have a striking example of the intrinsic coherence of legal practice and wisdom or proverbs . . ." and mentions that in other ancient cultures "proverbs have the force of legal maxims."[7] Richter sees Tamar's words to Amnon (thus precisely within ruling Jerusalem circles) concerning his proposed "foolishness" (*n^ebālâ*—2 Sam 13:12) as a reference to an established moral code of a particular group ("it is not done so in Israel"); he points to the use of *n^ebālîm* in the following verse and asks whether it is likely to be an accident that the same sort of terminology is found in Prov.[8] He sees the *Richtersspiegel* of Ex 23 addressed not to a specific profession but to the upper, ruling, class, to whom the office of judging pertained, and understands it not as a legal statement but as one of behavior—the *Ethos* of the ruling class.[9] It is obviously partly in reference to this that he says specifically of Isaiah: "Auch für Jesaja kann zusammenfassend gesagt werden: Die Vorwürfe treffen die führenden Stände besonders hart, weil sie Verfehlungen gegen ihr in Prohibitiven ausgedrucktes Berufsethos geisseln."[10] Other scholars have made similar assertions.[11]

Thus, while there is much uncertainty about what specific law tradition Isaiah may have known, there is wide agreement that he appeals to a commonly accepted social ethic, similar to or identical with that taught within the wisdom tradition. In the light of this it already seems inherently more probable that Isaiah's use of *tôrâ* would refer to the instruction of such ethical teaching than to the legal tradition.

It is not surprising, then, that some authors have suggested a wisdom meaning in Isaiah's use of *tôrâ*. Lindars says that in 30:9 the *tôrâ* which the

[6]F. J. Jasper, "Reflections on the Moral Teaching of the Prophets," *SJT* 21 (1968) 462-76, speaking of the prophetic teaching, makes this point (p. 472).

[7]B. Gemser, "The Importance of the Motive Clause in Old Testament Law," *VTSup* 1 (1953) 64f.; he quotes Henri A. Junod to the effect that certain proverbs are "as it were, a first codification of the common law."

[8]Richter, *Recht und Ethos*, 51.

[9]*Ibid.*, 122f.

[10]*Ibid.*, 186.

[11]Rankin, *Israel's Wisdom Literature*, 71; Whedbee, *Isaiah and Wisdom*, 110; see also p. 150.

king's advisers refuse may "be compared not only with priestly instruction, but also with the advice of the wise men."[12] Wildberger, with reference to Isaiah's use of *tôrâ*, remarks: "Dies relative häufige Vorkommen zeigt, dass Jesaja sein prophetisches Amt weithin in Analogie zu dem eines priesterlichen bzw. weisheitlichen Lehrers aufgefasst hat . . ."[13] However, in view of Isaiah's polemic against "the wise," it is unlikely that he would identify with them in this manner. In the preceding chapter it was suggested that the correlative of denying wisdom to the wise men is attributing all wisdom to Yahweh; here it may be suggested that Isaiah's use of *hôrâ-tôrâ* terminology, rather than saying something about his conception of his prophetic ministry, reveals his attempt to attribute all true instruction to Yahweh. In some cases, to be sure, the *tôrâ* in question may be difficult to distinguish from the word of the prophet (1:10; 8:16.20; 30:9), but it is designated *tôrâ* because it is considered Yahweh's instruction, not because the prophet is thought of as a sage (much less as a priest). In two of the texts *tôrâ* is not clearly related to the prophetic word at all (2:3, where both *hôrâ* and *tôrâ* occur; 5:24), while in another case such connection is excluded (28:26—God imparts instruction to the farmer); in the one text where *hôrâ* is used with reference to the prophet's teaching (28:9), it is part of a sneering criticism found in the mouths of his opponents.[14]

Isaiah always employs *tôrâ* in a favorable sense and always sees it deriving more or less immediately from Yahweh. Supposing that he does use it to mean "wise instruction" and that he attributes all such to God, is there any term that he employs to designate false, merely human, instruction? It seems to me that one text suggests that he used *miṣwâ* in that sense. Although 29:13, the only Isaiah text where *miṣwâ* is employed, is regularly interpreted in a cultic and priestly sense, and the use of *niggaš* and *kibbēd* would seem to commend it, this interpretation appears to be wholly at odds with the context. The following verse speaks of a judgment on the *ḥăkāmîm* and the *n*^e^*bônîm*, and since the two verses are closely joined (*lākēn*), continuity in the subject matter must be supposed; and there is much in vs. 13 to relate the reproach there to the *ḥăkāmîm*. The wisdom tradition does concern itself with reverence for God (even in *kibbēd*-terminology—cf. Prov 3:9; 14:31) and

[12]Lindars, "Torah in Deuteronomy," 121.

[13]Wildberger, *Jesaja*, 36.

[14]Although these are named as priests and prophets, the basic debate may well be over political policy. Donner, *Israel unter den Völkern*, 150f., says that the close of the oracle (he takes vss. 7-13 to be the unity) shows that Isaiah is not impelled to pronounce these words simply by the unworthy attitude of the priests and prophets; behind this lies the fact that they belong to the anti-Assyrian aristocratic party of Jerusalem that had neglected Yahweh's admonition to neutrality. Thus, he says, the occasion was taken from their drunkenness, but the real target was the deficient foreign policy. Thus, it may be suggested that whereas Isaiah spoke of Yahweh's instruction (as in all the other *hôrâ-tôrâ* texts), his adversaries, rejecting his claim to speak for Yahweh, attributed the "instructing" to him.

with the heart; fear of Yahweh is also at home in wisdom.[15] The term *miṣwâ*, in the singular, would be difficult as an expression covering ritual prescriptions; it makes better sense, especially in the light of the participle *m^elummādâ*, as instruction in the wisdom tradition, a sense which it frequently has.[16] Possibly this participle explains also the reference to "mouth" and "lips" earlier in the verse: the very lofty teachings of the wisdom tradition were carefully phrased and intended to be memorized, but unless they were put into practice they would remain purely verbal exercises. The wisdom tradition's dictum, "the fear of Yahweh is the beginning of wisdom," is of highest worth; but if such dicta do not become a basis for action, they remain but words hypocritically mouthed, teachings of men that have been learned by rote.[17]

It is now time to investigate the *tôrâ* texts of Isaiah; they are: 1:10; 2:3; 5:24; 8:16.20; and 30:9. We omit 24:5 because it is found in the non-Isaianic "Apocalypse." The verse refers to the inhabitants of the earth "who have transgressed laws (*tôrôt*), violated statutes (*ḥōq*), broken the ancient covenant." Such diction would fit very naturally into many areas of OT tradition, but it stands in striking contrast to Isaiah's use of *tôrâ*.

Isaiah 1:10

The use of *tôrâ* in this verse has been given the most varied interpretations;[18] some of them we have already had occasion to note. Thus, Beecher took it to mean "law" in the aggregate sense,[19] while for Smith, Lindblom,

[15]Derousseaux, *Crainte de Dieu*, 207n., 270f., 277, sees deuteronomic influence ("D ancien") in this verse on the basis of the use of the infinitive of *yr'* and the presence of *miṣwâ*. But the use of the infinitive of *yr'* in this text is quite different from its employment in the Dt texts he lists (pp. 206f.): (a) in Dt the infinitive is always used with *l^e* and normally complements a finite verb; (b) in Dt the infinitive never takes a pronominal suffix; (c) in Dt the sense of the verb is different than in this Isaiah text, as Derousseaux himself recognizes (p. 277n.).

[16]The discussion of Prov in Ch. 2, above, brought in the use of *miṣwâ* at several points. Usually the plural, *miṣwôt*, is found in Prov, but the singular also occurs as a synonym for wisdom instruction: cf. especially 6:20.23; the same meaning is possible in 13:13; 19:16.

[17]Heaton, *The Hebrew Kingdoms*, 176f., takes these verses to refer to the wisdom circle.

[18]Theodor Lescow, "Die dreistufige Tora: Beobachtungen zu einer Form," *ZAW* 82 (1970) 362-79, postulates the existence of a *tôrâ*-form in three parts (generalizing introduction, central core of material from cult and ethics, and conclusion) which was employed especially as an entrance liturgy. He attempts to fit Isa 1:10-17 into this scheme but can do so only by including vss. 18-20; even so, the piece (1:10-20) presents problems. Significant for the present study is the fact that vss. 10-17, taken as a unity, simply do not fit the pattern: "Die Struktur der Predigt Jes 1:10-17 darf nicht aus dem Dreistufenschema entwickelt und damit wohl auch nicht als Tora in dem geprägten Sinne dieses Wortes verstanden werden" (pp. 370-73). Yet Isaiah himself designates it as *tôrâ*! Incidentally, nowhere does Lescow justify the designation "Tora" for the form he is investigating.

[19]Beecher, "*Torah*: A Word-study in the Old Testament," 14.

and others, it is a designation for the prophetic word.[20] Duhm explained the term as priestly usage, Begrich lists it with other texts as "priestly *tôrâ*," and a number of others appear to be of the same opinion.[21] But some relate the term, though only in part, to wisdom usage.[22]

The compositional unity to which this verse belongs is taken to be 1:10-17; these are the limits as given by, e.g., Eichrodt, Eissfeldt, Gray, Fohrer, Hammershaimb, Lindblom, Marti, von Rad, Westermann, and Wildberger.[23] The procedure will be to show, through consideration of formal elements, content, and terminology, that *tôrâ* in this passage is best understood in the wisdom sense; then we will deal with an objection that might be raised by comparison of this piece with Ps 50.

Formal Elements: *Aufmerkruf*; Rhetorical Question

Our passage begins with a "call to attention" (*Aufmerkruf*), a form already encountered in our discussion of the wisdom "instruction" in Prov and in the broader ancient Near Eastern tradition:

šimᵉʿû dᵉbar yhwh *qᵉṣînê sᵉdōm*
haʾăzînû tôrat ʾĕlōhênû *ʿam ʿămōrâ*

Hear the word of the Lord, princes of Sodom!
Listen to the instruction of our God, people of Gomorrah!

The points to be made here are that this "call to attention" fits very well into

[20] Smith, "The Use of the Word *twrh* in Isaiah," 20f.; Lindblom, *Prophecy in Ancient Israel*, 156; Karl Marti, *Das Buch Jesaja* (*Kurzer Hand-Commentar zum Alten Testament* X; Tübingen: Verlag von J. C. B. Mohr, 1900), 10; Haldar, *Associations of Cult Prophets*, 124.

[21] Bernard Duhm, *Das Buch Jesaia* (*HKAT* III, 1; 4th ed.; Göttingen: Vandenhoeck und Ruprecht, 1922), 28; Begrich, "Die priesterliche Tora," 65, 66, 67, 72, 73, 75; Walther Zimmerli, *The Law and the Prophets: A Study of the Meaning of the Old Testament*, tr. R. E. Clements (Oxford: Basil Blackwell, 1965), 73; Walther Eichrodt, *Der Heilige in Israel: Jesaja 1-12 ubersetzt und ausgelegt* (Stuttgart: Calwer Verlag, 1960), 31; Fohrer, *Das Buch Jesaja*, I, 38; Otto Procksch, *Jesaia I* (*KAT* IX; Leipzig: A. Deichertsche Verlagsbuchhandlung, 1930), 38.

[22] See Gray, *The Book of Isaiah I-XXXIX*, I, 18f.; Edward Kissane, *The Book of Isaiah* (Dublin: The Richview Press, 1941), I, 5, translates *tôrâ* by "teaching," but gives no comment on the term; on Wildberger and others, see below.

[23] For Eichrodt, Gray, Fohrer, and Marti, see the commentaries cited in the preceding notes; Eissfeldt, *The Old Testament*, 309; E. Hammershaimb, "On the Ethics of the Old Testament Prophets," *VTSup* 7 (1959) 80; Lindblom, *Prophecy in Ancient Israel*, 250; von Rad, *Old Testament Theology*, II, 150; Claus Westermann, *Basic Forms of Prophetic Speech*, tr. H. C. White (Philadelphia: The Westminster Press, 1967), 203; Wildberger, *Jesaja*, 32-49.

the particular category of "the invocation of the teacher" of *Lehreröffnungsformel*[24] and that this opening followed by a rhetorical question is characteristic of the wisdom tradition.

The *Aufmerkruf* admits many variations in form, occurs in different types of contexts, and serves diverse purposes. For example, there is the simple prophetic call: "Hear this word" (Am 7:16), usually with specification of who is being addressed (Am 3:1.13; 4:1; etc.), or, more commonly, "Hear the word of Yahweh." Such a call introduces an announcement rather than a teacher's address. Again, it may be the heavens and the earth (Isa 1:2) or the mountains and the foundations of the earth (Mic 6:2) that are called to listen; such as these are obviously not called upon to be instructed but to serve as witnesses.[25] Thus, while it is basically the imperative verb (most frequently *šm'*, the hiphil of *'zn*, and the hiphil of *qšb*) which constitutes the *Aufmerkruf*, the subjects addressed can be instructive. Even more instructive may be the objects of the verbs. *Aufmerkrufe* that occur outside of wisdom contexts often have no noun objects at all or, at most, a pronoun referring back to the speaker.[26] In other cases there may be noun objects that so clearly designate "instruction" within the wisdom tradition that the verse is easily designated *Lehreröffnungsformel*; for example, *mûsār* and *tôrâ* (Prov 1:8), *tôrâ* and *miṣwôt* (3:1), *mûsār* and *bînâ* (4:1), *ḥokmâ* and *tᵉbûnâ* (5:1), *mišpāt* and *tôrâ* (6:20), *tôkaḥat* (Job 13:6), *tôrâ* and *'imrê pî* (Ps 78:1). When the terms themselves are ambivalent, the context can show that a call to receive instruction is intended; for example, *'ămārîm* and *miṣwôt* (Prov 7:1), *'imrê pî* (7:24), *millîm* and *dᵉbārîm* (Job 33:1),[27] *qôlî* and *'imrātî* (Isa 28:23).[28]

One might argue, on terminological grounds alone, that 1:10 deserves to be judged "the invocation of the teacher." Although *tôrâ* can be said to be ambivalent (or polyvalent), its use in *Aufmerkrufe* is found only in wisdom

[24]Term used by Hans W. Wolff, *Dodekapropheton 1: Hosea* (*BKAT* XIV/1; Neukirchen: Neukirchener Verlag, 1961), 123. Wolff is here commenting on Hos 5:1; he says: "Der dreigliedrige Aufruf zum Hören lässt ein solennes Wort erwarten. Mit solchen mehrgliedrigen Aufrufen beginnen die alten Sänger ihre Lieder (Ri 5:3; Gn 4:23) und vor allem die Weisheitslehrer ihre Sprüche" (p. 122). And he adds: "Wer als Prophet so zu reden beginnt, tritt mit dem Anspruch des (höfischen) Rechtslehrer auf" (p. 123). Boston, "The Wisdom Influence Upon the Song of Moses," 200, also connects the wisdom and prophetic use of the form.

[25]Dt 32:1f. is a peculiar exception, for though it is the heavens and earth that are addressed in vs. 1, the terms that are used in these two verses (*'imrê pî*, *liqḥî*, and *'imrātî*) clearly point to instruction. But vs. 3 begins to proclaim the Lord's renown.

[26]See Gen 49:2; Jgs 5:3; Jer 13:15; Mic 1:2; with pronouns referring back to the speaker: Is 49:1; 51:4.

[27]See also Job 13:17; 21:2; 34:2.16.

[28]Cf. also openings in Isa 28:23 ("Parable of the Farmer") and in 32:9 (on the "complacent ladies" of Jerusalem). The noun-objects are identical and the verbs are similar; but one quickly discovers that the former is a wisdom piece, the latter an oracle of judgment.

contexts.[29] When a prophet introduces a piece as *d^e^bar yhwh*, we are no doubt to think of the prophetic word; but when he goes on to specify it, within the context of a "call to attention," as *tôrat 'ĕlōhênû*, we should remember that *dābār* and *d^e^bārîm* are also used to designate the instruction of the teacher within the wisdom tradition.[30] No doubt the "instruction" that proceeds from Yahweh has all the authority normally attributed to the word of God spoken by the prophet.

The reference to Sodom and Gomorrah is undoubtedly the prophet's own twist, but the address to rulers and to the people occasions no surprise; while an address to rulers in a call to attention would seem to be specially related to the wisdom tradition, the nation (or all nations) can be addressed in various contexts.[31] But the specific term used by Isaiah for "ruler," *qāṣîn* is of some interest. Although some authors relate the term to the Arabic *qâḍî*, the OT usage does not usually suggest the function of judging. The distribution of the term is somewhat curious: it occurs only thirteen times in the OT, and wisdom and prophetic texts account for nine of them;[32] three of these uses are in *Aufmerkrufe* (Isa 1:10; Mic 3:1.9). The Micah texts suggest that the office of judging falls to them in their capacity as community leaders, and also, perhaps, that a recognized ethical schooling stood in their background. They are expected "to know what is right" (*lāda'at 'et mišpāṭ*—3:1), and behind the prophet's accusation that they "hate what is good, and love evil" (3:2), that they "abhor what is just, and pervert all that is right" (*w^e'^et kol hay^e^šārâ y^e'^aqqēšû*—3:9), we may perhaps see an inversion of the exhortations which were actually a part of their schooling. Micah was a contemporary of Isaiah and well versed in Jerusalem affairs.[33] It can hardly be accidental that both Isaiah and Micah address the leaders as *q^e^ṣînîm*, see them as responsible for the social order and particularly for just judgment, and reproach them in terminology reminiscent of the wisdom tradition. These facts would make Richter's suggestion that the youth of the ruling

[29]Ps 78:1; Prov 1:8; 6:20; see also Prov 4:1f., where the opening formula is carried forward with "For excellent advice (*leqaḥ*) I give you; my teaching (*tôrātî*) do not forsake."

[30]Fohrer, *Das Buch Jesaja*, I, 58, makes a somewhat similar point on the two terms, but for him the *tôrâ* is that of the priest. It is not at all clear that Isaiah here is giving answers to "ganz bestimmte Fragen," as he asserts. For a very ancient example of a *Lehreröffnungsformel* in which "instruction" and "word" (in the singular) are used in parallel, see the "Instruction of Ubartutu to Šuruppak," quoted above, in Ch. 2; the Akkadian version of this text (which uses "words," in the plural) employs the same parallelism (also cited there).

[31]Thus the address to rulers: Sir 33:19; Wis 6:1f.; to God's people: Ps 50:1; Is 51:4; to all peoples: Jer 6:18; Joel 1:2; Mic 1:2; Ps 49:2.

[32]Wisdom texts. Prov 6:7; 25:15; Sir 48:15; prophetic: Isa 1:10; 3:6f.; 22:3; Mic 3:1.9; the other texts are: Jos 10:24; Jgs 11:6.11; Dan 11:18.

[33]Although Mic 3:1.9 designate these leaders as of "Jacob" and of "the house of Israel," vs. 10 relates them directly to Jerusalem.

class underwent schooling in Jerusalem, with special emphasis on the ethical demands of their calling, exceedingly likely; these texts, along with the three wisdom texts that employ the term, make it probable that *qāṣîn* was specially employed in these circles. If Isaiah wishes to introduce Yahweh as one who imparts wise instruction and rebukes[34] those who neglect it, it is not surprising that he does so by means of a *Lehreröffnungsformel* in which this term is employed.[35]

Finally, the rhetorical question which follows this opening deserves attention as a formal element that again relates this piece to the wisdom tradition. This is not to suggest that the simple employment of rhetorical questions necessarily speaks of wisdom influence; some do, indeed, seem to hold this, but the device is too common to be evidence of a particular tradition. However, here we have a pattern of a call to attention followed by a rhetorical question; this is a more complex literary procedure, and a good case can be made for its being a characteristic wisdom device. This pattern is found at least four times in Job.[36] If vss. 4f. of Ps 49 are considered an explanatory expansion after the *Aufmerkruf* of vss. 2f., as they should be, then the argument of this wisdom psalm begins with a rhetorical question and the same pattern is found again. Most significantly, however, the "Parable of the Farmer," the clearest example of a wisdom composition by Isaiah, exhibits the same pattern: the call to attention (28:23), followed by a rhetorical question (vs. 24). This parable is classified by Westermann as a "disputation" (*Streitgespräch*),[37] and its intention is, in part at least, polemical. Thus there is some evidence that the pattern here described and illustrated was a wisdom

[34]Isaiah does not use *tôkaḥat*, but he does employ *yākaḥ* in hiphil three times: once with Yahweh as the subject (2:4) and twice with the ideal king of the future as the subject (11:3f.).

[35]Wildberger, *Jesaja*, 35, rejects the classification of *Gerichtsrede* for this oracle, pointing out that *tôrâ* "sich nicht als Bezeichnung einer Anklagerede eignet," and further that "Inhaltlich wird in diesem Jahwewort nicht auf Bundesbruch geklagt, und die für die Gerichtsrede charakteristische Topik fehlt. . . . Es wird nicht Gericht gehalten, sondern Unterweisung erteilt . . . ." He also relates much of the content to the wisdom tradition (p. 36). Nevertheless, he designates the piece as priestly *tôrâ*; his reasons for doing so will be questioned below, but here it may be asked if there ever occurs in the OT a priestly *tôrâ* that is introduced by an opening address such as this.

[36]Job 13:6; 21:2; 34:16; 37:14. One might conclude from the use of rhetorical questions in this book that they were a favorite means for beginning an argumentative discourse, with or without an *Aufmerkruf*. Thus, in the first cycle, each of the three friends begins his discourse with a rhetorical question (4:2; 8:2; 11:2); in the second cycle Eliphaz and Bildad begin this way (15:2; 18:2) and Job responds to the latter in like manner (19:2); in the third cycle Eliphaz begins with a rhetorical question (22:2). In our passage the Yahweh speech proper begins with a rhetorical question (Isa 1:11).

[37]Westermann, *Basic Forms of Prophetic Speech*, 201.

procedure,[38] particularly favored for debates.[39]

The content of Yahweh's *tôrâ* must be taken to be fairly broad and not restricted to the points covered in this piece. A passage like Prov 1:8-19 begins with a call to hear the father's instruction and then lays down advice against consorting with the wicked. The specific advice given does not exhaust the father's store of instruction but is, on a given occasion, a particularly relevant example of it. The same is probably true of Isaiah's use of *tôrâ* in a text like the present one. It must be noted that for all the employment of wisdom procedures, the prophet introduces Yahweh in the third person; thus there is a change of person in passing from the *Aufmerkruf* to the actual instruction—something that would not happen in a simple wisdom composition.

Content and Terminology

The remainder of the passage, that which follows the call to attention, begins by insisting on the uselessness of sacrifices, solemnities, and prayers to please God and then passes into a series of exhortations, first general and then more specific. Not only is such criticism of the cult (without, however, the prophetic fire and indignation) at home in wisdom, but the demands made wholly reflect wisdom concerns.

It is generally agreed today that the prophets did not condemn sacrifice as such; what they condemned was the substitution, in practice, of sacrifice for righteousness. Such judgment on the value of sacrifice in the light of the dispositions of the offerer is found also in the wisdom tradition, as is well known. Rankin even suggests that such teachings in the prophets owed something to the wisdom tradition.[40] An example of "the thought that righteousness was better than sacrifice" in a non-Israelite text (and one that Rankin gives) is found in "The Instruction for Meri-ka-Re": "More acceptable is the character of one upright of heart than the ox of the evildoer" (*ANET*, 417). This comes from one who does not despise the cult but who elsewhere recommends sacrifice (*ANET*, 416). A rather similar judgment is found in Prov 21:3:

> To do what is right and just (*ṣᵉdāqâ ûmišpāṭ*)
> is more acceptable to the Lord than sacrifice.

[38]The presence of this pattern in Mic 3:1 does not weaken this conclusion, for there is good reason to suppose that Micah, too, was turning the weapons of the wisdom school against its graduates, as pointed out above.

[39]The same procedure seems to be found at the beginning of "A Dialogue About Human Misery," *ANET*, 439, though the text is broken and somewhat obscure. That it is the opening shot in a debate becomes clear in the first lines of the friend's reply. The sufferer's reply (Stanza III) begins with a rhetorical question.

[40]Rankin, *Israel's Wisdom Literature*, 15; see also Johannes Hempel, *Das Ethos des Alten Testaments* (*BZAW* 67; Berlin: Verlag Alfred Töpelmann, 1964), 28, 224.

Since the Meri-ka-Re composition can be dated to the end of the twenty-second century,[41] there is no reason to attribute the similar statement in Prov to prophetic influence.

Of considerable interest is Isaiah's use of *tô'ēbâ* (vs. 13) in his judgment of the rites that Yahweh finds unacceptable, for it is a term that occurs frequently in Prov,[42] twice in passages that condemn the sacrifice of the wicked:

> The sacrifice of the wicked is *tô'ăbat yhwh,*
> but the prayer of the upright is his delight (*r^eṣônô*—15:8).
> The sacrifice of the wicked is *tô'ēbâ,*[43]
> the more so when they offer it with a bad intention (21:27).

Whether the *tô'ēbâ* expressions in Prov spring originally from wisdom usage or whether they come from other Israelite tradition (e.g., cultic) is disputed; a related question is that of a possible connection between the use of *tô'ēbâ* in Prov and in Dt,[44] where it also occurs frequently. Yet an equivalent term is used in "The Instruction of Amen-em-Opet", and it seems possible to build a good case for the expression coming into Israel's wisdom usage through the international wisdom tradition, especially through Egypt.[45] Three "abomination" passages in Amen-em-Opet have to do with falsehood:

> Do not talk with a man falsely—
> The abomination of the god (xiii, 15f.).
> God hates him who falsifies words;
> His great abomination is the contentious of belly (xiv, 2f.).
> Do not confuse a man with a pen upon papyrus—
> The abomination of the god (xv, 20f.).[46]

Two of the *tô'ēbâ* passages in Prov refer directly to the matter of falsehood in the spoken word:

> Lying lips are *tô'ăbat yhwh*
> but those who are truthful are his delight (*r^eṣônô*—12:22).

[41] According to John A. Wilson, *ANET*, 414.

[42] Twenty-one times in all: 3:32; 6:16; 8:7; 11:1.20; 12:22; 13:19; 15:8.9.26; 16:5.12; 17:15; 20:10.23; 21:27; 24:9; 26:25; 28:9; and 29:27 (*bis*). In most cases the term occurs in the phrase *tô'ăbat yhwh* or is otherwise related to Yahweh.

[43] It is possible that *tô'ăbat yhwh* should be read here with LXX.

[44] The term occurs seventeen times in Dt. Of special interest is the use of *tô'ăbat yhwh* (7:25; 12:31; 17:1; 18:12a; 22:5; 23:19; 25:16; 27:15), which occurs only here and in Prov; another text (24:4) has *tô'ēbâ hî' lipnê yhwh.*

[45] Egyptian terminology is probably reflected in the OT use of *tô'ēbâ* in Gen 43:32; 46:34; Ex 8:22 (*bis*), where, in each case, the phrase *tô'ăbat miṣrayim* is used to mean "that which is an abomination to the Egyptians." For reference to "abomination" texts in Egypt and Mesopotamia, see Gemser, *Sprüche Salomos*, 31.

[46] The three texts are found in *ANET*, 423.

There are six things the Lord hates,
yes, seven are *tô'ăbat*[47] *napšô*;
. . ., a lying tongue,
and hands that shed innocent blood;
. . . .
The false witness who utters lies,
. . . (6:16-19).[48]

Since there is such close similarity between these passages in the two compositions, and since the influence of Egyptian wisdom in Israel can be considered an established fact, there seems no point in looking outside of the wisdom tradition for the explanation of the term in Prov. (Since Isaiah's condemnation of incense as *tô'ēbâ* is certainly not because of the incense itself but because of the sins of its offerers, it is of interest to note that "hands that shed innocent blood" is among the things called *tô'ēbâ* in the second of the two passages from Prov quoted and that Isaiah climaxes his list of repulsive rites with the exclamation: "Your hands are full of blood!"—Isa 1:15c.)

While the two passages cited are the only places in Prov where *tô'ēbâ* is used of lying words, there are others in which it refers to or suggests deviousness or deceptive practices,[49] namely, 8:7; 11:1; 20:10.23. Since, therefore, the use of *tô'ēbâ* in such texts of Prov accords with wisdom usage attested even outside of Israel, there is no reason to attribute its employment there to cultic or other influence; and since the broader sense in which Isaiah employs *tô'ēbâ* in our present passage agrees very well with Prov 15:8 and 21:27, there is every reason to see wisdom influence in his usage. In fact, if we were to see an implied accusation in the *Aufmerkruf* that Judah has not been attending to Yahweh's *tôrâ*, we could propose another parallel from Prov:

When one turns away his ear from hearing *tôrâ*,
even his prayer is *tô'ēbâ* (28:9).

If one looks simply at the relevant expression in the Isaiah text (*qᵉṭōret tô'ēbâ hî' lî*), there is the possibility of understanding it in a cultic sense. Wildberger, having noted indications that Isaiah's *Opferkritik* is rooted in wisdom, appears to concede at least an equal possibility of cultic background.[50] Yet *tô'ēbâ* is far from being a typical cult expression, as Wildberger

[47]So with *Qᵉre*; *Kᵉtib* gives plural.

[48]Although these verses fall within Prov 1-9, they are part of a section (6:1-19) generally considered intrusive in their present position. There is no trace of late theologizing in these lines, and there is every probability that we are dealing with older materials utilized by the editor rather than with his own composition.

[49]McKane, *Proverbs*, 301, considers the parallel of Prov 12:22 with Amen-em-Opet "striking" and sees "three other occurrences which are directly comparable," namely, 11:20; 15:26; and 17:15.

[50]Wildberger, *Jesaja*, 35f.

asserts; what is more important, there is little to connect it with the cult of the Jerusalem priesthood. It occurs six times in H (Lev 18:22.26.27.29.30; 20:13), but not at all in P. All of the six texts in H refer to sins of sexual perversion, with no cultic overtones, and all but one (18:22) have the plural, *tôʿēbôt*. Ezekiel, who might be expected to witness to the practice of the Jerusalem priesthood on this point, uses *tôʿēbâ* forty-three times, but almost always in the plural, and never with a specifically cultic import. Dt alone uses *tôʿēbâ* in a cultic context, but there are only two texts (17:1; 23:19) which tell what is or is not acceptable in Yahweh's worship. Furthermore, it is questionable whether a practice attested in Dt but not in P was known in Jerusalem before the deuteronomic reform. Finally, it can even be argued that the use of *tôʿēbâ* in Dt derives from its use in wisdom[51] and, therefore, the wisdom influence on this point is the more widespread and pervasive.

Wildberger's suggestion that *tôʿēbâ hîʾ* is a cultic declaratory formula is impressive until the texts are examined. There are, in fact, only five texts (aside from Isa 1:13)[52] in which the expression occurs:[53]

1) "Egyptians may not eat with Hebrews *kî tôʿēbâ hîʾ lᵉmiṣrāyim*" (Gen 43:32).

2) "You shall not lie with a male as with a woman; *tôʿēbâ hîʾ*" (Lev 18:22).

3) "The images of their gods you shall destroy by fire. Do not covet the silver and gold . . . *kî tôʿăbat yhwh ʾĕlōhèkā hûʾ*" (Dt. 7:25).

4) "You shall not sacrifice . . . an animal with any serious defect; *kî tôʿăbat yhwh ʾĕlōhèkā hûʾ*" (Dt 17:1).

5) "her former husband . . . may not again take her as his wife after she has become defiled *kî tôʿēbâ hîʾ lipnê yhwh*" (Dt. 24:4).

Perhaps the most striking thing about these texts is the diversity of the matters they treat of—Egyptian customs, pagan idols, defective animals, and sexual taboos; only #2 and #5 have anything in common, and only #4 is related to the cult. The use of *hîʾ* or *hûʾ* for the copula is very common and it

[51]This is, in fact, the development traced by L'Hour, "Les interdits *toʿeba* dans le Deutéronome," 481-503. See also Weinfeld, *Deuteronomy and the Deuteronomic School*, 296. McKane, *Proverbs*, 301f., refers to a suggestion made by Humbert (*ZAW* 72 [1960] 224f.) that *tôʿăbat yhwh* in Dt is a borrowing from pre-exilic Israelite wisdom, adds arguments of his own, and then sums up: "My conclusion is that if a direct literary relationship is assumed between Deuteronomy and Proverbs in respect of this formula, the dependence is probably on the side of Deuteronomy, which, however, has pressed it into the service of a new cause . . ." It may be suggested, however, that the question is probably not one of *literary* dependence but a broader one of the influence of one traditionary circle on another, and he is inaccurate in saying that there is no "community of content" in the phrase in the two compositions.

[52]BH suggests the *hîʾ* in this text be deleted, but there seems no valid reason for doing so; BHS drops the suggestion.

[53]Wildberger's statement on this point is somewhat confusing, not to say misleading. He gives Lev 18:22 as an example of the formula, but then adds Dt 7:25; 17:1; 18:12; 22:5; 23:19; "u. ö.," as examples of an expanded form, *tôʿăbat yhwh ʾĕlōhèkā*; if the *hîʾ* is missing, however, as it is in many of these, the formula is an essentially different one. Dt 18:12 and 22:5 both have *kî tôʿăbat yhwh* (*ʾĕlōhèkā*) *kol ʿōśēh ʾēlleh*, but this is quite different from the *hîʾ*-formula and is rather comparable to the use of participles after *tôʿēbâ* in Prov 6:16-19 and to the *kol gᵉbah-lēb* of Prov 16:5. (On Dt 23:19, see text, below.)

is hardly possible to build any argument concerning a "declaratory formula" on the construction; the passage on Egyptian customs (#1), the only one which coincides with Isa 1:13 in the use of *l^e^*, finds parallels as to content in other passages in which the construction is entirely different (Gen 46:34; Ex 8:22).

It is really only #4, the one concerning sacrificial animals, that would be relevant as a cultic declaratory formula concerning what is (not) acceptable, and at first glance it would appear to be a possible parallel to the expression in Isa 1:13. However, as the phrase occurs in Dt, it is part of a motive clause and for that very reason cannot be simply a cultic declaration; this observation holds good also for #2, #3, and #5. It could be argued that the phrase originated as a declaration and was then adopted as a motivation; such speculations are difficult to disprove. However, the present meaning of the phrase, which is the only one we have to go on, appears to reflect a judgment on the *act* of offering an imperfect animal rather than a decision concerning the animal; thus the content is ethical and religious, as so often in Prov, rather than purely cultic.

Finally, it might be proper to include in this list, as an equivalent expression, Dt 23:19: "You shall not offer a harlot's fee or a dog's price as any kind of votive offering in the house of the Lord, your God; *kî tô'abăt yhwh 'ĕlōhèkā gam šᵉnēhem.*" The text has to do with votive offerings and the *šᵉnēhem* might be considered grammatically equivalent to *hî'*. But if this line of reasoning is followed, we can immediately see how little the formula demands a cultic context, for it is found exactly (except for the *kî*, which comes in only because we are dealing with the motive clause of an apodictic law) in two passages in Prov:

> He who condones the wicked, he who condemns the just,
> *tô'ăbat yhwh gam šᵉnēhem* (Prov 17:15).
>
> Varying weights, varying measures,
> *tô'ăbat yhwh gam šᵉnēhem* (Prov 20:10).

Thus the best parallels for Isaiah's use of *tô'ēbâ* come from Prov, especially passages like 6:16f.; 15:8; 21:3.27; 28:9. His phrase *qᵉṭōret tô'ēbâ hî' lî* is more closely paralleled by *zebaḥ rᵉšā'îm tô'ăbat yhwh* (Prov 15:8) than by anything in Dt or Lev.

Isaiah's exposition of the uselessness of Judah's sacrifices comes to a conclusion in vs. 15; Yahweh closes His eyes to their prayerful poses and His ears to their words. The concluding line of vs. 15 supplies the explanation in capsule form: "Your hands are full of blood!" Thus the sins condemned are those of social injustice and oppression rather than the political concerns that figure so largely in many of his other oracles. This is confirmed by the positive measures urged in vs. 17.

While Wildberger seems to find justification for speaking of a wisdom, priestly, or prophetic *tôrâ* in our passage,[54] it is largely the presence of what he considers to be cultic terms that inclines him to speak especially of priestly *tôrâ*. We have already discussed his claims concerning *tô'ēbâ* and its background; the two opening imperatives of vs. 16 (*raḥăṣû, hizzakkû*) are also given as arguments for a cultic context.[55] A preliminary observation to be made, however, is that it would seem poor psychology to insist on the uselessness of cultic observances and then to call for reform in terms that suggest a merely ritual purification; an *a priori* judgment would suggest that Isaiah would not be likely to deliberately choose such terminology. The first of the two terms, *rḥṣ*, certainly is used frequently in a ritualistic or cultic context—in approximately 70% of its sixty-nine occurrences; characteristic of this use, however, is the phrase "with water" (*bammayim*), which is found in about two-thirds of the cases. The texts which speak of washing the hands in a cultic or ritualistic context (Dt 21:6; Ps 26:6),[56] moreover, describe a ceremony by which the participants declare themselves innocent of guilt—something Isaiah surely didn't have in mind! However, the verb is also used in more than a score of texts to refer to other matters: it is frequently used for the washing of feet, either in a fairly literal manner[57] or in symbolic reference to bathing them in blood (Ps 58:11) or in milk (Job 29:6—literally "steps" rather than "feet"); Joseph washes his face (Gen 43:31); Pharaoh's daughter bathes (Ex 2:5), as do David (2 Sam 12:20), harlots (1 Kgs 22:38), and Ruth (Ru 3:3); etc. Thus the verb seems to have the general sense "to wash." Any cultic reference must be determined from the context, not from the employment of the word itself.[58]

There is even less reason for seeing *zkh* (used here by Isaiah in hithpael)[59] as a cultic term. The verb is not used elsewhere in the OT in the hithpael, so

[54]Wildberger, *Jesaja*, 36.

[55]*Ibid.*, 36, 46.

[56]The intent of the oath of the leaders in Dt 21:6 is clear enough. On Ps 26:6 Artur Weiser, *The Psalms: A Commentary*, tr. H. Hartwell (Philadelphia: The Westminster Press, 1962), 243, remarks: "The oath of purification, formulated positively in v. 3 and negatively in vv. 4f., is followed by the ritual ceremony of purification and its confirmation."

[57]Gen 18:4; 19:2; 43:24; Jgs 19:21; 1 Sam 25:41; 2 Sam 11:8 (perhaps euphemistically); Ct 5:3.

[58]It is worth noting that when *rāḥaṣ* is used in a cultic context and is accompanied by another verb that means "to be clean" (i.e., as the result of the washing), that verb is normally *ṭāhēr*; cf. Lev 14:8.9; 15:13; 2 Kgs 5:10.12.13. Obviously this is not the pattern found in Isa 1:15.

[59]Wildberger, *Jesaja*, 34, cites A. M. Honeyman, *VT* 1 (1951) 63-65, for the opinion that the word in our text is the niphal imperative of *zkk*; the significance of this, according to Wildberger, is that *zkk* is a cultic term, *zkh* a forensic one. However, the texts in which *zkk* occurs (in qal: Job 15:15; 25:5; Lam 4:7; in hiphil: Job 9:30) simply do not favor a cultic sense or even, in some cases, a forensic one. The noun *zak*, derived from this verb, is used to describe the pure quality of materials used in the cult in Ex 27:20; 30:34; Lev 24:2.7, but its other occurrences are in wisdom compositions: Job 8:6; 11:4; 16:17; 33:9; Prov 16:2; 20:11; 21:8; of these, only in Job 16:17, where there is reference to "sincere prayer," could the reference possibly be cultic. Walter Baumgartner, *Hebräisches und aramäisches Lexikon zum Alten Testament*, Lieferung I (Leiden: E. J. Brill, 1967), 258, takes note of Honeyman's view but identifies the form as the hithpael of *zkh*; on the development of the form, see Rudolf Meyer, *Hebräische Grammatik* (Berlin: Walter de Gruyter & Co., 1966), I, 107, 114f.

any light upon its range of reference and usual context will have to come from the other conjugations in which it occurs, namely, qal and piel. The piel should be the more instructive of the two since, ideally speaking at least, the hithpael is a reflexive of the piel. This form occurs in Ps 73:13; 119:9; and Prov 20:9; to these should probably be added Mic 6:11, which MT points as a qal. Two of these (Ps 73:13;[60] Prov 20:9[61]) belong to wisdom compositions, and characteristic wisdom expressions or concerns are found in the immediate context in the other two: Mic 6:11 condemns false scales and weights in terms similar to those in Prov,[62] while Ps 119:9 asks how a youth shall be "faultless in his way (*'orḥô*)." Since Ps 73:13 and Prov 20:9 are concerned with inner purity, purity "of the heart (*l*ᵉ*bābî, libbî*)," all four passages have to do with an inner, ethical rectitude that has little in common with merely cultic purity; the verb does not occur at all in a cultic context. The uses of the qal (Ps 51:6; Job 15:14; 25:4) do not appear to contribute much to our understanding of the Isaiah passage; in each case *zkh* is parallel to *ṣdq* and has a forensic sense.

Thus, these two opening imperatives do not suggest a cultic context.[63] Isaiah, having told his hearers that their hands are full of blood, urges them to wash and be clean, first with a verb that commonly signified washing or bathing and then with one that seems to have connoted especially an inner, ethical purity and that was particularly at home in wisdom contexts.

Westermann says that the words "Your hands are full of blood!" are the specific accusation standing between the reproof (vss. 11-15b) and the instruction (vss. 16f.).[64] While the first two imperatives seem to be closely joined to this accusation (and form a single poetic line with it), the string of imperatives that follow contain the instruction proper. The closing lines merit special attention:

[60]The second half of this verse, *wā'erḥaṣ b*ᵉ*niqqāyôn kappāy*, is (except for the waw-consecutive) identical with Ps 26:6a, a passage in which *rāḥaṣ* is clearly cultic. As employed in the present psalm, the phrase may well have been lifted from the liturgy; if so, it has been somewhat transformed in the process and does not weaken the interior, non-cultic reference of 73:13a, with its concern for the heart. This wisdom composition is the only text other than Isa 1:15 in which these two verbs are used together.

[61]Prov 20:9a manifests concern for interior morality with its reference to the heart. Vs. 9b uses *ṭāhēr*, a verb which, it is true, is used preponderately in cultic contexts; yet again it is proper to speak of a transposition, for in those passages the concern was almost exclusively with cleansing from ritual impurity, such as that which attends leprosy, seminal discharge, or touching a corpse. The present text, on the other hand, speaks explicitly of a cleansing from sin (*mēḥaṭṭā'tî*).

[62]*mō'znê reša'* and *'ab*ᵉ*nê mirmâ*; cf. Prov 11:1; 20:10.23.

[63]If Isaiah had wanted to imitate priestly or cultic diction we might have expected him to use a second term that is at home in the cult, such as *kibbēs* (usually used of garments, it is true, but see Jer 2:22; 4:14; Ps 51:4.9), *qiddaš*, or *ṭāhēr*.

[64]Westermann, *Basic Forms of Prophetic Speech*, 203f.

(16c-17a)	*ḥid*^{e}*lû hārēa'*	*lim*^{e}*du hēṭēb*
(17b)	*dir*^{e}*šû :mišpāṭ*	*'ašš*^{e}*rû ḥāmôs*[65]
(17c)	*šip*^{e}*ṭû yātôm*	*rîbû 'almānâ*

Cease doing evil; learn to do good.
Make justice your aim: redress the wronged,
hear the orphan's plea, defend the widow.

If the indications of the poetic structure may be followed, the general exhortation of vs. 16b ("Put away your misdeeds from before my eyes") has been specified with the double expression that sounds very much like a wisdom exhortation. This is seen both in that the positive command is to learn, and in the use of opposites, which is frequent in wisdom compositions. Exact parallels for these two commands and their terminology are not easy to find. There is however a good parallel as to sense in Ps 34:15:[66] "Turn from evil, and do good (*sûr mērā' wa'ăśeh ṭôb*)." Another parallel is found in Ps 36:4b:[67] "he has ceased to understand how to do good (*ḥādal l*^{e}*haśkîl l*^{e}*hêṭîb*)." Finally, according to Job 28:28, "avoiding evil is understanding (*sûr mērā' bînâ*)."[68]

The remaining exhortations, concerning right judgment and justice for the oppressed, for the orphan and the widow, are clearly directed to the ruling elements, to those with whom the responsibility for such matters rested. These are all concerns which are at home in the wisdom tradition; if we think of the ruling class as being the special recipients of the teaching of "the school," nothing could be more natural. These additional imperatives can be taken as more specific applications of the general command "learn to do good"[69] and have more to do with the ethical norms of the wisdom tradition than with individual commandments of Israelite law; thus they fit more easily into the category of wisdom *tôrâ* than into legal or priestly *tôrâ*. The vocabulary of these lines is, in the main, of too general a character to be

[65]So MT; the versions and most commentators read the passive.

[66]This is an acrostic psalm. Murphy, *JBC* 35:51, classifies it as a wisdom psalm; on vss. 12-22 he says that "the psalmist appears as a sage, inculcating typical wisdom lessons." Weiser, *The Psalms*, 297, sees a shift to wisdom emphasis in vss. 12-22. The wisdom character of at least this part of the psalm seems unassailable, especially in view of the *Aufmerkruf*: "Come, children, hear me;/I will teach you the fear of the Lord."

[67]Weiser, *The Psalms*, 305, distinguishes two parts to the psalm: "In mood and subject-matter the psalm is divided into two parts distinctly differing from each other. After the fashion of the Wisdom literature, vv. 1-4 contain a stern characterization of the man who is under the sway of sin." (The passage referred to is vss. 2-5 in the Hebrew.)

[68]The good-evil antithesis is found also in Amos (Am 5:14f.), but its presence there has been taken as an indication of wisdom influence on this prophet; see Wolff, *Amos' geistige Heimat*, 46-48.

[69]Fohrer, *Das Buch Jesaja*, I, 41f.

proper to one specific tradition; however, it is worth noting that the second verb in vs. 17b, *'šr*, to go straight (qal), to lead straight, reprove (piel), is found only in Isaiah (here and in 3:12; 9:15), in Prov (4:14; 9:6; 23:19), and, possibly, in Sir (4:18).[70]

The matters these verses deal with appear in Israel's legislation but with no great emphasis. The *Richtersspiegel* of Ex 23:6-9 enjoins just judgment for the needy, acquittal for the innocent, and punishment for the guilty; it forbids bribes and oppression of the alien. As already noted, Richter sees a special relationship of this passage to the class of men responsible for the order within society and to the school in which they received their training.[71] Ex 22:20-23 forbids the oppression of aliens and the wronging of widows and orphans, but otherwise there are no laws made in favor of the widow and the orphan outside of Dt. In Dt "the widow and the orphan" are mentioned eleven times,[72] regularly as needy persons to whom charity is to be shown. Although some of these passages are very probably old (24:17; 27:19), the fact that the Levites are often mentioned along with the widow and the orphan (14:29; 16:11.14; 26:12.13) suggests that many of them, at least in their present form, date only from the period of the deuteronomic reform; again, the fact that widow and orphan *always* occur together in Dt suggest that we are often dealing with a late stereotype rather than genuinely ancient provisions.[73] The special regard paid to oppressed or needy classes in Dt may well reflect the wisdom influence we have had occasion to note.[74]

In the wisdom tradition indications of concern for justice on the part of officials and for just, humane treatment of the oppressed and needy are ancient and widely attested. The following passage from "The Instruction of Meri-ka-Re" parallels our passage from Isaiah in the use of the imperative

[70]Baumgartner, *Hebräisches und aramäisches Lexikon zum Alten Testament*, I, 94, lists Sir 4:18 as a piel ("führen") of the *'šr* I root ("schreiten"), but it seems equally possible to relate the form to the *'šr* II; the Greek translation of the verse, in fact, seems to construe it *both* ways.

[71]Richter, *Recht und Ethos*, 66; see above, Ch. 3, n. 33.

[72]Dt 10:18; 14:29; 16:11.14; 24:17.19.20.21; 26:12.13; 27:19. The first of these references is in a purely homiletic section and speaks of the justice God exercises towards the widow and the orphan; 16:11.14; 26:12f. mention them only circumstantially.

[73]Richter, *Recht und Ethos*, 34, n. 80, asserts this to be the case (i.e., deuteronomic and late) for the combination stranger-orphan-widow; it is found in Dt 16:12.14; 24:17.19.20.21; Jer 22:3.

[74]On this point, at least, Weinfeld, "The Origin of the Humanism in Deuteronomy," 241-47, is on firm ground. He relates Dt's laws on landmarks (19:14) and on weights and measures (25:13-16) to the wisdom literature of the OT and the ancient Near East in general and then does much the same with Dt's concern for the Levites, the poor, the stranger, the orphan, the widow; in Weinfeld's opinion, this "humanism" comes from the wisdom rather than from the prophetic tradition: Dt represents the fusion of law and wisdom rather than of law and prophetic tradition; the arguments are more fully developed in *Deuteronomy and the Deuteronomic School*, 244-274. See also Gerstenberger, *Wesen und Herkunft*, 140.

and a general demand for justice (cf. *dirᵉšû mišpāṭ*) followed by others relating to specific classes, including the widow:

> Do justice whilst thou endurest upon earth. Quiet the weeper; do not oppress the widow; supplant no man in the property of his father; and impair no officials at their posts. Be on thy guard against punishing wrongfully.[75]

Amen-em-Opet provides for the widow in more than one text:

> Be not greedy after a cubit of land,
> Nor encroach upon the boundaries of a widow (vii, 14f.).[76]
> Do not recognize a widow if thou catchest her in the fields,
> Nor fail to be indulgent to her reply.[77]

Equally relevant is the following:

> Do not accept the bribe of a powerful man,
> Nor oppress for him the disabled (xxi, 3f.).[78]

These examples from Egyptian literature[79] are important because, coming from "instructions," they are imperative in form. The first examples from Prov, to which we now turn, are similar in both form and content. In the "Sayings of the Wise" (22:17-24:22) we read:

> Injure not the poor because they are poor,
> nor crush the needy at the gate;
> For the Lord will defend their cause,
> and will plunder the lives of those who plunder them (22:22f.).
> Remove not the ancient landmark,
> nor invade the fields of orphans;
> For their redeemer is strong;
> he will defend their cause against you (23:10f.).

Other examples in Prov come from the "sentence literature" and are declaratory in form, but the content is much the same. One of the Egyptian passages quoted above said that "God desires respect for the poor." This sentiment is met with frequently in Prov; cf., e.g.:

> He who oppresses the poor blasphemes his Maker,
> but he who is kind to the needy glorifies him (14:31).

God's concern for the poor is seen also in 15:25; 19:17 (and cf. 22:9; 29:14).

Within the structure of human society it was especially the king and other officials who were charged with the responsibility of safeguarding the rights

[75] *ANET*, 415.

[76] *Ibid.*, 422.

[77] *Ibid.*, 424.

[78] *Ibid.*

[79] See further F. Charles Fensham, "Widow, Orphan, and the Poor in Ancient Near Eastern Legal and Wisdom Literature," *JNES* 21 (1962) 129-39.

of the poor and needy;[80] one of the functions of instruction of youths shaped within the structures of the wisdom tradition was to inculcate an awareness of such responsibilities, as the very texts we have been discussing demonstrate. The wisdom tradition, then, did concern itself with *mišpāṭ*; and Isaiah, in presenting Yahweh as the imparter of a *tôrâ* that calls for right judgment for the oppressed and needy, introduces no novelty except to make Yahweh Himself the teacher. Prov 21:3 remains the best commentary on our passage:

> To do *ṣ^e^dāqâ* and *mišpāṭ*
> is more acceptable to the Lord than sacrifice.

Isa 1:10-17 and Ps 50

There are a sufficient number of elements found in both Isa 1:10-17 and Ps 50 for one to be tempted to postulate a common *Sitz im Leben* and to explain one from the other. In each Yahweh is introduced as a speaker, in each there is an *Aufmerkruf*, criticism of sacrifices, employment of the rhetorical question, and a stern rebuke for sinners. If the two are really comparable as to form and content, the interpretation of Isa 1:10-17 proposed above will be difficult to maintain, for the cultic and covenantal background of Ps 50 is beyond dispute.[81] Wildberger does, in fact, connect the two pieces.[82] In the course of attempting to prove that Isaiah knew the covenant tradition, he says: "Die Polemik gegen das Opfer in der zweiten Gerichtsrede[83] hat ein Parallele im 'Bundesfestpsalm' 50, der Schlusssatz jenes Abschnittes (1, 17) . . . gehört zu den grundsätzlichen Forderungen des amphiktyonischen Rechts."[84]

However, a closer look at Ps 50 shows that the apparent similarities to Isa 1:10-17, at least as they affect our discussion, are fairly superficial. Thus the *Aufmerkruf* of the psalm could never be taken for a *Lehreröffnungsformel*; not only does its introduction speak of summoning heaven and earth "to the trial of his people (*lādîn 'ammô*)" (vs. 4), but the words immediately following this address proclaim "I will testify against you (*w^e'ā'îdâ bāk*)" (vs. 7). The

[80]See Prov 29:14; Ps 72:4.12-14; Isa 11:3f.; Jer 22:15f.; Mic 3:1-4.9-12. E. Hammershaimb, "On the Ethics of the Old Testament Prophets," 75-101; Schmid, *Wesen und Geschichte der Weisheit*, 37-42.

[81]Weiser, *The Psalms*, 393; Murphy, *JBC* 35:66; Mowinckel, *The Psalms in Israel's Worship*, II, 70. However, Kraus, *Psalmen*, 372-74, expresses reservations concerning theories of the cultic setting of this psalm.

[82]Wildberger, "Jesajas Verständnis der Geschichte," 106f.

[83]In his commentary Wildberger now argues against the classification of 1:10-17 as a *Gerichtsrede* (see above, n. 35).

[84]In a footnote on this statement he refers to the article of Hammershaimb cited above in n. 80, and admits a particularly striking parallel adduced by him from a Ugaritic text, but his comment is: "aber sie beweist nur, dass auch das Gottesrecht des Alten Testaments schon früh in lebendigem Austausch mit seiner Umwelt stand." But then his reason for stating that the demands stem from amphictyonic law is based on presupposition rather than on demonstration. In his commentary Wildberger seems to be inconsistent on this point; see p. 48.

following verses do *not* reject sacrifices or say they are unacceptable, but criticize, apparently, the tendency to put too much trust in these externals to the detriment of a deeper acknowledgment of Yahweh's lordship;[85] the covenant was inaugurated in sacrifice (vs. 5) and the demand for sacrifice continues.[86] One could not imagine this author using the term *tô'ēbâ* to characterize the sacred rites or suggesting that God will not hear their prayer (cf. vss. 14.23). In the Isaiah passage there is no doubt that the condemnation of the sacrifices and the following rebuke and instructions are intimately linked, whereas in the psalm attention seems to shift from the people as a whole, who are addressed concerning sacrifice (vss. 8-15), to sinners within the covenant community who are rebuked in stern tones (vss. 16-21).

Thus the central teaching of the psalm is not close to our passage from Isaiah. None of those indications of cultic and covenant context which show up so clearly in the psalm are to be found in Isaiah. The psalm refers explicitly to covenant (vss. 5.16), displays elements of a covenant *rîb* (calling of heaven and earth, reference to a trial and to testimony—vss. 4.5.7), the people are addressed as "my faithful ones" (*ḥăsîdāy*—vs. 5), *ḥuqqîm* is used and stands in parallel with *bᵉrît* (vs. 16), and the reference to specific sins seems almost to come from the Decalogue.[87] On the other hand, those elements in Isaiah that we have seen as indications of wisdom influence, especially the use of *tôrâ*, the rhetorical question following the *Aufmerkruf*, and the demand directed to the ruling class of justice for the needy, have no counterpart in the psalm.[88]

ISAIAH 2:3

The compositional unity to which this verse belongs is taken to be 2:2-4. Agreement on these limits is almost unanimous.[89]

[85] Weiser, *The Psalms*, 396; Murphy, *JBC* 35:66.

[86] Murphy, *ibid.*, on vss. 22f.; Rowley, *Worship in Ancient Israel*, 165.

[87] Murphy, *ibid.*

[88] The point here is to emphasize the difference between the two compositions, not to assert that there was no contact between the cult and wisdom; one might be tempted to see wisdom influence in this psalm in its use of the hiphil of *ykḥ* in vss. 8.21 and in employment of *mûsār* and *dᵉbāray* together in vs. 17. Weiser, *The Psalms*, 305f., clearly supposes the utilization of a wisdom reflection in the cult in his explanation of Ps 36.

[89] The parallel form of the oracle in Mic 4:1-4 has its own conclusion (vs. 4), which some authors argue is the original ending of the piece; others, however, assert that Micah's ending cannot be original. See, e.g., Johann Fischer, *Das Buch Isaias, I. Teil: Kapitel 1-39* (Bonn: Peter Hanstein Verlagsbuchhandlung, 1937), 38; Volkmar Herntrich, *Der Prophet Jesaja: Kapitel 1-12* (*ATD* 17; 2nd ed.; Göttingen: Vandenhoeck & Ruprecht, 1954), 27. All agree that Micah's version of the oracle represents a better and more primitive tradition. The differences between the two forms in which this oracle has been transmitted are not great, consisting mainly in variations in orthography, transpositions, etc.; none of these variations directly affect the present study. One variant reading of potential significance is the plural verb (*wywrwnw*) in IQIsa^{a} instead of MT's *wᵉyōrēnû* in Isa 2:3; this is not given in the BH or BHS apparatus, but see Millar Burrows, *The Dead Sea Scrolls of St. Mark's Monastery*, I (New Haven: The American Schools of Oriental Research, 1950), pl. II. The LXX also reads the verb in the plural in Mic 4:2. See further below, n. 112.

Authenticity

The question of the authorship of this piece is a thorny one. Among those who deny Isaian authorship of it are Marti, Gray, Fohrer, Lindblom, and Eissfeldt;[90] Cheyne thinks it is an older composition which was utilized independently by Isaiah and Micah.[91] However, the great majority of scholars, including—or perhaps especially—more recent ones, attribute it to Isaiah, or at least find no reason for not doing so; these include G. A. Smith, Procksch, Duhm, Rankin, Fischer, Kissane, von Rad, Herntrich, Fichtner, Wildberger, Eichrodt, H. W. Wolff, Vriezen, Gottwalt, Clements, and Lindars.[92] It would be pointless to attempt here to find a sure solution to a problem which has already been so widely debated. It is, in fact, impossible to *prove* that any OT figure is responsible for a given composition; one must start with the traditional ascription of a piece (as, e.g., its inclusion in a prophetic collection) and ask whether its vocabulary, form, and doctrine are consonant with the ascription on the basis of what has been established as normative for that period, in that type of composition, for that person—a process in which there is no small leeway for subjectivism. All that will be attempted here is a brief discussion of the objections most frequently raised against Isaiah's authorship of the piece.

[90]Marti, *Das Buch Jesaja*, 27f.; Gray, *The Book of Isaiah*, I, 43f.; Fohrer, *Das Buch Jesaja*, I, 51. Fohrer is convinced that promises don't belong to the original Isaiah; see "Entstehung, Komposition und Uberlieferung von Jesaja 1-39," 119. Lindblom, *Prophecy in Ancient Israel*, 390; Eissfeldt, *The Old Testament*, 318.

[91]T. K. Cheyne, *The Prophecies of Isaiah*, I (London: Kegan Paul, Trench, & Co., 1889), 15.

[92]George Adam Smith, *The Book of Isaiah* (The Expositor's Bible; 2nd ed.; London: Hodder and Stoughton, 1889), I, 25-27; Duhm, *Das Buch Jesaia*, 36, expresses a judgment that is still valid: "Dass dieser Verf. Jes. sein muss, kann man schwerlich jemals beweisen, aber auch gegen ihn sind bisher noch keine durchschlagenden Gründe vorgebracht worden. Allgemeine Sätze wie: die Eschatologie ist rein literarischen Ursprungs, kommt erst mit dem Exil auf, sind willkürliche Behauptungen und zu vage, um Grundlagen der Kritik zu sein." Duhm thinks of the piece being composed by Isaiah after Sennacherib's invasion as part of his "swan song." Procksch, *Jesaia* I, 61-63; Rankin, *Israel's Wisdom Literature*, 128; Fischer, *Das Buch Isaias*, 36; Kissane, *The Book of Isaiah*, 22; Gerhard von Rad, "The City on the Hill," *The Problem of the Hexateuch*, 232-42 (originally published in German in *EvT* 8 [1948/49] 439-47), especially pp. 233f.; see also his *Old Testament Theology*, II, 294f.; Herntrich, *Der Prophet Jesaja*, 27; Fichtner, "Jahves Plan in der Botschaft des Jesaja," 31; Hans Wildberger, "Die Völkerwallfahrt zum Zion: Jes. II 1-5," *VT* 7 (1957) 62-81; see also "Jesajas Verständnis der Geschichte," 113f.; Eichrodt, *Der Heilige in Israel*, 44-48; Hans W. Wolff, "The Understanding of History in the Old Testament Prophets," *Essays on Old Testament Hermeneutics*, ed. Claus Westermann (Richmond: John Knox Press, 1963), tr. K. R. Crim (German original in *EvT* 20 [1960] 218-35), 347; Vriezen, "Essentials of the Theology of Isaiah," 134, 144f.; Norman K. Gottwald, *All the Kingdoms of the Earth*, 196; R. E. Clements, *God and Temple* (Philadelphia: Fortress Press, 1965), 81 n.; see also *Prophecy and Covenant*, 49; Lindars, "Torah in Deuteronomy," 121; see others referred to by Rowley, *Worship in Ancient Israel*, 193f.

A preliminary difficulty is that our oracle is attributed also to Micah (Mic 4:1-4). However, the prophet who foretold that Zion would be plowed like a field (Mic 3:12) is unlikely to have seen the same place as the center of the saving pilgrimage of the nations. On the other hand, Zion occupies an important and salvific place in the teaching of Isaiah.[93]

Objections to an eighth century date for the oracle and to its attribution to Isaiah are usually based on the universalism expressed in the piece, which is said to be like that of Deutero-Isaiah and of exilic and postexilic Judaism, its eschatology, and its alleged isolation from anything found in the genuine oracles of Isaiah.[94] All of these arguments appear to be defective. Whether or not one finds Isa 2:2-4 isolated from the rest of the teaching of Isaiah may depend on how one judges the authenticity of passages like 9:1-6 and 11:1-9; for those who accept these oracles as Isaiah's, 2:2-4 presents a picture of future blessedness that is not without analogy in the prophet's thought. Almost every element in 2:2-4 can be traced back to ancient traditions current in Isaiah's day and forming part of his thought world. Thus John H. Hayes, working especially with the Zion Psalms (particularly Pss 46; 48; 76), argues that many elements of the "election of Zion" tradition are pre-Israelite and are not to be attributed to Isaiah or his time or to the deliverance of Jerusalem from Sennacherib.[95]

An earlier study by Wildberger, utilizing these and other OT texts to investigate the background of Isa 2:2-4,[96] led to the conclusion that "In kein anderes Prophetenbuch fügt sich ein Abschnitt wie Jes. ii 2ff so leicht ein, wie gerade in das Jesajabuch!" (p. 72). This statement is based, of course, on the fact that the Zion tradition figures so largely in Isaiah's oracles.[97] The claim is that Isaiah simply applied these traditions to the concrete historical situation of the threat of Assyria. Wildberger investigates the vocabulary of 2:2-4 and finds that the words and phrases used there fit well with Isaiah's own usage or can be explained as coming from the *Traditionsbereich* of the

[93]Cf. especially von Rad, "The City on the Hill," 232f.

[94]For objections from the universalism of Isa 2:2-4, see Marti *Das Buch Jesaja*, 27f.; Fohrer, *Das Buch Jesaja*, I, 51; Eissfeldt, *The Old Testament*, 318. On objections from eschatology, see W. Staerk, "Der Gebrauch der Wendung *b'ḥryt hymym* in alttestamentlichen Kanon," *ZAW* 11 (1891) 247-53; Marti, 28; Fohrer, 52.

[95]John H. Hayes, "The Tradition of Zion's Invulnerability," 419-26.

[96]Wildberger, "Die Völkerwallfahrt zum Zion: Jes. II 1-5," 62-81.

[97]Wildberger lists as surely authentic the following relevant Isaiah passages: 1:8.27; 3:16.17; 8:18; 10:12.32; 28:16; 29:8; 31:4.9; he lists 10:24 as possibly authentic. Childs, *Isaiah and the Assyrian Crisis*, would not accept as authentic all of these references (cf., e.g., his discussion of 31:4-9, pp. 58f.); he does, however, admit that Isaiah knows an earlier Zion tradition and that, in spite of his reinterpretation, the prophet employs it in a positive manner (see especially his comment on 28:16-17a, p. 67).

Zion Psalms.[98] Many other scholars, too, have insisted that this text is based on ancient traditions.[99]

The whole range of questions connected with OT eschatology—its definition, its sources, its beginnings and development— is still so hotly debated[100] that it is difficult to see how firm arguments for dating or authorship can be based on the eschatology (if that's what it is!) of Isa 2:2-4. Mowinckel, for example, strictly relates the Messiah to eschatology ("To use the word 'Messiah' is to imply eschatology, the last things"), and eschatology is taken strictly to mean that belief in a divine act "which coincides with the end of the present world order, and introduces or fashions a new world of a different kind."[101] Clements, on the other hand, while admitting that "what is eschatological lies by definition on the other side of history," insists that this definition applies to a feature that is peripheral rather than central to Israel's hope; he adopts a broader definition of eschatology "which renders it suitable to describe the biblical ideas of God's purpose in history. Eschatology is the study of ideas and beliefs concerning the end of the present world order, and the introduction of a new order."[102]

Depending on what sort of definition of eschatology we adopt, the vision of future hope expressed in Isa 2:2-4 may be given or denied the adjective "eschatological." Von Rad, while seeing in this oracle "the earliest expression of a belief in the eschatological glorification of the holy mountain and of its significance for the redemption of the entire world," understands that the conversion of weapons into tools takes place only after the peoples have returned to their own land and that the oracle "ends with a strikingly sober and

[98]This part of his study (pp. 73-75) is a useful refutation of the claim that the diction of the piece is out of place for Isaiah or the traditions he knew. Siegfried Herrmann, *Die prophetischen Heilserwartungen im Alten Testament: Ursprung und Gestaltwandel* (Stuttgart: W. Kohlhammer Verlag, 1965), 141, reviews Wildberger's arguments and concludes: "Der Spruch ordne sich also in die Zeit Jesajas ein und habe auch dort seinen religionsgeschichtlichen Ort."

[99]E.g., von Rad, "The City on the Hill," 234f.; Eichrodt, *Der Heilige in Israel*, 47; Gottwald, *All the Kingdoms of the Earth*, 196, 199, relates the oracle to the enthronement tradition; Clements (see n. 92, above); Bruce Vawter, *The Conscience of Israel* (New York: Sheed & Ward, 1961), 155.

[100]One of the most recent studies on the problem is Hans-Peter Müller, *Ursprünge und Strukturen alttestamentlicher Eschatologie* (*BZAW* 109; Berlin: Alfred Töpelmann Verlag, 1969). See also Th. C. Vriezen, "Prophecy and Eschatology," *VTSup* 1 (1953) 199-229; A. N. Wilder, "The Nature of Jewish Eschatology," *JBL* 50 (1931) 201-206; Bruce Vawter, "Apocalyptic: Its Relation to Prophecy," *CBQ* 22 (1960) 33-46; A. S. Kapelrud, "Eschatology in the Book of Micah," *VT* 11 (1961) 392-405.

[101]Sigmund Mowinckel, *He That Cometh*, tr. G. W. Anderson (Oxford: Basil Blackwell, 1959), especially Ch. 5 and 8; the quotations are from pp. 3 and 125.

[102]Clements, *Prophecy and Covenant*, Ch. 6, "Prophecy and Eschatology," 103-118; the quotations are from pp. 104, 105.

realistic picture, and the scene remains in every sense a historical one wholly devoid of mythological overtones."[103] Eichrodt, too, insists on the basic realism intended.[104]

The suggestion that the phrase *b^e'aḥărît hayyāmîm* is post-exilic and eschatological has been refuted on more than one occasion. The phrase has generally been equated with the Akkadian *ana aḫrat ūmē*, which simply means "in the future."[105] An article by George Buchanan reaches the conclusion that in every OT occurrence the expression "makes perfectly good sense if translated by 'in the future,' 'in days to come,' 'after this,' or some expression with this meaning, which does not by itself have any eschatological overtones."[106] Most recently a study has been devoted to this phrase by Lipiński (see n. 104) to prove that the expression is not found exclusively in post-exilic texts.

The objection arising from the universalism of the passage can be dealt with briefly. To such objections Rowley remarks: "We have no reason to date this kind of universalism in the same age as the very different universalism of Deutero-Isaiah."[107] Fischer points out that "Israels Religion zielte von Anfang auf Universalismus hin (Gn 18, 18) . . ."[108] More relevant even than texts such as Gen 18:18, for present purposes, are some of the Zion Psalms, especially Ps 46; 48; 76; and 87; in these we find universalism combined with some of the other themes that are present in Isa 2:2-4. Ps 46:10f. proclaims that Yahweh "has stopped wars to the ends of the earth," speaks of His destruction of weapons of war, and quotes Him as saying:

> Desist! and confess that I am God,
> exalted among the nations (*baggôyim*), exalted upon the earth.

Clearly it is the nations, those who have been warring (against Jerusalem) and whose weapons have been destroyed, who are so addressed. Less clearly is this note present in Ps 48, though it may be suggested in that Zion is said to be "the joy of all the earth" and in that God's name, as also His praise, "reaches to the ends of the earth." The translation of Ps 76:11 is somewhat problematic because the text presents difficulties; the *NAB* revocalizes *'dm* and *ḥmt*

[103] G. von Rad, "The City on the Hill," 233f.; the final statement refers to the end of the oracle and not the exordium. Mowinckel quite correctly notes that the presence of mythological language does not necessarily imply eschatology (*He That Cometh*, 149, 261).

[104] Eichrodt, *Der Heilige in Israel*, 48. See also E. Lipiński, *"b'ḥryt hymym* dans les textes préexiliques," *VT* 20 (1970) 445-50; he does not discuss Isa 2:2-4 but says of the OT texts in which the phrase *b^e'ăḥarît hayyāmîm* occurs, except for Dan 10:14; "elle vise des événements de l'histoire" (p. 445). Gottwald, *All the Kingdoms of the Earth*, 147, 195f., 199-202.

[105] Cheyne, *The Prophecies of Isaiah*, 15; Wildberger, "Jesajas Verständnis der Geschichte," 114n.; Lipiński (see preceding note), 445; and Gray, *The Book of Isaiah*, I, 44.

[106] George W. Buchanan, "Eschatology and the 'End of Days'," *JNES* 20 (1961) 188-193; the quotation is from p. 190.

[107] Rowley, *Worship in Ancient Israel*, 193.

[108] Fischer, *Das Buch Isaias*, 36.

and emends the final verb in the light of the LXX in order to render it:

For wrathful Edom shall glorify you,
and the survivors of Hamath shall keep your festivals.

The procedure is reasonable, the translation makes sense, and the pattern that emerges in the psalm as a whole fits with what we found in Ps 36. Weiser's treatment of the text is somewhat different, but the conclusions he reaches support a similar interpretation.[109] Ps 87 displays a very universalistic spirit throughout.

There is no compelling reason for dating these psalms late; the fact that many of Isaiah's undoubtedly authentic oracles reflect the same traditions is a reason for dating them early, for it is impossible to believe that Isaiah "invented" these—often highly nationalistic—traditions.[110] In the case of Isa 2:2-4 we are undoubtedly justified in speaking of a reinterpretation and transposition of the earlier traditions; the weapons have disappeared and peace reigns, but this is the result of a marvelous act by which the nations have submitted themselves to Yahweh's *tôrâ* and learned His ways, not the result of carnage wreaked among those who have come up against Jerusalem to destroy it. In a similar manner Isaiah has reworked the picture of the Davidic king who would shatter the nations like an earthen dish (Ps 2:9), in the establishing of whose throne corpses would be heaped up and heads crushed over the wide earth (Ps 110:6), into a Prince of Peace whose birth would turn the raiment of war into fuel for flames (Isa 9:4f.) and in whose reign there would be no harm or ruin on all God's holy mountain (Isa 11:9). Our oracle can in good conscience be attributed to Isaiah.

Yahweh the Wise King; Wisdom Terminology

The argument in favor of the wisdom sense of *tôrâ* in this passage can proceed along two lines: the presentation of Yahweh as the King to whom the nations come for instruction and the terminology of the piece, much of which fits comfortably into the wisdom tradition. Other interpretations, it would seem, are actually less easy to defend: aside from the fact that Isaiah manifests no ascertainable interest in Israel's traditional law, it is difficult to defend the use of *tôrâ* in the aggregate sense in this period. Authors have, indeed, suggested priestly[111] or prophetic[112] *tôrâ*, but there is no hint of any

[109]Weiser, *The Psalms*, 528. See also Kraus, *Psalmen*, 527.

[110]G. von Rad, *Old Testament Theology*, II, 257.

[111]Begrich, "Die priesterliche Tora," 65.

[112]Beecher, "*Torah*: A Word-study in the Old Testament," 3, speaks of a prophet or a priest as the giver of *tôrâ* here; Gottwald, *All the Kingdoms of the Earth*, 147, 199, 201f. Wildberger, "Die Völkerwallfahrt zum Zion: Jes II 1-5," 79, also speaks of *tôrâ* imparted through prophets. In favor of this view it might be urged that a plural verb ought to be read in place of MT's *w^{e}yōrēnû* (see above, n. 89). But a plural would be at odds with the context, which speaks only of Yahweh and the nations, and the textual evidence for it is very slight. The variant reading in all likelihood envisions priests as imparters of *tôrâ* and is probably a late introduction under the influence of a text like Dt 33:10.

human or earthly mediator apparent in this vision, which rather stresses Yahweh Himself as source and imparter of *tôrâ*.

There can be little doubt that in this oracle Yahweh is conceived of as divine king. Clements, commenting on this passage, says: "From an early period . . . the presence of Yahweh in Jerusalem as the divine king, was the basis of a hope of a changed world in which the lordship of Yahweh would be acknowledged by all nations."[113] Yahweh's sovereignty as king extends not simply over Judah, of course, but over all nations; when the nations come streaming to His throne in Jerusalem, they are acknowledging Him as their rightful sovereign. We have already noted that the king in the ancient Near East enjoyed a special claim to wisdom and to being considered a source of wisdom. Moreover, according to vs. 4, one result of the pilgrimage to Zion is that Yahweh will judge between (*wᵉšāpaṭ bên*) them to settle their disputes. Now, it is particularly in this act of rendering judgment for those subject to him that the king is called upon to exercise his special gift of wisdom.[114] The parallel expression in our text says that "he will reprove many peoples (*wᵉhôkîaḥ lᵉʿammîm rabbîm*)," and both the content and terminology fit a wisdom context very well. Not only is *hôkîaḥ* frequently used in wisdom compositions,[115] but the best parallel is found in Ps 94:10, a passage that speaks of God instructing (cf. Isa 2:3) and reproving the nations (*hăyōsēr gôyim hălōʾ yôkîaḥ*) and which clearly exhibits wisdom traits.[116] Moreover, the construction *hôkîaḥ lᵉ* is elsewhere found only in wisdom compositions.[117]

Thus Yahweh is here presented as divine king to whom the nations come for judgment and correction; the first is the function of the wise king, the second of the wise teacher. It is because the nations are willing to receive judgment and correction from the one they now acknowledge as king that

[113]Clements, *God and Temple*, 82. See also Östborn, *Tōrā in the Old Testament*, 150.

[114]It was to enable him to judge his subjects rightly that Solomon was given "a wise and understanding heart" (1 Kgs 3:12), and his disposition of the dispute between the two harlots demonstrated that he had "the wisdom of God for giving judgment" (vs. 28).

[115]About half of the fifty-one occurrences are in wisdom compositions (Job and Prov) or in passages that betray wisdom influence; the latter include Isa 11:3.4 and Ps 94:10 (see following note).

[116]Ps 94 is not classified as a wisdom psalm, but vss. 8-11 clearly bring us into a wisdom context. The senseless and fools (*bōʿărîm, kᵉsîlîm*) are exhorted to understand and be wise (*bînû, taśkîlû*); two rhetorical questions which follow employ proverb-like expressions that argue from God's role as creator of man and from his role in instructing the nations and teaching man (*hamᵉlammēd ʾādām dāʿat*); the concluding statement says that Yahweh knows the thoughts (*yōdēaʿ mahšᵉbôt*) of men, that they are vain (*hebel*). See also vss. 6f.12. See Weiser, *The Psalms*, 623f.; Murphy, *JBC* 35:110: "8-11, an admonition to fools, in the wisdom style."

[117]The construction *hôkîaḥ lᵉ*, in the meaning "reproach, reprove, rebuke," is found only in Job 16:21; 32:12; Prov 9:7.8; 19:5; and in Isa 2:4 and the parallel Mic 4:3. In Gen 24:14 *lᵉ* is used with *hôkîaḥ*, but in a completely different sense.

war is no longer the means of settling disputes and that, therefore, weapons of war can be converted to tools of peaceful and constructive pursuits.[118]

If we now look back at vs. 3, the one in which *tôrâ* occurs, its interpretation can be seen to fit easily into this picture. The pertinent lines, which come just after the words of mutual exhortation to go up to the mount of Yahweh's house, are as follows:

w^e^yōrēnû midd^e^rākāyw *w^e^nēl^e^kâ b^e^'ōr^e^ḥōtāyw*
kî miṣṣiyyôn teṣe' tôrâ *ûd^e^bar yhwh mîrûšālāim*

That he may instruct us in his ways
and we may walk in his paths.
For from Zion shall go forth instruction,
and the word of the Lord from Jerusalem.

It is easy to see that there is a relatively dense concentration of words which are frequently found in wisdom contexts: *hôrâ*, *derek*, *'ōraḥ*, *tôrâ*, and *dābār*. None of them are employed exclusively in wisdom compositions, but the occurrence of several of them together is already suggestive; it remains to determine whether the manner of their employment points in the same direction.[119]

On the use of *hôrâ*,[120] the most instructive passages are undoubtedly those of Isaiah himself. He uses the term twice: in 28:9 (a text which relates the sneering question of his adversaries—who may well be of the party of the royal counselors: "To whom would he impart knowledge?") and 28:26. The latter is particularly significant, for it is in a wisdom composition, the "Parable of the Farmer," and it is Yahweh Himself who instructs. Thus the best parallel to our text from Isaiah's own teaching puts us squarely in a wisdom context. Perhaps the very closest text in the OT to the line we are discussing is Ps 25:8-12, another passage which shows strong wisdom influence.[121] Here it is said three times that Yahweh instructs man in the proper manner of life, employing *derek* three times (vss. 8.9.12) and *hôrâ* twice (vss. 8.12). In vs. 8 it is said that Yahweh instructs sinners in "the way" (*yôreh haṭṭā'îm baddārek*), in vs. 9 that He teaches the humble "his way" (*wîlammēd 'ănāwîm darkô*), and in vs. 12 that He will instruct the one who fears the Lord in the "way" he should choose (*yôrennû b^e^derek yibḥār*). In this context even the covenant is introduced as a means of instruction (*ûb^e^rîtô l^e^hôdî'ām*—vs. 14). Earlier in the psalm, in vs. 4, the same kind of diction is

[118]See Eichrodt, *Der Heilige in Israel*, 47.

[119]See Fichtner, "Jahves Plan in der Botschaft des Jesajas," 31n.

[120]The participle of this verb, of course, means "teacher" and is used of God in Job 36:22. Although in the plural in Isa 30:20 (a non-Isaian text which exhibits wisdom traits), its use there is taken by most to refer to Yahweh (cf. the *NAB* "Teacher"); see Murphy, *A Study . . .*, 13n.

[121]This psalm is not classified as a wisdom psalm, but it is an acrostic and wisdom traits in this section of it are unmistakable. See Weiser, *The Psalms*, 238; Murphy, *JBC* 35:42.

found, as the psalmist prays God to make known to him his ways (*d^e^rākèkā yhwh hôdî'ēnî*) and to teach him His paths (*'ōr^e^ḥôtèkā lamm^e^dēnî*); the passage from prayer (vs. 4) to statement (vss. 8ff.) may mark a difference in the form (lament, instruction), but in diction and content they would both seem to be equally wisdom. Similar language is found in Ps 32:8, this time as a promise or a statement in the mouth of the teacher: "I will instruct you and show you the way you should walk (*'aśkîl^e^kā w^e^'ôr^e^kā b^e^derek zû tēlēk*)." This passage, too, manifests wisdom influence both in its content and language,[122] and displays a special similarity to Isa 2:3 not only in that one instructs (*hôrâ*) concerning the *derek*, but also in that the one instructed responds by walking (*hlk/ylk*) in it.[123] The combination of *hôrâ* and *derek* occurs also in Ps 27:11; 86:11, in neither of which are there strong indications of wisdom influence. These texts do not weaken the argument for a wisdom sense for *tôrâ* in the Isaiah text, nor do they point to any source (e.g., priestly, prophetic, legal) of the instruction sought other than Yahweh Himself. Curiously, and possibly significantly, *derek* is used as a direct object of the verb, without a preposition, in both these cases, whereas it was used with *b^e^* in all the other cases discussed above, in which the combination occurred in wisdom contexts.[124]

This raises the inevitable question of the significance of the preposition *min* which is used with *d^e^rākāyw* in the Isaiah (and Micah) text—inevitable, though in fact many commentators do not deal with it. Marti says that it should be understood as "partitiv=das, was zu seinen Wegen gehört."[125] Murphy, too, takes it as a partitive.[126] Cheyne, however, translates the expression literally by "teach us out of his ways"; "ways" he explains as "rules of moral and religious conduct" and comments: "These rules are described as a store out of which the divine teacher draws his instruction

[122]This again is a psalm that is not usually classified as a wisdom psalm but which clearly manifests wisdom traits. This is seen not only in the diction of this verse, but also in the parabolic animal imagery in vs. 9. See Weiser, *The Psalms*, 281, 286. Murphy, *JBC* 35:49, however, is willing to classify this as a wisdom piece: "Although this is usually classified as a thanksgiving Ps, perhaps it is better considered as a wisdom Ps. The wisdom elements (1-2, 8-11) serve as a wrapper for a thanksgiving testimony (3-7)."

[123]The difference is that in Ps 32:8 *derek* does double duty as designating both that concerning which the teacher instructs and the manner in which the pupil responds, so that only one noun is used with the two verbs; in Isa 2:3 two nouns, *derek* and *'ōraḥ*, are used in parallel, one with each verb.

[124]It would seem that this observation can also be extended to the couple of cases in which *derek* is qualified by some noun or adjective and is used with *hôrâ*. Thus, in Prov 4:11 we have *b^e^derek ḥokmâ hōrêtîkā*, but in 1 Kgs 8:36 it is *tôrēm 'et hadderek haṭṭôbâ*. The parallel text in 2 Chr 6:27 has *'el* in place of *'et*, but this would seem to be a textual error rather than a variant usage.

[125]Marti, *Des Buch Jesaja*, 25.

[126]Murphy, *A Study . . .*, 8.

(comp. Ps. xciv. 12 Del.)."[127] Obviously this interpretation pictures Yahweh as a wisdom teacher. Gray's interpretation is quite similar to this.[128] He translates the phrase here discussed "that he may instruct us of his ways," and comments: "of (*mn*)=*out of* (the treasure of), not concerning: cp. Ps 94:12, cp. Ec 7:10."[129] The passages he cites as parallels are instructive. In Ps 94, the context immediately preceding vs. 12 speaks of Yahweh as the one who instructs the nations and who teaches men knowledge (see discussion above); thus, when vs. 12 says "Happy the man whom you instruct, O Lord, *ûmittôrātᵉkā tᵉlammᵉdennû*," it is likely that *tôrâ* here should be taken in the wisdom sense and that *min* suggests an abundant store of wisdom from which the Lord brings forth that which is appropriate to the situation.[130] In Eccl 7:10 Qoheleth exhorts his pupil not to ask "How is it that former times were better than these? *kî lōʾ mēḥokmâ šāʾaltā ʿal zeh*." Here the construction suggests mode or manner, having almost adverbial force ("wisely"); however, the idiom could conceivably derive from a literal "out of (your store of) wisdom." The term *derek* is used so often in the wisdom tradition as a figurative expression for the sort of ethical conduct that the teacher strives to lead the student to that it would not be surprising if the term (especially in the plural) was sometimes used as a metonym for the teacher's own doctrine. Something like this can be seen in at least a couple of passages. In Prov 8:32b, Wisdom personified says: "Happy those who keep my ways (*dᵉrākay*)." Wisdom's "ways" here are hardly distinguishable from her teachings on conduct and are unlikely to be alluding to her own behavior, as the expression might if it referred to a human teacher; the case is similar to that of Yahweh's "ways" in Isa 2:3. See also Ps 86:11, where Yahweh's "way" is parallel to His "truth" (*ʾĕmet*). Thus it is possible to make a case for the interpretation of Cheyne and of Gray for *middᵉrākāyw*.

Marti has already suggested that *derek* and *ʾōraḥ* in Isa 2:3, which stand in parallel as in Ps 25:4 and in Prov 2:8, should be taken to mean "die von Gott gewollte Lebensweise."[131] In fact, the use of *derek* and *ʾōraḥ* in parallel as

[127]Cheyne, *The Prophecies of Isaiah*, I, 16.

[128]Gray, *The Book of Isaiah*, I, 46; his reference to Ps 94:16 is probably a typographical error for Ps 94:10.

[129]*Ibid.*

[130]Cf. what was said on *tôrâ* above, p. 73; see also Mt 13:51f.

[131]Marti, *Das Buch Jesaja*, 25. Wildberger, *Jesaja*, 85 (see also "Die Völkerwallfahrt zum Zion: Jes. II 1-5," 79), rejects this interpretation, apparently agreeing with Marti that such usage is late; instead of citing Ps 25:5 along with Prov 2:8 for Marti's opinion, he gives Ps 1:6 as the other text—although, in fact, *ʾōraḥ* does not even occur there. His own opinion is that "Die *drk* ist vielmehr z. B. der 'weg', den Jahweh im 'Heilsorakel' dem schuldlos Angeklagten oder sonstwie Bedrängten eroffnet (Ps 25:8.12; 27:11; 32:8; 86:11; u.ö., anders, d. h. dem späteren Verständnis von *twrh* entsprechend, Ps 1:6; 119:33 vlg. 102). Ebenso sind die *drkym* und *ʾrḥwt*, welche die Völker gehen möchten, diejenigen Pfade, die Jahwe ihnen je und dann in seinem Orakelwort weist." But it appears impossible to read *any* of the psalm citations given, which relate pleas or statements concerning Yahweh's instruction in "the way," as references to a "Heilsorakel." They are obviously concerned with an illumination that is more interior and more difficult to apprehend.

figurative terms to designate manner of life or behavior seems to be almost exclusively a wisdom usage. They occur together eight times in Prov; since the usage is not restricted to the introductory chapters, there is no reason to claim that it is recent.[132] The two terms are seldom found together outside of wisdom contexts; in the whole of the Psalter, where *derek* is so common and parallelism the rule, they occur together only in Ps 25:4 and 27:11. Both of these texts have been discussed above; the first of them, at least, is clearly wisdom usage. The terms occur together in a figurative sense also in Isa 40:14, a text packed with wisdom terminology. Of the four[133] remaining passages, namely, Gen 49:17; Joel 2:7; Isa 3:12; 30:11, the first two employ the terms in a literal, not a figurative, sense; the same is true of Isa 30:11, but it is likely that in both the Isaiah texts the prophet's polemic against the wise has influenced his choice of terminology.[134] Jeremiah, who uses *derek* some fifty-six times, and Ezekiel, who uses it more than one hundred times, never use it with *'ōraḥ*; in fact, aside from Joel 2:7 and the parallel to Isa 2:3 in Mic 4:2, *'ōraḥ* is not found at all in prophetic texts outside of Isa 1-41, where it appears eight times.[135] To sum up: the use of *'ōraḥ* and *derek* together in a figurative sense occurs ten times in wisdom compositions or in texts that show clear wisdom influence (eight times in Prov; Ps 25:4; Isa 40:14), once where wisdom influence is probable (Isa 3:12),[136] and only once where such influence is not apparent (Ps 27:11). Thus it can be argued that the usage is typical wisdom procedure; as such it should carry weight in our understanding of *tôrâ* in the line of Isa 2:3 that immediately follows it.

The statement that *tôrâ* shall go forth from Zion is introduced by a *kî*-causal ("for," "because") that refers back to what immediately precedes, i.e., to the reasons given for the ascent to the Mount of Yahweh—to receive the instructions He will give. This is expressed in typical wisdom terminology,

[132] Prov 2:8.13.20; 3:6; 4:14; 9:15; 12:28; 15:19.

[133] Following MT strictly, Job 6:18 should also be listed; however, the *orᵉḥôt* of this text needs to be emended to *'ōrᵉḥôt*.

[134] On Isa 3:12, see Wildberger, *Jesaja*, 130; Marti, *Das Buch Jesaja*, 40. In 30:11 the two terms are used in their literal sense, or almost so, much as in Gen 49:17; however, these are words Isaiah puts into the mouths of his adversaries, who, given the context, may well be his political enemies of the royal circle of advisers.

[135] This distribution of the term is rather remarkable and tends to confirm the assertions of those who speak of the whole collection of Isa 1-66 as "Isaianic"; the surprising fact that *'ōraḥ* occurs only in Joel 2:7 (and in Mic 4:2//Isa 2:3) in all the vast body of prophetic literature and eight times in the Isaiah collection deserves an explanation. The occurrences in Isa are 2:3; 3:12; 26:7.8; 30:11; 33:8; 40:14; and 41:3. In four of these texts (2:3; 3:12; 30:11; 40:14) *'ōraḥ* and *derek* appear together. These data lend further support to the argument that the text we are studying should be attributed to Isaiah rather than to Micah.

[136] It should be pointed out that, in any case, this text is not typical in that the two terms are not used in parallel, *'ōrᵉḥōtèkā* being used to qualify *derek*.

and *tôrâ* ought to be understood in the same sense.[137] This fits perfectly with the picture as a whole, namely, of the King who imparts instruction in the proper way of life and who renders just and saving judgment for those subject to him. There is no hint that any of this is mediated through prophet or priest; to the extent that Isaiah attributes any of these functions to a human mediator, it is to Yahweh's *Stellvertreter* and *alter ego*, the ideal king of the future (11:1-9). The use of *d^ebar yhwh* in our text, then, does not include the suggestion that Yahweh's *tôrâ* is delivered in the words the prophet speaks as it did in 1:10, where Isaiah's own formula introduced the *tôrâ* of Yahweh; rather it must be taken as the *dābār* of the teacher (see n. 30), though it is a *dābār* that contains not only the wisdom of the wise king of the wisdom tradition, but also boundless might of the Lord of all the earth.

Isaiah 5:24b

The treatment of this passage, despite its brevity, presents a number of difficulties. As in the case of Isa 2:2-4, the question of Isaian authorship arises. There are the further problems of whether it is related to its present context and, if that is answered affirmatively, just what the "present context" is. All of these matters will affect to some extent the interpretation of the piece.

Authenticity

Doubt about the Isaian authorship of this line can arise from the fact that it seems to be a superfluous, generalizing conclusion to a development that already has a satisfactory conclusion in vs. 24a. If the ordering of the series of woes it concludes is taken to be the work of a redactor, this conclusion can easily be attributed to him. This is in fact the approach taken by Duhm, Marti, and others,[138] but the logic is by no means compelling; Wildberger is sure the woe-series is the work of an editor but nevertheless defends vs. 24b as an authentic word of Isaiah from another context.[139] Marti compares the line with Isa 1:4b (whose authenticity he rejects), saying that the *'āzab 'et yhwh* "ist eine deuternomistisch Wendung"; Duhm asserts that the use of *'imrâ* in 5:24b "schmeckt nicht nach seinem Stil."[140]

[137]Wildberger, *Jesaja*, 85, takes *tôrâ* here in the sense in which it is used in Dt 17:11; this interpretation would be possible if it were only a question of rendering verdicts, but it does not adequately regard the much broader concept present in our text of instructions in God's ways, nor does it suit well the parallel term *d^ebar yhwh.*

[138]Duhm, *Das Buch Jesaia*, 61; Procksch, *Jesaia I*, 97, follows Duhm; Marti, *Das Buch Jesaja*, 59.

[139]Wildbeger, *Jesaja*, 197.

[140]Duhm, *Das Buch Jesaia*, 61; Marti, *Das Buch Jesaja*, 4f., 59.

Nevertheless, most authors (including Fischer, von Rad, Herntrich, Wildberger, Eichrodt, Lindars, McKane, Kissane, Gray, Lindblom, Vawter, and Pedersen) comment on the passage or cite it without challenging its authorship. I believe that its vocabulary fits well into Isaiah's usage and that its meaning accords with the view proposed in this study; these points will emerge in the section that follows and no attempt will be made here to defend its authenticity.

However, since arguments against its authenticity have been drawn from a comparison with 1:4b, and since that piece will not figure largely in our later discussion, a few words about it here are in order. This text presents problems, too, but most of them need not concern us. The third member of the line is missing in some of the ancient versions and most recent commentators consider it a gloss; however, it is only the terms in the first two members that are of special interest for the present study. And since one of them (*n'ṣ*) will be discussed in the following section, only the remaining verb, *'zb*, need be dealt with. This verb occurs almost two hundred times in the MT and is very broadly distributed; it is found seven times in Isa 1-39.[141] The phrase in question, *'zb 'et yhwh*, though not occurring in Dt, is found seven times in the following books in passages which should probably be attributed to the deuteronomic historians; if to these are added another five passages (two of them in Dt) in which the near equivalent *'ăzabtānî* or similar construction (in the mouth of Yahweh) occurs and an additional text in which *'zb* is followed by *'et 'ĕlōhênû*, the case for this phrase being deuteronomic looks very good indeed.[142] Moreover, in only one of the other Isaiah passages is *'zb* employed with Yahweh as its object, and there the construction is somewhat different (*wᵉ'ōzᵉbê yhwh yiklû*—1:28b); elsewhere the object is land, cities, wealth, or eggs. Therefore, the assertion that the phrase is an interpolation in Isa 1:4b has some force. However, the same cannot be said of the assertion concerning the line as a whole, for *n'ṣ* is not a typical deuteronomic term (see below).[143] The point that can be made here is that the similarity between 1:4b and 5:24b is minimal, consisting in the employment in both texts of *yhwh*, *n'ṣ*, and *qᵉdôš yiśrā'ēl*. Not only is the verb parallelism different in the two texts (*'zb*, *n'ṣ*; *m's*, *n'ṣ*), but the objects of the verbs are different: in 1:4b they are terms for God, while in 5:24b they are terms for God's teaching. Thus no argument can be drawn from 1:4b concerning the authenticity or meaning of 5:24b.

[141] Isa 1:14.28; 6:12; 10:3.14; 17:2.9.

[142] See Jos 24:16.20; Jgs 2:12; 10:6; 1 Sam 12:10; 1 Kgs 9:9; 2 Kgs 21:22; also Dt 28:20; 31:16; Jgs 10:10; 1 Sam 8:8; 2 Kgs 22:17.

[143] It can be argued that *'āzᵉbû 'et yhwh* is an interpolation, that the LXX translators recognized that the line should have had only two members instead of three, but that they dropped the wrong one.

Isaiah 5:24b Considered Apart from its Context

Since the question of the relationship of this line to its present context is so uncertain, it is best not to draw any primary arguments concerning its meaning from the context. The first step will be to see what can be established concerning its meaning without regard to present context.

The line, which presents no textual difficulties or uncertainties, stands as follows:

> *kî māʾăsû ʾēt tôrat yhwh ṣᵉbāʾôt*
> *wᵉʾēt ʾimrat qᵉdôš yiśrāʾēl niʾēṣû*
>
> For they have spurned the *tôrâ* of the Lord of hosts,
> and scorned the word of the Holy One of Israel.

The attempt to determine the meaning of *tôrat yhwh* in this passage naturally begins with a consideration of the verb with which it is used. Any temptation to suppose that *mʾs tôrat yhwh* is a deuteronomic interpolation, and therefore has a "legal" sense, can be quickly allayed by a glance at the evidence: *mʾs* does not occur at all in Dt and is found only once with a legal term (2 Kgs 17:15, with *ḥuqqîm*) in the deuteronomic history.[144] It occurs with *tôrat yhwh* in Am 2:4 in what may be a deuteronomic interpolation, but it is not the presence of this phrase that determines the matter; strong arguments can be drawn only from the context and from the parallel expression, (*lōʾ*) *šmr ḥuqqîm*.[145] The verb *mʾs* is found with *tôrâ* in Jer 6:19, a passage discussed earlier,[146] and with legal terms in a half-dozen other passages.[147] All these passages are probably later than Isaiah and may represent a subsequent development.

This frequently used verb is employed most commonly with a personal object (Yahweh, the people Israel, Saul, etc.), less commonly with a variety of concrete material objects (land, city, idols, rod, stone, etc.). However, it is also employed with terms that signify instruction of some sort from God or knowledge of God. Thus it is used with *dᵉbar yhwh* in 1 Sam 15:23.26; Jer 8:9 (a reproach directed against the wise); and with *baddābār hazzeh* in Isa 30:12. In Hos 4:6 it is used with *daʿat* (by which is surely meant the same as the *daʿat ʾĕlōhîm* of 4:1). It also occurs in wisdom contexts with a wisdom term: with *mûsar šadday* in Job 5:17 and with *mûsar yhwh* in Prov 3:11. In all these passages it is a question of reproaching those who reject, or of exhorting the hearers not to reject, the word, knowledge, or discipline of the Lord. The verb is also used, in what can be argued to be wisdom contexts, with a term for that which *should* be rejected, namely, evil (*rāʿ*). This combination is found in

[144] See above, Ch. 1, n. 58.

[145] See above, Ch. 1, n. 57 and the accompanying text.

[146] See above, p. 22.

[147] Lev 26:15.43; Ezek 5:6; 20:13.16.24.

Ps 36:5, a passage whose wisdom traits we have already noted (see above, n. 67). The other text is Isa 7:15, in which there is reference to learning to choose the good and to reject the evil (*mā'ôs bārā'*); if we extend the comments of Alonso-Schökel on similar phraseology in Gen 2-3 to this text, we again find ourselves tantalizingly near the world of wisdom.[148]

Thus the expression *m's tôrâ*, taken by itself, is ambiguous; in different contexts it could have different meanings. Fortunately, we do have a context for *m's tôrâ* in Isa 5:24b in the parallel expression *n'ṣ 'imrâ*, and this would seem to favor strongly a wisdom sense. On Duhm's assertion that the use of *'imrâ* in our passage "schmeckt nicht nach seinem Stil," Wildberger justly comments that it "ist wirklich Geschmackssache."[149] Duhm's suggestion seems particularly groundless because Isaiah himself uses the word in 28:23; 29:4 (*bis*); and 32:9. Of special significance is Isaiah's use of the term in 28:23, for this verse is the *Lehreröffnungsformel* of the "Parable of the Farmer" and the exordium of a wisdom composition. This relatively rare word is employed five times in *Aufmerkrufe* in the OT, two of them in Isaiah.[150] Of special interest is its use in Dt 32:2, for there it stands parallel to the wisdom word *leqaḥ*; the wisdom features of the opening lines of this poem have already been referred to.[151] There is little evidence that *'imrâ* was employed as a legal term. In Dt 33:9 it is said that the Levites keep (*šmr*) God's *'imrâ*, a term which there stands parallel to *b^erît*. The use of *b^erît* suggests the likelihood of a legal sense of *'imrâ*, though it is also possible that *'imrâ* stands strictly as a synonym for *b^erît* (the fact that it is singular, not plural as *mišpāṭîm*, *miṣwôt*, or *ḥuqqîm* would be if employed parallel to *b^erît*, perhaps suggests this), the term being chosen because it can suggest something that is sure and true (cf. Ps 12:7; 138:2; 147:15; Prov 30:5). In any case, this is probably a late passage.[152] Again, no firm conclusions can be drawn from the fact that *'imrâ* is employed nineteen times in Ps 119 as one of the synonyms for "law"; in his quest for parallel terms the author may have pressed into service a word that did not normally function in this manner—and this word

[148]Luis Alonso-Schökel, "Motivos sapienciales y de alianza en Gn 2-3," *Bib* 43 (1962) 295-315, especially 301-304. "Ante todo, la *ciencia del bien y del malo* nos traslada al ambiente sapiencial: tardíamente lo formuló Jesús ben Sira, describiendo al sabio que viaja para 'conocer el bien y el mal de los hombres' (39,4); pero la práctica es antigua entre los *ḥakamim*" (p. 301). Ps 36:4f. contrasts good and evil. We have already discussed the "good-evil" terminology found in Isa 1:16f., one of the *tôrâ* passages.

[149]Wildberger, *Jesaja*, 197.

[150]Gen 4:23; Dt 32:2 (if not strictly part of the *Aufmerkruf*, for the verbs are not imperative, this is at least an expansion thereof); Isa 28:23; 32:9; Ps 17:6. Aside from its use in Ps 119, where it occurs nineteen times, *'imrâ* is found only eighteen times in the MT; this could be accurately described as only fifteen passages, for 2 Sam 22:31 is parallel to Ps 18:31, and in two places it appears twice in the same verse (Isa 29:4; Ps 12:7).

[151]See above, n. 25. The term *leqaḥ* occurs only in wisdom compositions or in passages that clearly exhibit wisdom traits: Dt 32:2; Isa 29:24; Job 11:4; Prov 1:5; 4:2; 7:21; 9:9; 16:21.23.

[152]See above, Ch. 1, n. 18 and text.

may have come to him from the wisdom tradition.[153] Thus even if Isa 5:24b is considered to be an interpolation, *'imrâ* is unlikely to have a legal import. But the evidence from Isaiah's oracles indicates that he could have used *'imrâ* here as a wisdom term, as he did in 28:23; as such it is a good parallel for *tôrâ*, also taken in its wisdom sense.

These conclusions receive striking and unambiguous confirmation from the manner in which *n'ṣ*, the verb here used with *'imrâ*, is employed in the OT: it is often used with wisdom terms but never with a legal term. Wildberger asserts that *n'ṣ* and *'zb* are "zwei Verben, die in der Bundestradition beheimatet sind," but the statement goes beyond the evidence.[154] The verb is most frequently used with a personal object, usually Yahweh Himself or the people Israel.[155] Once the object is the offering made to Yahweh (*minḥat yhwh*—1 Sam 2:17) and once the prophetic word (Jer 23:17). However, there are at least four clear cases in which the object is a wisdom term: Ps 107:11 (*'ăṣat 'elyôn*); Prov 1:30 (*tôkaḥat*); 5:12 (*tôkaḥat*); 15:5 (*mûsār*); the first of these is particularly interesting because the parallel to *'ăṣat 'elyôn* is *'imrê 'ēl*. On the basis of these texts it appears that the best parallels for the diction of our passage come from texts employing wisdom terms.[156]

To conclude this section it may be said that the arguments presented, which prescind from the present context of the line, favor both the authenticity of the piece and a wisdom interpretation of its terms; in fact, these two aspects can be said to cohere. If our passage is conceded to be Isaiah's, a legal meaning for the terms is almost certainly excluded. One might argue, on the basis of the *n'ṣ* d^e*bar yhwh* in Jer 23:17, that our text

[153] See A. Robert, "Le sens du mot loi dans le Ps CXIX," *RB* 46 (1937) 182-206, who insists that the "law" in this composition is not to be taken in a narrowly nomistic sense but includes elements from the prophetic and wisdom traditions; see also his "Le psaume CXIX et les sapientiaux," *RB* 48 (1939) 5-20. See also Johannes Fichtner, "Zum Problem Glaube und Geschichte in der israelitisch-jüdaischen Weisheitsliteratur," *TLZ* 76 (1951) 148.

[154] Wildberger, *Jesaja*, 22f. Dt 31:20 has Yahweh say that Israel 1) served other gods, 2) despised me (w^e*ni'ăṣûnî*), and 3) broke my covenant. The verb is used with Yahweh as object in many different contexts (Num 14:11.23; 16:30; 2 Sam 12:14; Isa 1:4; Ps 10:3.13), and not much significance can be attributed to the fact that the covenant is mentioned in the same context in this passage, nor even to the fact that Jer 14:21, which Wildberger also cites, refers to the covenant in the same verse in which *n'ṣ* is used. This latter text presents difficulties; here Yahweh is admonished not to spurn (*'al tin'aṣ*), but the object is not expressed; it could conceivably be, not the people, but the object expressed in the second half of the line, "the throne of your glory." The LXX suggests some textual uncertainty.

[155] See preceding note; also Dt 32:19; Isa 60:14; Jer 14:21; 33:24; Lam 2:6.

[156] One might object that these four texts have *n'ṣ* in qal while it is used in piel in Isa 5:24b; the objection, however, can easily be met. There is almost perfect consistency in the use of the piel when God or something identified or closely connected with Him is the object (the only exception being Isa 60:14, where Israel is the object). In all other cases it is the qal that is used (the only exception being Ps 107:11, where the object is *'ăṣat 'elyôn*); Jer 33:24 is not really an exception, for the object is clearly Israel, even though designated "my people." Ernst Jenni, *Das hebräische Pi'el: Syntaktisch-semasiologische Untersuchung einer Verbalform im Alten Testament* (Zurich: EVZ-Verlag, 1968), 225, notes as striking "dass das Object im Pi'el immer Gott oder etwas Göttliches ist, im Qal degegen nur einmal in Ps. 107, 11 . . ."

refers to the prophetic word, but this is most improbable. It has already been shown (Ch. 1) that there is no basis for considering *tôrâ* a term for the prophetic word outside of Isaiah, and the evidence so far considered indicates that the same is true also for Isaiah's own oracles. The parallel *tôra-'imrâ* is not normal terminology for the prophetic word; it does, however, fit very well into a wisdom context and also suits preoccupations of Isaiah that have already been established.

Isaiah 5:24b and its Context

It is possible to argue that 5:24b is an original part of the composition in which it is found and that this context considerably strengthens the case for a wisdom understanding of *tôrâ* as used there. The verse comes as the conclusion of a series of woes, several of which are clearly directed against Isaiah's adversaries of the wisdom school; it is to them, primarily, that Isaiah utters the reproach that they have spurned the wise instruction of Yahweh. It is obviously in this sense that McKane, who interprets 5:19-24 as a unit, understands the piece.[157]

Commentators usually find a series of six or seven woes intentionally strung together, though the calculations often do not agree, and some of them join material from other chapters (especially 10:1-4) to complete the series. Those who find here a deliberate series of six or seven do not usually attribute the arrangement to Isaiah himself, though some, more cautiously, hesitate to deny at least the possibility.[158] No attempt will be made here to argue that Isaiah is responsible for the present arrangement of the woes in this chapter or that they all belong together; yet a case can be made for taking vss. 18-24 as an original, single, development. Wildberger apparently holds that the individual woe is the unity, for he says that "jeder einzelne Weherufe ist von Propheten zu seiner Stunde vor einem bestimmten Hörerkreis in die jeweilige Situation hinein gesprochen worden."[159] The argument that immediately follows, that the contents of vss. 11 and 22 are too similar to belong in the same development, persuades that we are dealing with more than one collection, but not that the individual woes must be taken separately, as self-contained unities. Some of the woes in this chapter, such as vss. 21 and 22, would seem very brief as prophetic speeches and, taken by themselves, almost banal in content. In fact, the prophetic woes do not stand as such brief sayings but are virtually always developed in some manner into longer oracles.[160] One possible type of development, the one which is in fact found in Isa 5:18-24, is a series of woes concluded with a single threat to

[157]McKane, *Prophets and Wise Men*, 65f.

[158]E.g., Herntrich, *Der Prophet Jesaja*, 80f.

[159]Wildberger, *Jesaja*, 180.

[160]Isa 5:8f. (at least). 11-13; 10:1-3.5ff.; 28:1-4; 29:1ff.15f.; 30:1-5; 31:1-3; 33:1ff.; 45:9f.; Jer 23:1-4; Ezek 13:3ff.18-21; 34:2ff.; Am 5:18-20; 6:1-7; Mic 2:1-3; Nah 3:1-7; Hab 2:6b-8.9-11. 12-14.15-17.19f.; Zeph 2:5-7; 3:1-5; Zech 11:17.

cover the series; the procedure is particularly suitable if all the woes are directed at more or less the same group of men.[161]

Even if this is conceded, however, there is still the difficulty that the threat in vs. 24a, introduced by *lākēn*, seems to be an adequate conclusion to the series, and a new conclusion, introduced by *kî* is unexpected. This is the reason Marti gives for rejecting the authenticity of vs. 24b, saying that it brings "noch eine sehr allgemein Begründung der Drohung, als ob sie durch v. 22f. nicht genügend motiviert wäre."[162] But the line is neither a new motivation nor is it "quite general." It acts, rather, as a summary of the indictments that are contained in the woes, as will be seen. The procedure is not without parallel in the prophetic writings. In Jer 7:5-12 we find descriptions of sexual immorality (vss. 8f.), a prophecy of punishment to come (in the imperative—vs. 10), and then a summarizing expression introduced by *kî*: "For they have openly rebelled against me . . ." (vs. 11). Within the context of Isaiah's own book we might see an analogy in the use of the summary-appraisal form (see above, Ch. 3), for both procedures have a similar pedagogical function and might easily have been employed by one who knew well how to play the part of the teacher.

These woes, as well as others in this chapter, manifest in part an interest in concerns common to the wisdom tradition and in part Isaiah's special polemic against the wise. Gerstenberger, Whedbee, and others hold that the woe-form originates in the wisdom tradition, and it must be admitted that arguments in favor of this view have some force; nevertheless, although the position would be most helpful for the point I am here trying to establish, it seems that the opinion should be rejected.[163] What can be maintained, however, is that in these particular woes Isaiah accuses the wise of falling into the sins they especially condemn and of failing in true wisdom through their opposition to his teaching.

[161]Cheyne, *The Prophecies of Isaiah*, I, 33, among others, takes this to be the unit.

[162]Marti, *Das Buch Jesaja*, 59.

[163]Gerstenberger, "The Woe-Oracles of the Prophets," 249-63, is the basic study in this area. He argues that the prophets, in using the woe-form, were adapting a form that had long existed; as found in the prophets, woe passages generally combine two or more forms which can easily be distinguished. The woe-form itself is stereotyped, consisting, in its simplest form, of *hôy* plus a participle characterizing the evil-doers against whom the woe is directed; this simple form the prophets complete in a variety of ways: with threat, lament, proverb, rhetorical question, etc. The simple woe-form, which is impersonal (regularly third person) and stereotyped, is easily distinguished from its prophetic completions and from prophetic speech in general, which is usually direct, personal, and often highly emotional. In arguing for an origin of the woe-form in the wisdom tradition, Gerstenberger looks to both content and form. There is no doubt that an impressive percentage of the prophetic woes are concerned with social matters and find their best parallels in the wisdom literature; this observation forms the basis of his argument from content: if the woe-form ever existed independently of the prophetic preaching, then an integral part of it was its concern for social justice. He sees the woe-saying as a sort of mitigated, non-official, private form of the curse and finds an analogy between the curse-blessing and woe-happy (*'ašrê*) antithesis; the similarity in form (and, occasionally, in content) between the *'ašrê*

The passage preceding vs. 24, namely, vss. 18-23, contains four woes. Although the characterization in vs. 18 is vague, vs. 19 indicates that those addressed are the ones who make light of Isaiah's words concerning the *'ēṣâ* of Yahweh—that *'ēṣâ* which Isaiah opposed to that of the royal advisers; it has already been argued that the scoffers are the royal advisers.[164]

Those indicted in vs. 20 are accused of inversion of values; the prophet is no doubt concerned with ethical values and with what really constitutes truth and wisdom, but it is the pairs evil-good, darkness-light, and bitter-sweet that he uses. The employment of antithetical pairs such as these was a common procedure in wisdom circles,[165] and it is probably because Isaiah here addresses himself to the sages that he uses them. Cheyne,[166] commenting on this verse, gives reference to Job 17:12; the text, in which Job

formula and the *hôy* formula suggests that they had a common origin and pertained originally to the same (i.e., wisdom) circles.

These arguments are not very compelling. Social concerns are found in the legal and prophetic, as well as in the wisdom, traditions; further evidence is needed before this can link the woe-formula to wisdom circles. The formal similarities between *hôy* and *'ašrê* formulas are minimal, consisting mainly in the use of the participle after the opening term; this is not much, especially if one takes *'ašrê* to be a plural construct and *hôy* to be, at least in origin, an exclamation. The distribution of the terms does not favor the theory, for *hôy* (taken strictly) is not found outside the prophets, while *'ašrê* is confined mainly to Pss and Prov, occurring only three times in prophetic texts (Isa 30:18; 32:20; 56:2). Even if the *'î* of Eccl 10:16 is emended to *'ôy* and the *'imrû* of Isa 3:10 to *'ašrê*, the picture does not change much. On the disribution of these terms, see especially Waldemar Janzen, "'AŠRÊ in the Old Testament," *HTR* 58 (1965) 215-26; and on the whole problem, his more recent *Mourning Cry and Woe Oracle* (*BZAW* 125; Berlin: Walter de Gruyter, 1972), in which he proposes a view similar to that given earlier by R. Clifford (see below). E. Lipiński, "Macarismes et Psaumes de congratulation," *RB* 75 (1968) 321-67, holds with good reason that the opposition *'ašrê-hôy* is late and rare and argues that the *'ašrê* formula does not originate in wisdom, but belongs first of all to the language of the psalms. Any argument drawn from Lk 6:20-26 is bound to be weak; the antithetical woes are lacking in the parallel text of Mt 5:3-12, and this construction, along with the transposition from the third to the second person may well be Luke's own work. Furthermore, if Klaus Koch, *The Growth of the Biblical Tradition: The Form-Critical Method*, tr. S. M. Cupitt (New York: Charles Scribner's Sons, 1969), 17, is followed, these beatitudes belong to the apocalyptic tradition of eschatological blessings, rather than to the wisdom tradition.

A more likely origin of the prophetic woe-form is that proposed by Richard Clifford, "The Use of *HÔY* in the Prophets," *CBQ* 28 (1966) 458-64. He argues that the prophets have adapted the funeral lament for their own purposes, a cry which comes as the prophet's automatic reaction upon hearing the word of God's judgment. Yet in describing the funeral lament, taken over by the prophets, as simply *hôy* plus a substantive and so making it possible to set together 1 Kgs 13:30 (*hôy 'āḥî*) and prophetic woes, Clifford apparently fails to note the regularity with which the prophets use the participle (usually plural) and the role this plays in turning the cry from a lament over one or more specific persons to an indictment of a group characterized by the behavior indicated by the participle. Thus the prophets may well have taken the use of the woe-cry from the funeral lament, but in doing so they have really forged a new form.

Whedbee, *Isaiah and Wisdom*, 82-90, defends Gerstenberger's view, but the attempt is not convincing. See my review, *CBQ* 34 (1972) 128.

[166]Cheyne, *The Prophecies of Isaiah*, I, 33.

addresses his "wise friends," is an apt comparison and suggests that this was a favorite manner of reproaching an adversary in wisdom circles:

> Such men change the night into day;
> where there is darkness they talk of approaching light.

Fohrer identifies those addressed here as the sages and sees the source of conflict in the differing political policies of prophet and wise man.[167] No doubt that is at least part of the reproach (see vs. 19), but the expression is very general and it is difficult to exclude the possibility that the inversion condemned embraces also the reversal of right judgment that is the subject of vs. 23.[168]

The woe of vs. 21, directed against those who are wise and prudent in their own eyes (and probably in the eyes of the people—but not, it is implied, in the eyes of Yahweh and His prophet), recalls wisdom sayings such as Prov 3:7 ("Be not wise in your own eyes . . ."); 26:5 (". . . lest he become wise in his own eyes").12 ("You see a man wise in his own eyes?/There is more hope for a fool than for him"); 28:11 ("The rich man is wise in his own eyes,/but the poor man who is intelligent sees through him"). That it is the sages and royal advisers Isaiah has in mind is widely agreed;[169] he is turning against them ammunition from their own magazine. To examples from Prov, Wildberger adds one from Ptah-hotep: "Sei nicht hochmutig auf dein Wissen und vertraue nicht darauf, dass du kenntnisreich bist." He supposes that in speaking of the presumption of the wise Isaiah is referring to the politicians who, trusting to their own lights, can find the right answers without listening to Yahweh or His prophet.[170]

The similarity of vss. 20 and 21, in that both turn traditional wisdom material against the sage, strengthens the contention that these woes stand in a series. To this may be added not only the brevity of vs. 21, but also the fact that both of them are rather vague as to content, i.e., regarding the precise ways the wise have reversed true values and have been guilty of presumption. Unless these woes had been accompanied by some context which gave further precision, their intent would have been difficult to determine. In fact, however, the needed context is provided by the first woe (vss. 18f.) and the last woe (vss. 22f.) of this series.

[167]Fohrer, *Das Buch Jesaja*, I, 87.

[168]Richter, *Recht und Ethos*, 185, relates this verse to wisdom teaching, but in a very general way.

[169]See, e.g., Fohrer, *Das Buch Jesaja*, I, 87f.; Scott, "Solomon and the Beginnings of Wisdom," 276f.; McKane, *Prophets and Wise Men*, 65; Gerstenberger, "The Woe-Oracles of the Prophets," 259; Richter, *Recht und Ethos*, 185; Fichtner, "Jesaja unter den Weisen," 78.

[170]Wildberger, *Jesaja*, 193f.

Wildberger rearranges several verses and places vs. 23 directly after vs. 30, but there seems no need to do this; the drunkenness referred to in vs. 22 provides a natural explanation, along with a general moral bankruptcy (including willingness to accept bribes), for the perversion of judgment that vs. 23 speaks of. Israelite law insists on just judgment, of course (cf. Ex 23:6-8), but does not concern itself with sobriety. In the wisdom literature we find not only a number of passages which warn of the dangers of drinking to excess (e.g., Prov 20:1; 21:17; 23:29-35; Sir 18:33; 19:2; 31:25-31) and of the evil of unjust judgment (Prov 17:15; 24:24), but one in which rulers are advised of the connection between sobriety and judgment: Lemuel's mother warns that wine is not for kings:

> Lest in drinking they forget what the law decrees,
> and violate the rights of all who are in need (Prov 31:4f.).

There is, therefore, every reason to hold that the four woes of Isa 5:18-23 belong together as a series and are directed at those that Isaiah designated, sarcastically, as "the wise." The first and the last woes are specific, blaming them for their failure as royal counselors and for moral turpitude, respectively; the two woes in the middle of the series are couched in more general terms and need to be defined by what precedes and follows. The fact that this arrangement is artistic and intelligible is no reason for attributing it to an editor! After the threat of vs. 24a there follows a summary of what this group has been accused of: they have spurned the wise instruction (*tôrâ*) of Yahweh. If *tôrâ* is given its wisdom sense in vs. 24b, the line fits perfectly into both its remote context (the teaching of Isaiah and his polemic against the wise) and its proximate context in this chapter; none of the other possible meanings of *tôrâ* suit so well or even at all. It is important to note, for the sake of later discussion, that *tôrâ* in this text includes both what pertains to Yahweh's *'ēṣâ* (as revealed through Isaiah) and those more general items of behavior that make up the riches of the wisdom tradition.[171]

Isaiah 8:16.20

Isa 8:16 stands in MT as follows:

ṣôr t^{e}'ûdâ ḥătôm tôrâ b^{e}limmudāy

The *NAB* translates it: "The record is to be folded and the sealed instruction kept among my disciples."

[171]Although I have argued that the context of vs. 24b is vss. 18-24, essentially the same conclusions concerning *tôrâ* can be drawn even if the unity is taken to be vss. 22-24. Fischer, *Das Buch Isaias*, 57, for example, seems to relate vs. 24 exclusively to the final woe.

Preliminary Problems

This verse presents a series of grave difficulties. There are the questions of the verb forms in vs. 16 and of their interpretation, of the sense of the preposition in *b^elimmudāy*, and even of the textual certainty of the word; there is the further problem of the nature of the connection between vs. 20 and vs. 16, in both of which the terms *tôrâ* and *t^eʿûdâ* occur; there is also the question of whether the "binding" and "sealing" imply a written document or are to be taken in a figurative sense. An exhaustive discussion of these problems does not seem called for here; no definitive solutions could be imposed, and some of these matters are of only marginal importance to this study. If it could be established that the verbal forms in vs. 16 are imperative (and assuming this is not a prayer of Isaiah), then "my disciples" would be words in the mouth of Yahweh. However, what evidence there is indicates that the verbs are infinitives; and this is the view of almost all modern commentators.[172]

Whether these verbs and their objects refer to a written document or are to be taken figuratively is a question of greater importance, but nothing crucial to this study hinges on the answer. Many have argued that this passage stands related to the development begun in Isaiah's vocation narrative and that the content of the "document" in question, whether written or symbolic, contains the salient points of this development. It will be sufficient for our purposes to defend this view. The verb *ḥtm* is, indeed, most easily understood of a written document,[173] but Wildberger has special difficulty with the preposition *b^e* in the expression *b^elimmudāy*,[174] for it does not seem to fit well with the sealing and handing over of a written document.[175] He refers to the use of *ṣwr* and *ṣrr* (and cf. the substantive *ṣ^erôr*, purse"), which are sometimes used with *b^e* to speak of "binding" gold, etc., in a purse or some other container. The second verb, *ḥtm*, can be used in the same manner (cf. Job 14:17 and,

[172]The masoretic pointing, which reads the words as *ṣôr* and *ḥătôm*, takes the words to be imperatives; but the plene scriptum form of the second, which on the evidence from Qumran goes back at least to the first century B.C., suggests that earlier tradition read the two verbs as infinitive absolutes, and most scholars do not hesitate to repoint the text. Cheyne, *The Prophecies of Isaiah*, I, 55, is one of the few who retain the imperatives. Wildberger, *Jesaja*, 343, repoints the second verb as an absolute infinitive and insists that *ṣôr* does not come from *ṣrr* but from the related form *ṣwr*. Kissane, *The Book of Isaiah*, I, 107, repoints and emends to produce the passive participles *ṣārûr* and *ḥātûm*, but the suggestion has not won acceptance.

[173]See 1 Kgs 21:8; Isa 29:11; Jer 32:10.11.14.44; Est 8:8.10; Dan 12:4.9; Neh 10:1.2.

[174]Some, basing themselves on signs of uncertainty in LXX and Peshitta traditions, have tried to eliminate this word from the text; Fohrer, *Das Buch Jesaja*, I, 120f., argues also on metrical grounds. But the LXX's *tou mē mathein* indicates that something similar to our MT lay before the translators, and the Syriac read the term but placed it at the beginning of vs. 17. Wildberger, *Jesaja*, 344, unhesitatingly holds that the MT tradition is to be preferred and that no excuse exists for striking the word.

[175]Wildberger, *Jesaja*, 344.

especially, Dt. 32:34: "Is not this . . . sealed up in—*ḥātum b*^{e}—my storehouse?"). His conclusion: Isaiah safeguards his teaching by depositing it with his disciples like a precious treasure sealed in a purse.[176] The commentators are divided on this point, though the majority seems to favor a figurative interpretation. Duhm carefully notes that the figurative interpretation does not exclude the possibility that Isaiah also committed writings to his disciples.[177]

The question of the relationship of vss. 19f. to vss. 16-18 is quite an important one, for if these verses belong together, the total context must be taken into account in explaining the import of *tôrâ* in vs. 16. One is immediately struck by the strangeness of the reference to consulting necromancers after the verses which precede it, dealing as they do with Isaiah's teaching during the Syro-Ephraimitic War. Then, too, vss. 17f., with their reference to waiting and signs and portents whose fulfillment are expected, appear to be a conclusion, not a transition or introduction to something else; this impression is strengthened by the solemn formula that closes vs. 18: "he who dwells on Mount Zion." In fact, virtually all modern commentators take vss. 16-18 as a distinct unit; these include Duhm, Cheyne, Marti, Gray, Fischer, Fohrer, Eichrodt, Lindblom, and Wildberger.[178] Another problem is the difficult nature of vs. 20 and the apparent disorder of the text.[179] What seems necessary to assert, however, although some commentators appear to ignore it, is that the phrase *l*^{e}*tôrâ w*^{e}*lit*^{e}*'ûdâ* in vs. 20 can hardly be thought to have originated independently of the *t*^{e}*'ûdâ* and *tôrâ* of vs. 16—the more so since *t*^{e}*'ûdâ* occurs in only one other text in the OT (Ru 4:7). Thus a number of commentators consider the words to be a late editorial addition,[180] and at least two scholars have suggested that they are a marginal gloss or rubric that has found its way into the text.[181]

It is hardly possible, therefore, to build useful arguments on the supposition that vss. 16 and 20 belong to the same compositional unit or that the use

[176] *Ibid.*, 344f.

[177] Duhm, *Das Buch Jesaja*, 85.

[178] Duhm, *Das Buch Jesaia*, 84-86; Cheyne, *The Prophecies of Isaiah*, I, 56; Marti, *Das Buch Jesaja*, 87-90; Gray, *The Book of Isaiah*, I, 154-57; Fischer, *Das Buch Isaias*, 81f.; Fohrer, *Das Buch Jesaja*, I, 119-21; Eichrodt, *Der Heilige in Israel*, 95, 103, compiles a unity of vss. 1f.16f.3f.18 and treats 19f. separately; Lindblom, *Prophecy in Ancient Israel*, 160f., 162n., 368; Wildberger, *Jesaja*, 343, 349.

[179] The reconstruction and rendering of Patrick W. Skehan, "Some Textual Problems in Isaia," *CBQ* 22 (1960) 47f., shows how good sense can be made of the difficult vss. 19f. The interpretation is just as consistent with the theory that supposes vss. 19f. to be a fragment that has been tacked on as with Isaian authorship of vss. 16-20 as a unit.

[180] Of the commentators mentioned in n. 178, above, Marti, Fohrer, and Wildberger suggest a later addition, while Gray seems to incline to that opinion.

[181] Herntrich, *Der Prophet Jesaja*, 157; Lindblom, *Prophecy in Ancient Israel*, 162n.

of *tôrâ* in vs. 16 is illumined by vss. 19f. However, this does not lead to any grave disadvantages. If it is conceded that *tôrâ* and *tᵉʿûdâ* in vs. 20 are dependent on the same words in vs. 16, there are only two alternatives: either the two verses are part of the same development, in which case *tôrâ* would certainly have the same meaning in each; or, by far the more likely case, the *tôrâ* in vs. 20 is part of a gloss of some sort and is not relevant to the present study. We will therefore deal with the *tôrâ* of vs. 16, taking vss. 16-18 to be its immediate context; if the *tôrâ* in vs. 20 is authentic, the discussion will be equally relevant to the meaning it has there.

The Context

The first step in attempting to understand vss. 16-18 is to identify their broader context; the terms "attestation" (*tᵉʿûdâ*) and "instruction" (*tôrâ*) obviously refer to teaching of some sort that has already been given and now awaits confirmation and verification, and their meaning will be clear only to the extent that we can identify the teaching in question. A related question is that of why these particular terms are used; they must refer by and large to Isaiah's teaching, but since neither *tᵉʿûdâ* nor *tôrâ* are technical terms for the prophetic word, it must be asked why they were chosen.

There is broad scholarly agreement that the context against which 8:16-18 must be understood is all, or at least much, of the material that begins with the call narrative in Isa 6 and ends with 8:15. Fohrer holds that the call narrative is not isolated autobiography but that it, taken with 8:16-18, forms the framework of the intervening material; the two passages must be understood together.[182] Moreover, Isaiah himself is responsible for the collection of the materials in these chapters; referring to the call narrative, he says: "Er selbst hat ihn den in Kap. 7-8 gesammelten Worten aus dem zweiten Zeitraum seiner Tätigkeit vorangestellt, wahrscheinlich um seine damalige Verkündigung aus seinem Auftrag 6, 9ff. heraus deutlicher zu machen."[183] The essential elements of this view had been proposed earlier by Duhm and Budde.[184] All three of these scholars extend the collection to 9:6, but Fohrer holds the final, messianic, oracle to come from a later hand, while Duhm and Budde take it to be authentic; yet these two also agree that 8:18 marks the conclusion of a period in Isaiah's ministry. Not all scholars concur in assigning the prophet a role in the writing and arranging of these materials, but many do date them to the period of the Syro-Ephraimitic War and assign

[182]Fohrer, "Entstehung, Komposition und Überlieferung von Jesaja 1-39," 124f.; see also Sellin-Fohrer, *Einleitung in das Alte Testament*, 401f.

[183]Idem, *Das Buch Jesaja*, I, 21.

[184]Duhm, *Das Buch Jesaja*, 64, 85; Karl Budde, "Über die Schranken, die Jesajas prophetischer Botschaft zu setzen sind," *ZAW* 41 (1923) 165-77.

a similar role to 8:16-18; among others may be listed Marti, Gray, Buber, Wildberger, Wolff, and Gottwald.[185]

The basic elements of this theory, namely, that the materials of 6:1-8:18 (with the exception of some disputed verses in the latter part of Ch. 7 and 8:9f.) are organically connected and chronologically ordered and that they come to form a document of some sort at an early period, possibly through the literary activity of Isaiah himself, can be said to rest on a firm foundation. The events related, except for the call narrative (on which see below), are easily dated to the period of the Syro-Ephraimitic War, and the use of the first person in 6:1-13; 8:1-4.5-8.11-15.16-18, often in introductory verses, indicates that we are not simply dealing with random oracles collected and arranged by some late editor. The relationship of 8:16-18 to the preceding materials is made firm by the reference to Isaiah's sons,[186] described, along with Isaiah himself, as "signs and portents in Israel," for the reference can only be to Shear-jashub (7:3) and Maher-shalal-hash-baz (8:1-4) and to the related events and teachings. The hypothesis that the call narrative of Isa 6 was composed some time after the event as an introduction to the materials in 7:1-8:18 seems a very probable one. The fact that the call narrative is in Ch. 6 and not at the beginning of the book suggests that it already formed part of one of the smaller collections. It might not be completely fanciful to see the whole of Isaiah's "Memoirs" marked off by a sort of inclusion, beginning with the prophet's vision of Yahweh enthroned in the Temple and concluding with the reference to Him "who dwells on Mount Zion."[187]

Thus there is a firm basis for taking 6:1-8:15 as the proper context for understanding 8:16-18. The general theme of the section is Isaiah's attempt to bring the policy makers of Judah to trust in Yahweh rather than in foreign alliances, power politics, and other machinations promoted by human wisdom; inseparable from this theme, and running like an undercurrent throughout the section, is the prophet's struggle with the royal advisers. I have already suggested that this is reflected in the fact that his call narrative

[185]Marti, *Das Buch Jesaja*, 87; Gray, *The Book of Isaiah*, I, 1; Buber, *The Prophetic Faith*, 126; Wildberger, *Jesaja*, 241. Just as some of the others mentioned above, Wildberger traces the collection through 9:6, but of 8:16-18 says, "Der Prophet zieht einen Schlussstrich unter eine gewisse Periode seiner Wirksamkeit" (p. 344); Wolff, *Frieden ohne Ende*, 11; Gottwald, *All the Kingdoms of the Earth*, 202.

[186]It does not seem advisable or even possible to identify these sons with the "disciples" of vs. 16, as do Budde, "Über die Schranken . . .," 174, and Lindblom, *Prophecy in Ancient Israel*, 160f., 367f. The fact that these sons are called "signs" and "portents" would seem to clearly identify them with Shear-jashub and Maher-shalal-hash-baz; Wildberger, *Jesaja*, 347, adds the further objection that there is no example of *y^elādîm* being used in this transferred sense (the case is quite other with *bānîm*).

[187]Cf. Gray, *The Book of Isaiah*, I, 156.

highlights the mission of binding, deafening, and hardening;[188] I have further suggested that this struggle also lies behind Isaiah's demand that Ahaz ask for a sign, this being the only way to resolve the conflict between the prophet who proclaims God's word and the sage who impugns the prophet's credentials.[189] Although the term *'ôt* does not appear in 8:1-4, the narrative obviously deals with a "sign" in a manner very reminiscent of 7:14f.;[190] this sign was given by Isaiah in support of his message in the same conflict situation. The passage 8:11-15[191] appears to indicate that the opposition sought to discredit Isaiah by alleging that his denunciation of their policies was tantamount to conspiring with the enemy. The prophet, turning to his disciples, tells them not to consider conspiracy everything "this people" calls conspiracy;[192] let their "conspiracy" be with the Lord!

Although Isaiah's message went unheeded, he knew that the word he had spoken was genuine; since it concerned, in part at least, specific events in the immediate future, it was only a matter of time until it was vindicated. That this is the situation in 8:16-18 is clear from the reference to trustful waiting (*ḥkh*, *qwh*—vs. 17) and to the children who are "signs and portents in Israel" (vs. 18). Although the exact import of the presence of Shear-jashub during Isaiah's encounter with Ahaz is uncertain, he was present at Yahweh's command (7:3) and so undoubtedly added a dimension or impact to the prophet's message on that occasion; the giving of the name (probably early in Isaiah's ministry) and its precise significance for the contemporary scene may have been public knowledge. The sign-value of Maher-shalal-hash-baz is clearer: within a short time Syria and Israel will fall before the might of Assyria. The very presence of this oddly-named infant asserts that the policy Isaiah advocated against that of the royal advisers could be safely followed.[193]

[188]See above, p. 56. Wildberger, *Jesaja*, 255, does not seem to be far from this position.

[189]See above, p. 57.

[190]So close is the resemblance that many authors relate both narratives to the same birth; see, most recently, Herbert M. Wolf, "A Solution to the Immanuel Prophecy in Isaiah 7:14-8:22," *JBL* 91 (1972) 449-56. One grave difficulty with this author's attempt to relate the *t^e'ûdâ* of 8:16 to the *gillāyôn* (which he takes to be a wedding contract) of 8:1 is his failure to explain (or even mention) the *tôrâ* that is so closely joined to it.

[191]The introductory verse (vs. 11), in which the prophet is admonished not to walk in the way (*hlk b^ederek*) of "this people" employs good wisdom terminology and seems to present Yahweh as a teacher; admonitions concerning "the way" are frequent in wisdom literature and many of them are intended to turn one from the way of the wicked (cf. Prov 1:15; 2:12; 3:31; 4:14; 7:24; 22:5). Although many wish to derive the principal verb from *swr* instead of *ysr*, a position supported by the reading of 1QIsa^a, the latter verb fits the context well.

[192]It is difficult to see what other meaning can be arrived at, for every other OT occurrence of *qešer* (2 Sam 15:12; 1 Kgs 16:20; 2 Kgs 11:14//2 Chr 23:13; 2 Kgs 12:21; 14:19//2 Chr 25:27; 2 Kgs 15:15.30; 17:4; Jer 11:9) has this meaning; the meaning of the verb *qšr* (which should be read in vs. 13), except where it means simply "to bind," points in the same direction.

[193]The inclusion of Isaiah himself among the "signs and portents" does not seem to have been satisfactorily explained, unless we are to assume the reference is to the meaning of his name.

Interpretation

It is against this background that Isaiah's use of *t*^{e}*'ûdâ* and *tôrâ* in 8:16 must be understood. The sense of *t*^{e}*'ûdâ* here is "testimony, witness, attestation." The only other use of the term in the OT (Ru 4:7), where it refers to an act which testifies to an agreement, is enlightening but certainly not a close parallel. The employment of the hiphil of *'wd*,[194] at least in some of its uses, is more instructive, for it has to do with calling someone to witness with an eye to testifying at a later date to what had been said or done.[195] That the employment of *t*^{e}*'ûdâ* here is to be explained in this way is assured by the use of the hiphil of *'wd* in 8:2. Now that it is clear that the battle with the royal advisers has been lost, that the king is determined to follow their counsel (or already has), Isaiah commits to his disciples the record of all he has done in these days. The term *t*^{e}*'ûdâ* reflects the polemic, for it is a claim that there are signs and witnesses to attest to what he has asserted in the name of Yahweh and he has now only to wait for the One who truly controls events to bear witness in deeds to His own holiness and truth.

The term *tôrâ* reflects the same polemic, but in another way. That it cannot mean "law" is obvious, and there is no more reason to think it is simply a term for the prophetic word than there is to think *t*^{e}*'ûdâ* is; *tôrâ* here means "instruction" and it is used because Yahweh's teaching is being opposed to that of the sages, just as Yahweh's "way" is implicitly opposed to the "way" of "this people" in vs. 11.[196] In immediate conjunction with *tôrâ* here stands the term *limmudāy*, and the two words go naturally together as scholastic terminology. Too little attention has been paid to the use of *limmudāy* in this text. The term has been almost universally translated as "disciples," but the influence of the NT and early Christianity may have come into play here; Isaiah and his followers are pictured, no doubt rightly, in a relationship similar to that of Jesus and His immediate followers (disciples). But it would not be pedantic to insist that the term would more naturally be taken to mean "students, pupils" (*Schüler, Lehrlinge* as opposed to *Jüngern*);[197] as such it would have been taken over, with deliberate intent,

[194]Cf. Paul Joüon, *Grammaire de l'hêbreu biblique* (Rome: Pontifical Biblical Institute, 1947), 206. In fact, *'wd* is employed but seldom outside of the hiphil.

[195]Dt 4:26; 30:19; 31:28; Isa 8:2; Jer 32:10.25.44.

[196]Gray, *The Book of Isaiah*, I, 155: "The *testimony* . . . more particularly refers to such sides of Isaiah's public utterances as his assertions that Ephraim and Syria would do Judah no harm, but would be speedily destroyed: cp. the *attesting* of the name Maher-shalal-hash-baz in 8:1f.: the *teaching* . . . is more particularly his insistence on the need for quiet confidence and faith in Yahweh" (in this Gray follows very closely the position of Duhm, *Das Buch Jesaja*, 64). I do not believe, however, that it is possible to distinguish the content of the two terms in this fashion.

[197]The fact that the common Greek NT term for "disciple," *mathētēs*, is derived from *manthanein*, "to learn," should not obscure the legitimacy and necessity of the distinction; originally it meant "student, pupil" and it was only through usage that it came to include the idea of a special relationship to a master. Likewise, the meaning of "disciple" that now attaches

from the terminology of the school. It is not used as a substantive elsewhere in the OT, nor is it found at all before Isaiah. Duhm suggests that it originates with Isaiah:

> Viellicht ist der Ausdruck erst von Jes. geschaffen worden. Schulen, in denen man lesen und schreiben lernte, muss es längst gegeben haben. Nun hat Jes. gleichsam eine Schule um sich errichtet, indem er denen, die sich ihm anschlossen . . . die Zeichen der Zeit deutete und statt der "eingelernten Menschensatzung" den wahren Gottesdienst predigte.[198]

Duhm's words, in fact, seem to imply that Isaiah has taken the term over from "the school"; the quotation even suggests a conscious opposition on the part of Isaiah to the current scholastic education. Even after Isaiah the term *limmūd* does not become current nor is it used again of the followers of a prophet. When it is used, adjectivally, it suggests either simple instruction (Isa 54:13) or the proficiency in good or evil which comes from training and practice (Jer 13:23; Isa 50:4). Thus, it is a word which fits more naturally into the realm of education than of discipleship. In using the term for his followers, Isaiah opposes his instruction—ultimately Yahweh's—to that of the sages. An essential ingredient of true wisdom, when its religious character is preserved, is "fear of the Lord," and in 8:12f. Isaiah sedulously warns his followers that Yahweh shall be their fear, not that which is feared by "this people."

To sum up briefly: the first and primary of the two terms in 8:16 is *tᵉʿûdâ*; it is used because Isaiah's message has been rejected but has still to be vindicated. In all probability this "attestation" is a written document which

to the term *talmîd* (found in the OT only in 1 Chr 25:8) comes from its employment in the rabbinic schools rather than from its etymology. K. H. Rengstorf, "*mathētēs*: The Term in the Old Testament and Judaism," *TDNT* IV, 426f., attempting to explain the virtual absence of OT terms in this area, argues that *lmd* refers always to the revealed will of God and man's conforming to it and that it is always the whole of the chosen people as such that is the subject of this "learning"; he reaches the conclusion that "it is quite impossible for it [the OT community] to use a noun formed from *lāmad* to denote the individual who gives himself especially to *lāmad* and thereby to differentiate him from the other members of the chosen people." But both assertions concerning the employment of *lmd* on which this conclusion is based are false. Looking simply to the qal of *lmd*, it is possible to point to a whole series of texts in which it is not a question of learning God's revealed will and/or in which the subject is not the chosen people as such: Dt 18:9; Isa 1:17; 2:4//Mic 4:3; Jer 10:2; Ezek 19:3.6; Ps 106:35; Prov 30:3; 1 Chr 5:18. With reference to Isa 8:16 he stresses the textual uncertainty and suggests that even if the text is to be accepted as it stands, we would speak rather of a "community of faith" (*Glaubensgemeinde*) than of a "fellowship of disciples" (*Jüngergemeinde*)—p. 430. See the discussion of Aelred Cody, *A History of Old Testament Priesthood* (*AnBib* 35; Rome: Pontifical Biblical Institute, 1969), 20n., of the meaning of *lmd* in a Ugaritic text given by Gordon (*Ugaritic Textbook*, 62:53ff.); either of the alternatives offered (i.e., whether *lmd* refers to an "apprentice" of the chief priest or whether it refers to the chief priest himself, who then has "a role in which he ensures the conservation of his people's literary heritage") could provide relevant background for our text.

includes his call narrative and much of the other material now in 6:1-8:15. It is an "attestation" because it bears witness to words and signs from Yahweh that have in part already been realized (the "blinding, deafening, and hardening" and Shear-yashub—the latter finding at least a preliminary fulfillment in Isaiah's circle) and are in part still to be fulfilled. The document is also called *tôrâ* because even as "attestation" it consists of teaching and instruction of Yahweh, opposed to that put forward by the royal sages and advisers. Neither of these two nouns have pronominal suffixes or other specification, for both are to be referred immediately to Isaiah,[199] but ultimately to Yahweh. Yet it may be suggested that attestation is more properly the human task of witnessing the divine act, whereas Isaiah would have insisted that Yahweh alone is the source of instruction and that the prophet is only its bearer.

Isaiah 30:9

Following Duhm, Marti, Fischer, and von Rad, the unity to which this verse belongs is taken to be 30:8-17.[200] Cheyne takes these verses together but expands the unity to include vs. 18.[201] Eissfeldt and Donner hesitate on whether vss. 15-17 should be joined to vss. 8-14 or taken as a separate piece, but offer no firm arguments for the separation.[202] Fohrer separates vss. 15-17 from vss. 8-14, but the reason he gives, that vs. 15 has an introduction,[203] is not compelling. The *kōh-'āmar 'ădōnāy yhwh* is introduced by a *kî* which links it to the preceding words; if the verb is translated as a normal perfect ("For thus said the Lord God"—see the *NAB*), it fits very well with the preceding development. The fact that vs. 15 does not fit into the classical pattern of a judgment oracle constitutes an objection only for those who conceive the prophets as rigidly bound to standard forms. Westermann, discussing the progressive relaxation of the form of the "judgment against the nations," sees a beginning of this relaxation already in the eighth century prophets. He insists that, especially in the oracles of the eighth century prophets, such expansions cannot be considered secondary and that they often contain the most distinctive compositions of the prophets in question; and he adds that all of Isaiah's statements about faith are found in such expansions.[204] He lists 30:15 as just such an expansion (p. 187). Childs finds

[199]Gottwald, *All the Kingdoms of the Earth*, 202.

[200]Duhm, *Das Buch Jesaja*, 218-21; Marti, *Das Buch Jesaja*, 221-24; Fischer, *Das Buch Isaias*, 200-203; von Rad, *Old Testament Theology*, II, 40.

[201]Cheyne, *The Prophecies of Isaiah*, I, 176-78.

[202]Eissfeldt, *The Old Testament*, 316; Donner, *Israel unter den Völkern*, 159-62.

[203]Fohrer, *Das Buch Jesaja*, II, 98; "Entstehung, Komposition und Überlieferung von Jesaja 1-39," 130.

[204]Westermann, *Basic Forms of Prophetic Speech*, 181f.

30:8-17 "clear and straightforward from a form critical perspective."[205]

There are some surprising similarities between this passage and 8:16-18, the one just studied. In each case there is a probable reference to a written document which serves the purpose of attestation or witness.[206] In the present passage the people are blamed for forsaking the *tôrâ* of Yahweh, while in the earlier one the *tôrâ* which Isaiah preserves among his disciples referred to a teaching which has been rejected. Both texts can be referred to broader contexts in which Isaiah warns against foreign alliances and calls for quiet trust in Yahweh alone (7:4.9; 28:12.16; 30:15). And in each case, it can be argued, his polemic is directed primarily against the royal advisers who advocate the expedient course of seeking outside military aid.

It would be exceedingly useful to know what Isaiah was commanded to write down. If 30:8 is taken to be the beginning of the passage, there is no expressed antecedent for the pronoun contained in *kotbāh*. The commentators' conjectures on what the "it" is have varied widely. Some have thought of something quite brief, such as the "Rahab quelled" of vs. 7.[207] Others suggest something very extensive, even including much of the material of Isa 28-30,[208] and thus a composition similar to that supposed to be referred to in 8:16-18. Cheyne and Fischer seem to relate their assertion of a brief message to the fact that it is to be written on a tablet (*lûaḥ*) and both refer back to the brief inscription of 8:1 as an illuminating parallel. However, Duhm, Marti, and Fohrer treat *'al lûaḥ 'ittām* as a gloss introduced under the influence of 8:1.[209] The remaining term, *sēper*, is consistent with the theory of a longer composition; but Fohrer points to the verb *ḥqq* as arguing for an inscription and thus for a short text. Although the argument is not absolutely compelling (Marti had already pointed to Isa 49:16 and Ezek 23:14 as texts in which *ḥqq* has a meaning other than "to engrave, inscribe"), it does have some force—despite the fact that one of the examples Fohrer gives (Jos 8:32) was probably a lengthy text. But this raises the further question, one of those which led Duhm to confess he didn't understand the line,[210] of why *ḥqq*, rather than *ktb*, stands with *sēper*. Fohrer's suggestion that *sēper* here means "inscription" rather than "scroll" can find support in the use of the term in Job 19:23, which he cites, and in the Ahiram inscription, which he does not; but the preposition used in the present text (*w*^e^*'al sēper ḥuqqah*) appears to me to render that interpretation exceedingly improbable.

Because of such problems and because the context of the command to write is unclear, it seems impossible to give any definite answer to the question of what Isaiah was to write down. Kissane thinks that the command is a purely rhetorical figure and that the content of the "inscription" is the

[205]Childs, *Isaiah and the Assyrian Crisis*, 36; see also p. 64.

[206]Repointing the *lā'ad* of 30:8b to read *l*^e^*'ēd* with the Targum, Peshitta, and Vulgate.

[207]Cheyne, *The Prophecies of Isaiah*, I, 176; Fischer, *Das Buch Isaias*, 201.

[208]Duhm, *Das Buch Jesaia*, 218f.; Marti, *Das Buch Jesaja*, 222.

[209]For Duhm and Marti, see preceding note; Fohrer, *Das Buch Jesaja*, II, 95. In 8:1, the term is not *lûah*, of course, but *gillāyôn*.

[210]Duhm, *Das Buch Jesaia*, 218.

following vs. 9 rather than anything that has preceded.[211] Although Fohrer understands the command to write more literally, he comes to much the same conclusion as to content.[212] It is probably not possible to determine the content of this "document" any more closely than to say that it was intended as a summary of Isaiah's preaching during the period ca. 705-701.

If Kissane and Fohrer are correct, the reproach in vs. 9, that they have refused to hear the *tôrâ*,[213] is part of the summary of which the "document" in question consists. Whether that is the case or not, there is every reason to hold that *tôrâ* here refers in a general way to Isaiah's teaching during this period. In support of this suggestion is the fact that *'bh* appears as a sort of catchword, occurring three times in oracles from this period (elsewhere in Isaiah only in 1:19); in the other two places it clearly refers to the people's rejection of Isaiah's demand for faith and *Stillsein*. In 28:12:

> This is the resting place,
>   give rest to the weary;
> Here is repose—
>   but they would not listen (*w*^{e}*lō' 'ābû' š*^{e}*môa'*).

[211] Kissane, *The Book of Isaiah*, I, 344.

[212] Fohrer, *Das Buch Jesaja*, II, 93.

[213] Donner, *Israel unter den Völkern*, 160, suggests that *tôrat* should be dropped from the text; in "Tafel XIII" (p. 188) it appears that the reason is his reconstruction of the oracle in a very rigid 3/2 meter (except for vs. 8a, which stands outside the meter, and vs. 11, whose meter is 2/2/2/2). His reconstruction necessitates, restricting ourselves to vss. 9f.: a) elimination of *tôrat* (vs. 9); b) elimination of *'ăšer* (vs. 10); c) emendation of *'āmrû* to *'ōm*^{e}*rîm* (vs. 10); d) elimination of *lānû n*^{e}*kōḥôt*. These verses then go as follows:

9)	*kî 'am m*^{e}*rî hû'*	*bānîm keḥāšîm*
	bānîm lō' 'ābû	*lišmôa' yhwh*
10)	*'ōm*^{e}*rîm lārō'îm lō' tir'û*	*w*^{e}*laḥōzîm lō' teḥĕzû*
	dabb^{e}*rû lānû ḥălāqôt*	*ḥăzû mahătallôt*

But (aside from the small change in the infinitive of vs. 9, which has a basis in IQIsa^{a}) there is no justification in the textual tradition for the changes he makes. There is the further difficulty that *tir'û* and *teḥĕzû* are left without any object, and this introduces a glaring inconsistency between *lo' teḥĕzû* and the *ḥăzû mahătallôt* which follows shortly after. With somewhat different divisions of the phrases it is possible to come up with the same regular meter, except for a 2/3 line at vs. 10b, without departing from MT for vss. 9-10. If *'al lûaḥ 'ittām* is deleted from vs. 8, as has been suggested by a number of commentators (see above n. 209), that verse, too, falls easily into this meter.

8)	*'attâ bô' kotbāh*	*w*^{e}*'al sēper ḥuqqāh*
	ût^{e}*hî l*^{e}*yôm 'aḥărôn*	*l*^{e}*'ēd 'ad 'ôlām*
9)	*kî 'am m*^{e}*rî hû'*	*bānîm keḥāšîm*
	bānîm lō'▪'ābû š^{e}*môa'*	*tôrat yhwh*
10)	*'ăšer 'ām*^{e}*rû lārō'îm*	*lō' tir'û*
	w^{e}*laḥōzîḿ*	*lō' téḥĕzû lấnû n*^{e}*kōḥốt*
	dabb^{e}*rû lānû ḥălāqôt*	*ḥăzû mahătallôt*

If *tôrâ* were to be eliminated from this passage, of course, it would simply mean the text is not relevant to this study. However, there seems no need to eliminate the term.

And in 30:15:

For thus said the Lord God,
  the Holy One of Israel:
By waiting and calm you shall be saved,
  in quiet and trust your strength lies.
But this you did not wish (*w^elōʾ ʾăbîtem*).

Thus the basic content of *tôrâ* in 30:9 is much the same as in 8:16 and many of the things that were said concerning that text apply here. In that earlier period the indications of Isaiah's struggle with the royal advisers were less obvious, his words being usually addressed to the king or the people, surfacing only occasionally, as in some of the woe-oracles. In the present period the struggle is much more explicit, as his words more frequently and more directly concern the forgers of the royal policy. In 28:14-22 Isaiah criticizes those responsible for the pact with Egypt, a "covenant with death," calling them "arrogant" (*ʾanšê lāṣôn*);[214] the parallel expression, *mōš^elê hāʿam hazzeh*, Fohrer translates "ihr Sprüchemacher dieses Volkes da" and renders more literally as "Spottredner" in a note. While this translation may be questioned, it is likely that Isaiah intended a word-play involving the two identical *mšl* roots (to rule, and to speak a proverb or mock) in relating the terms used both to the "Beamtenkreise" and to the "Weisheitslehre."[215] If the idea of scoffing or mocking is contained in these expressions (and in the use of *lyṣ* in vs. 22), then this oracle ought perhaps to be closely related to 28:7-13,[216] from which it is clear that priests and prophets, too, were among those who rejected the prophet's message and attempted to discredit him by ridicule; along with the officials more directly pertaining to the court, they helped determine and support the royal policy. From vs. 9 (*ʾet mî yôreh dēʿâ w^eʾet mî yābîn š^emûʿâ*) it is clear that Isaiah's teaching could be characterized as "instruction" and even as *tôrâ*. Although its precise import is difficult to determine, the "Parable of the Farmer" (28:23-29) probably belongs in the context of this debate; Yahweh's *ʿēṣâ* is being defended in terms that are calculated to appeal to (or refute) the wisdom circles, and the wonderful, incomprehensible, manner of His action is emphasized (vs. 29). In this context belongs also 29:13f., which speaks again of the wonderful nature of God's action and of the overthrow of the wisdom of the wise,[217] and 29:15f., a woe

[214]The same expression is found in Prov 29:8; the only other occurrence of *lāṣôn* is in Prov 1:22.

[215]Cf. Fohrer, *Das Buch Jesaja*, II, 56.

[216]It is possible that vss. 7f. do not belong with the following vss. 9-13; Marti, *Das Buch Jesaja*, 205f., separates them. In that case, vss. 9-13 refer to scoffers who are unidentified but who surely belong to the royal court.

[217]I have already argued that these verses are directed against the wise; see above, p. 67. See also Fohrer's comment, *Das Buch Jesaja*, II, 78.

pronounced against those who hatch out plans in secret and completed with a series of parabolic sayings in the wisdom style.[218] Relevant here, too, are the woes pronounced in 30:1-5 and 31:1-3; the first of these speaks of the *'ēṣâ* which has been worked out independently of Yahweh, and the second condemns trust in Egyptian might rather than in Yahweh.[219]

It is clear, therefore, that, in this period too, Isaiah preached against a foreign policy of alliances and revolt, advocating instead quiet reliance on Yahweh's might and governance; that the circle of royal advisers attempted to discredit him and his message through mockery and scorn and that in this they were supported and seconded by priests and prophets who were connected with the Temple and the royal court; and that Isaiah countered by reference to divine revelation he had received (cf. 28:22) and by condemning the self-styled "wise" and their wisdom for their short-sighted policies and the inability of their system to take account of the authentic word of God. Since the verb *hôrâ* is used twice in these texts, once of the prophet's teaching (28:9) and once of the instruction imparted by God to the farmer (28:26), there is reason to suppose that Yahweh's teaching through Isaiah could be designated as *tôrâ*; to this must be added the evidence from the *tôrâ*-texts already discussed.

It is against this background that Isaiah's complaint that the people have refused to hear the *tôrâ* of Yahweh (*lō' 'ābû šᵉmôa' tôrat yhwh*) in 30:9 must be understood. Although the debate was immediately concerned with *'ēṣâ*, something far broader was at stake. The call to renounce plans to seek help from Egypt and to revolt against Assyria is but part of a broader and deeper teaching concerning Yahweh's lordship and providence and concerning the trustful confidence that could be the only adequate response to these ("This is the resting place, . . . Here is repose"; "See, I am laying a stone in Zion; . . . he who puts his faith in it shall not be shaken"; "By waiting and calm you shall be saved, in quiet and trust your strength lies"); *'ēṣâ*, at least in Isaiah's usage,[220] was too narrow a term to cover such teaching, but Isaiah could and did designate it as *tôrâ*. His choice of the term was a function of his polemic against "the wise": true teaching comes from Yahweh alone, not from those whose wisdom has degenerated into mere human scheming.

This discussion of the background would alone seem sufficient to justify the assertion that *tôrâ* is used as a wisdom term in 30:9,[221] for those he

[218]See Whedbee, *Isaiah and Wisdom*, 130f.; Fohrer, *Das Buch Jesaja*, II, 79-81.

[219]On the dating of the oracles discussed in this paragraph, as well as 30:8-17, see Fohrer, *Das Buch Jesaja*, I, 9-11 (and the commentary on each passage), and "Entstehung, Komposition und Überlieferung von Jesaja 1-39," 129f.

[220]See above, p. 59.

[221]It should be obvious that *tôrâ* here does not refer to the law or priestly *tôrâ*. And the discussion should have made it clear that although the instruction at issue was mediated through the prophetic word, this alone is no adequate explanation for the use of the term.

primarily addresses are surely the royal policy makers[222] who have rejected his message and wish to hear no more of it (vs. 11). But there is also a series of indications in this oracle that point still more clearly to a wisdom usage. The first of these is the fact that *tôrâ* stands in close relation to *bānîm*[223] (a term that occurs twice in this line): it is as "sons" or "children" that Judah is reproached for failure to hear Yahweh's *tôrâ*; it is precisely in the wisdom tradition, from most ancient times, that instruction is addressed to "sons." It is significant, too, that the sin is a refusal[224] to *hear*. Although *šm'* can mean "to obey," it is natural to take it in the more literal sense when there are references in Isaiah's oracles from this period (28:9.12; 29:9f.), and even in the immediate context (30:10f.15), to mockery, perversity, and the unwillingness to listen. The call to "hear instruction" is, of course, an ancient and characteristic element of the wisdom tradition and one regularly addressed to "sons." The call to hear instruction no doubt includes the expectation (or at least the hope!) of obedience, but there is, nevertheless, a clearly discernible difference in the meaning of the verb *šm'* in its use in, e.g., Prov 1:8a (*šᵉma' bᵉnî mûsar 'ābîkā*) and in, e.g., Dt 28:1 (*'im šāmôa' tišma' bᵉqôl yhwh 'ĕlōhèkā lišmōr la'ăśôt 'et kol miṣwôtāyw . . .*). Isaiah employs *šm'* in the "hear and obey" sense in 1:19, but in his call narrative, a passage more relevant to the present context, the "listen and understand" is quite explicit: *šim'u šāmôa' wᵉ'al tābînû* (6:9).

The expression *šm' tôrâ* is quite rare. Dt, which uses both words frequently, never combines them in this way.[225] We find *šm' 'et tôrâ* in Zech 7:12, but there is reason to believe that Zechariah is reflecting the usage of Isaiah.[226] The only other OT text which has *šm' tôrâ* is Prov 28:9, a passage already discussed in detail.[227] This usage fits in well with a whole series of other wisdom texts in which *šm'* is used with terms for the wisdom teacher's

[222]The terminology in vs. 9 (*'am, bānîm*) shows that the oracle is directed to a wider audience and that the people share in the guilt of their leaders in that they concur in their acts and applaud their decisions and sentiments; but to the extent that Isaiah is waging a polemic concerning the policies adopted (cf. vss. 15f.), it is directed primarily against those responsible for it. See Duhm, *Das Buch Jesaia*, 221; Lindars, "Torah in Deuteronomy," 121.

[223]Note the similar conjunction of *tôrâ* with *limmudāy* in 8:16; there *tôrâ* was committed to obedient pupils, while here disobedient sons are accused of failure to hear *tôrâ*.

[224]Although the distribution of *'bh* is quite broad in the OT, it is worth noting that it is used with wisdom terms in Prov 1:25 (*tôkaḥat*) .30 (*'ēṣâ*).

[225]In Dt 31:12 *tôrâ* is the unexpressed object, but the reference is to the physical act of hearing the law read; so also in Neh 13:3.

[226]See above, Ch. 1, n. 74 and text.

[227]See above, p. 39.

instructions.[228] Isaiah's usage accords well with wisdom phraseology.[229]

The words put into the mouths of Isaiah's adversaries in vss. 10f. and the specification of the accusation in vs. 12 contain further indications that Isaiah is deliberately using wisdom terminology in order to bring the battle into the enemy's camp. In vs. 10 Isaiah has the people saying to the prophets (*ḥōzîm*), "Do not descry for us what is right (*n kōḥôt*)." Terrien, arguing for wisdom influence in Amos, points to the use of this term (in the singular) in Am 3:10.[230] Wolff argues in like manner, calling this term "das in der Weisheit mehrfach belegte Wort für 'das Recht' " and referring to Prov 8:8f.; 24:26; and Sir 11:21.[231] He refers (as does Terrien) to Isaiah's use of it: "Bei Jesaja taucht das Wort 30,10 auf, in der Auseinandersetzung mit den Kreisen höfischer (diplomatischer) Weisheit . . ." [232] The evidence for calling this a wisdom term, however, is rather weak. The two texts from Prov can stand as evidence, but the term occurs also in 2 Sam 15:3; Isa 26:10; 57:2; and 59:14. Since 2 Sam 15:3 gives the words of Absalom, "Your suit is good and just," it might be argued he is using terminology that the ruling class learns in "the school," but the texts from the later Isaiah collections do not exhibit any obvious wisdom influence. Nevertheless, Crenshaw, who shows himself to be rather critical of many of the arguments for wisdom influence in Amos, is willing to admit some force to this one.[233] Given numerous other, far firmer, indications of wisdom terminology in this context, the term can perhaps bear a little weight.

Somewhat clearer is the use of *derek* and *'ōraḥ* in the following verse. It has already been pointed out that the use of these two terms in parallelism, in a figurative sense, is a typical wisdom procedure.[234] The present text does not employ them in a figurative sense, i.e., to designate a way of life or a manner of behavior, it is true, but there is another factor to be taken into account. Isaiah is clearly not repeating words actually spoken by his critics, but is putting into their mouths words that express his estimate of their real dispositions and sentiments: he is saying that they wish to have no more to do with

[228] Prov 1:8 (*mûsār*—parallel with *tôrâ*); 4:1 (*mûsār*); 8:33 (*mûsār*); 12:15 (*'ēṣâ*); 15:31 (*tôkaḥat*); 19:20 (*'ēṣâ*) .27 (*mûsār*); 22:17 (*dᵉbārîm*).

[229] It is worth recalling that another passage in which Isaiah designates Judah as Yahweh's "sons," 1:2f., is also stamped with wisdom terms and imagery; see above, p. 49. In the more immediate context of our passage, in 30:1, Isaiah again uses the designation "sons," and again a wisdom stamp is quite likely; the complaint that they "carry out a plan (*'ēṣâ*) that is not from me" sounds very much like the words of a wisdom teacher whose teaching and advice has been abandoned by his erstwhile pupils. See Loewenclau, "Zur Auslegung von Jesaja 1,2-3," 299.

[230] Terrien, "Amos and Wisdom," 112.

[231] The citation from Sirach, in which the term does not have moral overtones, does not appear to be apposite. It occurs also in Sir 6:22, but again without a moral connotation.

[232] Wolff, *Amos' geistige Heimat*, 30.

[233] Crenshaw, "The Influence of the Wise upon Amos," 46.

[234] See above, pp. 93f.

God and His governance. A very keen and biting sarcasm can be seen in the prophet's words as he expresses the royal advisers' desire to be quit of God's directing influence in those very terms which they familiarly (but hypocritically!) used to teach about the proper way of life. It is precisely the sort of artistic irony we would expect of this most articulate prophet.

But it is when Isaiah further specifies their crimes in vs. 12 that he most clearly turns against them their own terminology: they are accused of[235] putting their trust in "what is crooked and devious (*b*e*'iqqēš*[236] *w*e*nālôz*[237])." The first of these two words is used seven times in Prov, in Dt 32:5, and in only two other texts;[238] thus it is almost exclusively a wisdom term. The second, the niphal participle of *lwz*, is found, aside from this text, only in three passages in Prov (2:15; 3:32; 14:2) and in Sir 34:8. The terms occur in parallel in Isa 30:12 and Prov 2:15 and nowhere else. The most reasonable explanation for this is that Isaiah is deliberately using the vocabulary of wisdom against its practitioners.

Finally, and most surprisingly, Isaiah apparently incorporates a wisdom term into the brief recapitulation of the heart of his message that we find in vs. 15: "By waiting and by calm you shall be saved (*b*e*šûbâ wānaḥat tiwwāšē'ûn*) . . ." On the basis of its distribution it would appear that *naḥat* was a term especially, or even exclusively, employed as wisdom diction. Aside from this text of Isaiah, it is found only in wisdom compositions; the term is not frequent but its appearance in four different books in a total of eight texts seems enough to be significant and too much to be chance. The texts are

[235]The phrase *mo'oskem baddābār hazzeh* could easily be taken as wisdom terminology; see above, pp. 97f.

[236]Emended from MT's *b*e*'ōšeq* with most commentators. Support for the emendation comes mainly from the context, but LXX's *pseudei* is more easily explicable from *'iqqēš* (see Prov 28:6 where the same Gk root is used to render *'iqqēš*) than from *'ōšeq*.

[237]The discussion supposes that *w*e*nālôz* is the correct reading, though some of the early witnesses raise problems, especially LXX's *kai hoti egoggysas* and IQIsa^a's *wt'lwz*. But these two variant readings do not agree with one another nor is one easily explicable from the other. Furthermore, it does not seem possible that either reading could be correct, and so they bear mutual witness to a disturbed text. A singular verb does not fit the context grammatically, nor does the Gk *goggyzein* suit the context as to meaning. LXX almost certainly supposes the reading to be the niphal of *lwn*, but, aside from the problem of fitting "murmuring" into this context, the OT use of *lwn* is restricted almost exclusively to the tradition of the murmuring in the wilderness in Ex 15-17 and Num 14-17 (the only exceptions being Jos 9:18 and—conjectural—Ps 59:16). A possible solution might be to suppose that the Qumran reading is basically correct but that the last two letters should be reversed to yield *wt'lzw*; the meaning would suit the context and with the emendation it would fit grammatically, too. But what evidence the LXX affords is against the emendation. In view of the fact that the early witnesses do not point in any clear direction, the MT is to be preferred, especially since the witnesses give at least indirect support: LXX seems to have read a niphal form of *lwn*, while IQIsa^a reads the final radical as *z*.

[238]Dt 32:5; 2 Sam 22:27//Ps 18:27; Ps 101:4; Prov 2:15; 8:8; 11:20; 17:20; 19:1; 22:5; 28:6.

Prov 29:9; Job 36:16; Eccl 4:6; 6:5; 9:17; Sir 11:19; 12:11; 31:21.[239] The fact that most of these texts are late is more than overbalanced by another consideration, namely, the lack of any OT evidence (leaving Isa 30:15 aside) from any period, for its employment outside the wisdom tradition. Furthermore, Prov 29:9 may well be early and two of the Eccl texts (4:6 and 9:17) are citations of proverbial sayings that may equally well be early; and it is relevant to recall here what was said in a previous chapter of the basic conservatism of the wisdom movement in its forms and terminology.

What is striking about the employment of this term by Isaiah is that he uses it to express his characteristic call to trust and *Stillsein*. If the formula "For thus said the Lord God" means that Isaiah is here quoting an oracle that he had spoken earlier, as seems to be the case, then the use of *naḥat* may indicate an attempt to deal with "the wise" in a more positive fashion than simply by polemic: a term that they could recognize as their own was used by the prophet in his call for trust in Yahweh that enabled one to renounce the deceptive props of foreign alliances.[240] But by the time 30:8-17 is spoken, it is clear that the appeal has fallen on deaf ears; since they formed their own plans (30:1) and have attempted to keep them hidden (29:15), the prophet has no choice but to brand them as deceitful children who have refused to heed Yahweh's instruction and to foretell the total collapse of the edifice they have constructed (30:13f.).

Summary

In the case of each *tôrâ* text of Isaiah it has been possible to bring forward strong arguments in favor of the wisdom sense of the term, i.e., the meaning "wise instruction." Supposing that there is any consistency at all in Isaiah's use of the word, this meaning seems to be virtually imposed. It does not appear possible to argue for any other conceivable meaning of *tôrâ*, such as the priestly or the legal, for all these texts—if, indeed, it is possible to argue for such meaning with equal cogency for even one. In Chapter One I argued that no text, leaving aside those of Isaiah, used *tôrâ* as a technical term for the prophetic word. Now that conclusion can be extended to Isaiah's use of the term. Isaiah uses *tôrâ* because it was a term of the wisdom tradition that he wished to appropriate for his continuing debate with wisdom circles. In two instances the prophet's attack was wholly concerned with foreign policy (8:16; 30:9), once with a breakdown of the social order (1:10), and once with a

[239]The term is found in the MT of Job 17:16, but that needs to be emended to *nēḥāt*. In view of the corrupt condition of the text, the presence of *naḥat* in Job 36:16 cannot bear too much weight; but it is found there in the MT and the Vulgate so read it.

[240]Mitchell Dahood, "Some Ambiguous Texts in Isaias," *CBQ* 20 (1958) 41-43, while touching the question of etymology only lightly, points to the collocation of *yšb* and *nwḥ* forms in non-Israelite texts as an argument for the derivation of *šûbâ* from *yšb* in our text. Supposing that Isaiah chose *naḥat* because of its wisdom overtones, the collocation of the otherwise unattested *šûbâ* would thus find an explanation.

combination of the two (5:24). In the remaining instance (2:3) the presentation was visionary and irenic; but even here the polemic was probably not absent, for there could not have been lacking an implied contrast between the peace among nations that would prevail when Yahweh's wisdom held sway and the carnage the prophet saw and foresaw as a result of that human wisdom which went its own way.

5

CONCLUSIONS

If the position argued in the preceding chapters has been established, it has some obvious implications for the translation and exegesis of Isaiah's authentic *tôrâ* passages. In addition, Isaiah's use of *tôrâ,* as set forth here, casts light on other Isaiah passages, helps to define more closely his relationship to the wisdom circles of his own day, and possibly serves as a starting point for estimating Isaiah's long-term influence on the wisdom tradition.

With regard to the second of these three points, Isaiah's relationship to the wisdom circles of his own time, the general thrust has been to confirm Fichtner's observation of a special relationship of Isaiah to the wisdom tradition, especially as manifested in his use of wisdom terminology, and the assertions of von Rad, McKane, Whedbee, and others who say that this usage was a function of Isaiah's polemic against "the wise." No support was found for Fichtner's "converted sage" theory. Isaiah's ability to utilize the forms and vocabulary of wisdom should probably be attributed, rather, to that genius by which he was able to master Israel's traditions and to use them in an original and creative manner in the presentation of his message; it is with reason that he has always been recognized as one of the greatest of the prophets. On the other hand, the possibility that Isaiah underwent the same sort of training as his opponents of the wisdom circles is not to be excluded. Many of the elements of Isaiah's polemic seem to find their best explanation in the supposition that there was a Jerusalem "school" in which the sons of the ruling classes received their training. If Isaiah came from a noble line, as is often supposed, he might well have received the same training; in this case, his familiarity with their traditions and the ease with which he utilized them would be readily intelligible.[1] But this is something quite other than exercising the function of teacher, royal counselor, judge, etc., that would have identified him with the wisdom circles.

I have suggested that Isaiah's polemic against the sages is more explicit during his ministry under Hezekiah than under Ahaz.[2] The reason for this is

[1]One might argue in this direction from the fact that at times Isaiah uses wisdom techniques where there is no obvious polemic against wisdom circles, as, e.g., 1:2f.

[2]See above, Ch. 4, p. 115.

possibly related to the different characters of the two kings. Hezekiah, in contrast to Ahaz, is depicted as a man of piety and faith, as enjoying friendly relations with Isaiah, as willing to accept and even to request a sign from the prophet (Isa 38:7f.22//2 Kgs 20:8-11; cf. Isa 37:30//2 Kgs 19:29); presumably he was also more willing to listen to and to act on Isaiah's revealed message. But in the crucial events of 705 he disregarded the prophet's urgent advice, and it would not be surprising if Isaiah laid a relatively greater share of the blame on the royal counselors and on their ability to persuade and influence the king.[3]

On the question of the point of conflict between Isaiah and the sages, neither McKane's nor Whedbee's solution can be accepted without reserve. Against McKane it can be asserted that there are no indications that Isaiah ever questioned the legitimacy of the role of the royal counselors, much less of the wisdom tradition itself. On the contrary, there is much to show that he regarded them not as mortal enemies of all that was good and holy, but as unworthy practitioners of a noble calling. His use of wisdom forms and vocabulary must be considered primarily as an attempt to enter into debate with them, though not simply on their own terms. Isaiah was aware that those who exercised the function of judges had been trained in a tradition that taught them to despise bribes, practice sobriety, esteem justice, and exercise special care of the weak and helpless members of society; to complain of the absence of these qualities in those who judge, using the language of the school itself to do so,[4] was a forceful way of challenging them to live up to their authentic traditions.

In the matter of the debate over national policies, the possibility of a parallel challenge did not exist; the very need to investigate the advantages and disadvantages of the available options transferred the operation from the realm of principles to that of pragmatism. Yet this should not have necessarily excluded the influence of the prophet and his revealed message. All those involved accepted the same Yahwistic faith; all, and the wise men in particular, shared the conviction that Yahweh was capable of overruling the plans that were made contrary to His will. In spite of Whedbee's claim, there is no indication of dispute on these matters; it was rather a question of their refusing to believe that that word could be true which would force them to set aside their well-wrought plans. In these circumstances, Isaiah's use of *'ēṣâ* to designate Yahweh's future act may well have been intended to inject his word more forcefully into the deliberative procedure as well as being a reminder

[3]The story of Hushai and Ahitophel (2 Sam 17:1-14) reminds us that one of the esteemed qualities of the professional counselor was the ability to present his plan persuasively and reveal the weaknesses of rival plans. The cynical were aware that the wise man could easily find reason for any course of action—and its opposite; cf. "A Pessimistic Dialogue between Master and Servant," *ANET*, 437f.

[4]Cf. Isa 1:10-17; 5:7.22f.; 10:1-3.

that Yahweh's *'ēṣâ* (if they were willing to accept the prophet's witness that it could be known) would surely prevail.[5]

Isaiah's use of *tôrâ*, on the other hand, would seem to have been much deeper, more far-reaching, in its implications. The term, as employed in his oracles, always looks back to Yahweh as its source, never—it is otherwise with his use of *'ēṣâ*—to man. This can only mean that he recognizes Yahweh alone as the source of wise instruction and that man can only be wise by receiving such instruction from Yahweh. In view of Isaiah's reasons for being disappointed with the practitioners of wisdom in his own time, this development is not surprising. To the extent that the term includes the traditional values of the wisdom circles, especially the obligation of the ruling class to establish and defend social justice (1:10-17; 5:22-24), Isaiah recognizes their excellence and gives them a lasting authority under Yahweh's aegis. But beyond this, in that he employs the term in contexts that relate to broader matters, most especially those that pertain to national policy, he is saying that true wisdom must begin by asking about Yahweh's will, both as contained in Israel's religious traditions and as revealed in a particular situation. Revelation, in this view, becomes the ultimate source of wisdom, and the old empiricism is given a much restricted role; empiricism is not excluded, of course, but is subordinated to revelation in its functioning.

These implications we find in Isaiah's oracles, of course, not in the behavior or attitude of those contemporary sages he jousted with. Yet something like this did come to be accepted as the true approach to wisdom in Israel's later wisdom tradition, and I suggest that the influence of Isaiah in bringing this to pass was great. That he did battle with the wisdom circles of his time can be taken as an established fact; that the source of the conflict was their unwillingness to submit empiricism to the demands of faith seems easy to establish; that Isaiah's attempts to call them to a truer understanding of wisdom, one more consonant with Israel's faith, did in fact bear fruit is suggested by the subsequent history of the wisdom tradition. This did not come to pass in his own day but is to be attributed to the lasting power of his word and to the instruction committed to his disciples. More will be said of this in the concluding section of this chapter.

The conclusion argued here, that for Isaiah true wisdom must stem from Yahweh, finds confirmation in what he has to say of the ideal king of the future, most especially in the characterization in 11:2[6] of the charismatic

[5]To this extent Whedbee's thesis is probably correct, that Isaiah's use of this term may have been intended to call to mind traditional sayings about Yahweh's *'ēṣâ* prevailing over that of men.

[6]No new defense of the authenticity of Isa 11:1-9 will be attempted; the discussion in the text will show how well the oracle suits Isaiah's thought, especially when viewed against his experience with Judah's sages. Although the question of authorship is far from settled, a goodly majority of modern scholars suppose or defend Isaian authorship of the piece; among these may be listed the following: Cheyne, ***The Prophecies of Isaiah***, I, 75; Duhm, ***Das Buch Jesaia***, 104 (Duhm actually defends Isaian authorship of only vss. 1-8); Fischer, ***Das Buch Isaias***, 101;

gifts he will be endowed with. The verse runs as follows:

w[e]*nāḥā ʿālāyw rûaḥ yhwh*	*rûaḥ ḥokmâ ûbînâ*
rûaḥ ʿēṣâ ûg[e]*bûrâ*	*rûaḥ daʿat w*[e]*yirʾat yhwh*

In view of Israel's early traditions and in view of what can be known of Isaiah's teaching and ministry, hardly any element of this characterization need occasion surprise. Israel's earliest leaders were charismatic figures, raised up and endowed by Yahweh's spirit,[7] including her first kings, Saul (1 Sam 10:10; 11:6) and, especially, David (1 Sam 16:13). Dynastic succession in Judah gave a certain degree of stability to the kingdom, but the historical kings were something less than instruments in the hand of Yahweh: "It was only Isaiah who in his prophecy moved the picture of the anointed one who was coming very definitely in the direction of the charismatic . . ."[8]

Some authors have concluded that the endowments of the spirit here described constitute the "equipment" of the messianic king along more or less traditional lines. Mowinckel, for example, says, "In every point the

Kissane, *The Book of Isaiah*, 132f.; Fichtner, "Jesaja unter den Weisen," 80; Herntrich, *Der Prophet Jesaja*, 205-16; Rankin, *Israel's Wisdom Literature*, 128; Hammershaimb, "On the Ethics of the Old Testament Prophets," 82; Robert Koch, "Der Gottesgeist und der Messias," *Bib* 27 (1946) 241-68, 376-403; Eichrodt, *Der Heilige in Israel*, 136-42; Kaiser, *Isaiah 1-12*, 155; Vawter, *The Conscience of Israel*, 188; Weiser, *Introduction to the Old Testament*, 189 (he is less inclined to defend the authenticity of vss. 6-9 than of vss. 1-5); Vriezen, "Essentials of the Theology of Isaiah," 142; *idem*, "Ruach Yahweh (Elohim) in the Old Testament," 57; J. L. McKenzie, "Royal Messianism," *CBQ* 19 (1957) 42f.; von Rad, *Old Testament Theology*, I, 323; II, 46, 168f.; Herrmann, *Die prophetischen Heilserwartungen im Alten Testament*, 137; Walter Harrelson, "Nonroyal Motifs in the Royal Eschatology," *Israel's Prophetic Heritage*, 154; Helmer Ringgren, *The Messiah in the Old Testament* (*SBT* 1/18; London: SCM Press, 1956), 31.

Those who reject the authenticity of an oracle such as this often appear to be led by an *a priori* judgment that the early prophets did not make promises of salvation. For example, Georg Fohrer, "Die Struktur der alttestamentlichen Eschatologie," *Studien zur alttestamentlichen Prophetie [1949-1965]* (*BZAW* 99; Berlin: Verlag Alfred Töpelmann, 1967), 32-58, finds that Haggai and Deutero-Isaiah divide history into two periods, the present moment being the turning point to the new period of salvation; but, says Fohrer, the pre-exilic prophets didn't think of two successive ages, but of the "Entweder-Oder" of destruction or deliverance through repentance. Fohrer's analysis finds that all oracles of promise in Isaiah 1-39 fall at the end of the smaller collections to which they pertain; commenting on this, he says: "Während Jesaja selbst das Entweder-Oder von Strafgericht oder Rettung durch Umkehr verkündigt hat, deutet die eschatologische Theologie die zu dem Vorher-Nachher von vorübergehendem Unheil und ewigem Heil um" (p. 138). The truth of such assertions is apparently believed to be self-evident, for little attempt is made to justify them; that they accord very well with Fohrer's own interpretation of the prophets is clearly seen in his "Prophetie und Geschichte," 481-500, in which he rejects revelation in history and *Heilsgeschichte* in favor of an existentialistic "history of decision." It is not surprising, then, to find that in his commentary (*Das Buch Jesaja*, I, 151) his treatment of the authorship of Isa 11:1-9 is rather off-handed.

[7]Moses: Num 11:17; Judges: Jgs 3:10; 6:34; 11:29; 13:25; 14:19; 15:14.

[8]Von Rad, *Old Testament Theology*, I, 323.

description of the future king corresponds with the ideal of the royal psalms."[9] No doubt all that is said of the future king in vss. 1-5 is consonant with the idealized personage imaged in the Royal Psalms,[10] but it may be asked where in these psalms the king is characterized by the terms found in Isa 11:2. In fact, none of these six qualities are predicated of the king in any of the Royal Psalms.

Thus, although there are antecedents in the traditions about David's and Solomon's wisdom, Isaiah is here not following earlier messianic traditions, but producing a new formulation. Moreover, this formulation reveals strong influence from the wisdom tradition. With the exception of *g^ebûrâ*, these words are characteristically wisdom terms. Taken individually, most of them occur often enough in the OT in non-wisdom passages, but the concurrence of all of them in one verse can hardly be explained apart from wisdom influence.[11] The wisdom connections of this verse and of Isa 11:1-9 as a whole have been widely recognized.[12]

While the first two terms, *ḥokmâ ûbînâ*, evidently have a special reference to the king's role as judge[13] (cf. vss. 3-5) and to other royal functions, this is a pair very much at home in wisdom contexts and in Isaiah's polemic against the wise. As we have seen, Isaiah frequently indicted the ruling class for their failure to judge justly, most especially in their failure to vindicate the rights of the poor; he says that only in their own eyes are they wise and understanding (*ḥăkāmîm, n^ebônîm*—5:21) and that on the day of Yahweh's judgment their wisdom and understanding (*ḥokmâ, bînâ*) will perish (29:14).[14] It is not

[9]Mowinckel, *He That Cometh*, 175.

[10]The compositions in this category are taken to be Ps 2; 18; 20; 21; 45; 72; 89; 101; 110; and 132.

[11]Thus four of these words occur together in Prov 9:10, while all six are found in Prov 8:12-14. (The latter example is complicated, however, for vs. 13a seems to be intrusive and the whole passage—8:12-16—is probably influenced by Isa 11:1-5; see below.) Three, four, or five of these words are found in Prov 1; 2; 10; 14; 15; 16; 23; 30; Job 15; 28; 38. Similar concurrences of these terms outside the wisdom writings are rare and can usually be connected with wisdom traditions in some way.

[12]Fichtner, "Jesaja unter den Weisen," 78; Fohrer, *Das Buch Jesaja*, I, 151; van Imschoot, "Sagesse et esprit dans l'Ancien Testament," 40; Martin-Achard, "Sagesse de Dieu et sagesse humaine chez Ésaie," 137, 143; Joseph Bourke, "The Wonderful Counselor," *CBQ* 22 (1960) 134-38; Porteous, "Royal Wisdom," 254f.; Wildberger, *Jesaja*, 15, 189; Blanchette, "The Wisdom of God in Isaia," 421; McKane, *Prophets and Wise Men*, 110; Whedbee, *Isaiah and Wisdom*, 162.

[13]Scott, "Priesthood, Prophecy, Wisdom, and the Knowledge of God," 13; Porteous, "Royal Wisdom," 254.

[14]The criticism here concerns especially the role of counseling rather than judging, but it would be unwise to compartmentalize too neatly the functions of those responsible for the public order; Isaiah seems to bind his criticism in these two areas rather closely together in 5:18-24.

surprising that Isaiah sees these qualities especially invested in the ideal king to come, in whose reign the abuses of the past would be unthinkable, for the king was the one primarily responsible for this function[15] and for the public order in general;[16] this is the positive correlative of the judgment by which Judah's wise men are stripped of even the appearance of possessing these qualities.

Although *g^e^bûrâ* is not basically a wisdom term, its collocation with *'ēṣâ*, as here, makes it very relevant to Isaiah's conflict with the sages. Indeed, McKane has declared that the question of who has the *g^e^bûrâ* to establish his *'ēṣâ* is basic to the struggle between prophet and wise man;[17] although his statement appears to go too far, there is no doubt that Isaiah believed that Yahweh's *'ēṣâ* alone would be effective. The words form a natural pair (and are found together in 2 Kgs 18:20//Isa 36:5; cf. also Job 12:13), for *g^e^bûrâ* is the power to give effect to *'ēṣâ*. In the Judah of Isaiah's day the question of where the power lay exercised a profound influence on the formulation of national policy; it lay, so Judah's wise men thought, in the horses and chariots of Egypt. Yahweh can grant *g^e^bûrâ* to the men of Judah, Isaiah says, but only to those who wait for Him "in quiet and in trust" (30:15). The future king will have the *g^e^bûrâ* which comes to him from Yahweh's own spirit and will be thus enabled to effect the policies he formulates. And he will have no need for the royal advisers that Isaiah had found to be so baneful an influence on even the relatively well-disposed Hezekiah. That these gifts come from Yahweh's spirit guarantees that the king's *'ēṣâ* will be Yahweh's *'ēṣâ*. A very similar conception, it would seem, is expressed in the characterization of the ideal king as "Wonder-Counselor" in 9:5.[18]

[15]See Hammershaimb, "On the Ethics of the Old Testament Prophets," 91f.

[16]It is difficult to see why the promise of restoration of the public order implied here is any more unconditional, any more "Vorher-Nachher" (the schema Fohrer insists on eliminating from the pre-exilic prophets), than in 1:26, in which Isaiah promises restoration of Jerusalem's judges and counselors "as in the beginning." If it is replied that this promise presupposes the judgment of 1:25, it may be pointed out that 11:1 also supposes that judgment precedes the restoration.

[17]See above, Ch. 3, n. 48.

[18]The debate concerning the authenticity of 9:1-6 proceeds along much the same lines as that over 11:1-9 (see above, n. 6), and few who accept the one reject the other. Jochen Vollmer, "Zur Sprache von Jesaja 9:1-6," *ZAW* 80 (1968) 343-50, has argued that many terms and expressions used in these verses are late—usually exilic or later—including *ṣalmāwet*, *nāgah*, *haggîlâ*, *'ōl*, *sōbel*, *s^e^'ôn*, and *qin'â*. The evidence is not convincing, as even a brief examination can show. Thus *ṣalmāwet* is found, e.g., in Jer 2:6; the hiphil of *ngh* occurs in 2 Sam 22:29//Ps 18:29; *'ōl* appears in Dt 21:3; 1 Sam 6:7; 1 Kgs 12:4.9.11.14 and other texts that can be dated early; etc.; on *s^e^'ôn*, see Wildberger, *Jesaja*, 376. No more compelling is Vollmer's "Jesajanische Begrifflichkeit?" *ZAW* 83 (1971) 389-91. On *pele' yô'ēṣ*, see Harrelson, "Non-royal Motifs in the Royal Eschatology," 151; G. R. Driver, "Isaiah I-XXXIX: Textual and Linguistic Problems," *JSS* 13 (1968) 40; Wildberger, *Jesaja*, 381f.; George Jeshurun, "A Note on Isaiah 9:5," *JBL* 53 (1934) 384f. There is an obvious similarity between this name of the future king and what is said of the wonderful aspect of Yahweh's *'ēṣâ* and action, as in 28:29 and 29:14.

The first question concerning the final pair, *da'at w^{e}yir'at yhwh*, whether *da'at* is construct and takes *yhwh* in the same manner as *yir'at*, is probably to be answered in the affirmative.[19] The balance would be better served if the first term thus corresponded to its partner, *yir'at yhwh*. It is true, however, that at a later period *da'at* alone could stand in parallel to *yir'at yhwh* (Prov 1:29), and even Isaiah uses *da'at* alone in a sense apparently equivalent to *da'at 'ĕlōhîm* (5:13);[20] that is probably the sense it has here, whether it is taken as a construct or not. If, on the evidence from Hosea (see n. 20), we think of *da'at 'ĕlōhîm* as originally a prophetic term, then the present verse combines, perhaps for the first time, this prophetic conception with the wisdom term *yir'at yhwh*.

That *yir'at yhwh* is a wisdom term is clear both from its distribution in the OT and the content it has in this passage. It occurs nineteen times in MT in addition to the two occurrences in Isa 11:2f.:[21] fourteen times in Prov;[22] three times in Pss (19:10; 34:12; 111:10); once each in Isa 33:6 and 2 Chr 19:9. Since Ps 111 is a wisdom psalm, all but four of these nineteen occurrences are clearly in wisdom contexts. Even this margin can be reduced, for Ps 34 deserves to be classed as a wisdom psalm,[23] and some authors will say the same of Ps 19:8-15;[24] wisdom influence is also evident in Isa 33:6.[25] Thus *yir'at yhwh* emerges as a formula employed almost exclusively in wisdom texts.

The concept of the fear of the Lord is, of course, much broader than the use of this formula, but its specific content as employed here tends in the same direction. Becker finds an evolution in the "fear of God" concept that goes from numinous to moral to nomistic.[26] The moral content of the concept does not derive from the prophets but from the wisdom tradition; it was under the influence of the wisdom movement that the moral connotation of "fear of God" entered other streams of Israel's religious tradition.[27] Now the whole context of Isa 11:1-5 shows that the "fear of God" concept here is moral rather than numinous. Becker's comment is: "Unter der Voraussetzung der Echtheit, ist Is 11,2-3 ein relativ frühes Zeugnis für den

[19] Joüon, *Grammaire de l'hébreu biblique*, 386n.

[20] Hosea uses *da'at* alone in 4:6, but it is probably to be identified with the *da'at 'ĕlōhîm* in 4:1; in 6:6 he uses *da'at 'ĕlōhîm*.

[21] The phrase "and his delight shall be the fear of the Lord" in vs. 3 is usually taken to be a gloss.

[22] Prov 1:7.29; 2:5; 8:13; 9:10; 10:27; 14:26.27; 15:16.33; 16:6; 19:23; 22:4; 23:17.

[23] Weiser, *The Psalms*, 296f., 298; Murphy, *JBC* 35:51.

[24] Eissfeldt, *The Old Testament*, 127.

[25] See Becker, *Gottesfurcht im Alten Testament*, 259f.

[26] *Ibid.*, 84.

[27] *Ibid.*, 82f., 192, 209.

sittlichen Begriff der Gottesfurcht."[28] Wisdom in Israel, in Isaiah's experience, had slipped its moorings because it gave only lip service to the pride of place *yir'at yhwh* should hold (29:13; cf. 8:12f.). The future king would not be seduced from true wisdom because this last gift is given as the crown and complement of the first.

The six terms we have been discussing do not so much characterize the spirit as describe the qualities it bestows. In the light of Isaiah's experiences with the kings of Judah and the professional wisdom circles, it is clear why he believed that these qualities were precisely the ones needed by the ideal king of the future and why they are bestowed as charismatic gifts.[29] In this passage Isaiah has brought together some of Israel's most important traditions, those of royal messianism, charismatic leadership, and wisdom; the themes are united not by juxtaposition but by a thorough-going synthesis.

All of this agrees with and lends support to what has been said above of Isaiah's attitude to the wisdom tradition. It should be clear that what Isaiah expected as Yahweh's gift in the future also contained his teaching concerning the ideal that men of his day were obliged to strive for. The necessary conclusion is that Isaiah did not repudiate the wisdom tradition; on the contrary, he sought to reform it, partly by challenging it to return to its own high principles, partly by offering it insights of his own.

Although Isaiah's portrait of the ideal king does not directly involve *tôrâ* terminology, it does lend support to the interpretation set forth in this study, and that from two complementary points of view. On the one hand, the future king is raised up and endowed by God. The fact that his wisdom is a charismatic gift accords with Isaiah's bitter experience with human "wisdom" and with the assertion that he attributed all wisdom activity to Yahweh. On the other hand, there is a quasi-identification of the functions of the ideal king and Yahweh Himself; the king if Yahweh's *alter ego*, his *Stellvertreter*.[30] As such, he becomes the focus of wisdom on earth and exercises

[28]*Ibid.*, 285f. Derousseaux, *Crainte de Dieu*, disputes this development. Moreover, he holds that the "fear of the Lord" concept (in *yr'* terminology) is rooted primarily in northern traditions and came to be known in Judah with the migration there of northern traditions, primarily those of Dt (cf., e.g., p. 303); only by this route did it enter the wisdom tradition. Isaiah knew Dt and Isa 11:2 reflects deuteronomic influence (p. 275). But see above, Ch. 4, n. 15. There is also the fact that the phrase *yir'at yhwh* never occurs in Dt or the deuteronomic history.

[29]McKane, *Prophets and Wise Men*, 110, holds that the representation that wisdom derives from the spirit is exilic or post-exilic. But the spirit as source of the charismata needed by those who ruled Israel is an old tradition, and it remains to be explained why Isaiah could not have conceived of the spirit as a source of wisdom, etc., just as earlier ages had conceived of the spirit as a source of strength, prophetic activity, etc. The wisdom derived from experience alone, Isaiah knew, led to national bankruptcy; what was needed was wisdom that was rooted in Israel's Yahwistic faith and came from Israel's God. What Isaiah has done is to adapt Israel's ancient charismatic tradition to the needs of his own day.

[30]Fohrer, *Das Buch Jesaja*, I, 153; Johannes H. Scheepers, *Die Gees van God en die Gees van die Mens in die Ou Testament* (Kampen: J. H. Kok, 1960), 313 (from the English summary at the end); Wildberger, "Die Völkerwallfahrt zum Zion: Jes. II 1-5," 74.

those wisdom activities Isaiah otherwise attributes to Yahweh.[31] Would Isaiah have considered the ideal king as one who imparts *tôrâ*? In terms of the wisdom qualities bestowed on him in vs. 2, especially *ḥokmâ* and *bînâ*, he would be admirably equipped for this, and an affirmative answer seems indicated. Furthermore, Wildberger has pointed out that just as *šāpaṭ* and *hôkîaḥ* are used in parallel for the activity of Yahweh in 2:4, so are these terms used in the same manner for the activity of the ideal king in 11:4;[32] and the first text is one in which Yahweh is presented as giver of *tôrâ*. Another parallel element in 2:2-4 and 11:1-9 is the concluding vision of peace. In the former text this peace is the result of the instruction, judgment, and admonition of Yahweh the wise king. In the latter text the connection between wisdom activities of the king and the final state of peace is not so clearly drawn, but it is present, nevertheless. The idyllic peace has come about because the earth is filled with the knowledge of Yahweh. It should not be difficult to believe, especially in view of the other parallels with 2:2-4, that the universal knowledge which brings peace is imparted by the king upon whom Yahweh's spirit of wisdom has rested.

It has been said often that there is no *sachlich Verbindung*[33] between Isaiah's "genuine" oracles on the one hand and 2:2-4; 9:1-6; and 11:1-9 on the other. But, in fact, an element common to these three passages, the belief that it is Yahweh's will to bring peace and that He will do so if men will but "be still and listen," accords perfectly with some of the most important of Isaiah's undoubted oracles: "Take care you remain tranquil and do not fear" (7:4); "the waters of Shiloah that flow gently" (8:6); "Here is repose—but they would not listen" (28:12); "By waiting and calm you shall be saved, in quiet and in trust your strength lies" (30:15). The prophet who spoke such words passionately desired peace and believed that the way to peace was not through plans for making war most effectively but through submission to the saving will of God as revealed in His word—a word the prophet chose to designate as *tôrâ* because it contained a wisdom far deeper than that of the sages. No doubt Isaiah spoke much of war, weapons, and violence and related them to Yahweh's strange and alien "work," but these came by way of judgment on a people that would not listen to Yahweh's *tôrâ*. If Isaiah's vision of future peace seems to contrast with his words rooted in the historical situation, the difference lies not in the means to peace, which remains always submission to Yahweh's word, but consists in this, that in his historical situation men were unwilling to listen to the *tôrâ* of Yahweh, whereas in the future time they would hear it gladly; it is the difference between "This is a rebellious people . . . who refuse to listen to the *tôrâ* of Yahweh . . . because

[31] Wolff, *Frieden ohne Ende*, 78.

[32] Wildberger, "Die Völkerwallfahrt zum Zion: Jes. II 1-5," 74.

[33] See, e.g., Vollmer, "Zur Sprache von Jesaja 9:1-6," 344.

you reject this word . . . this guilt of yours shall be like a descending rift . . . It crashes like a potter's jar, smashed beyond rescue" and "Come, let us climb the Lord's mountain . . . that he may instruct us in his paths . . . For from Zion shall go forth *tôrâ* . . . They shall beat their swords into plowshares . . ."

Isaiah recognizes an intrinsic connection between peace and social justice: the walls of the city that harbors oppression will be broken down (5:1-7). Both are concerns of Yahweh's *tôrâ*; judges and counselors are condemned together for having scorned it (5:18-24), but when Isaiah thinks of better days, he sees judges and counselors restored together "as in the beginning" (1:26). And for all the similarities between 2:2-4 and 11:1-9, the former emphasizes world peace, the latter social justice.

Earlier I posed the question of Isaiah's long-term influence on the wisdom tradition. No attempt will be made to demonstrate such influence, but it may be possible to point to some indications that it did, in fact, make itself felt.

Isaiah's use of *tôrâ* indicates that he recognized Yahweh alone as the source of wise instruction and believed that man could only be wise by receiving such instruction from Yahweh; this has the effect of situating the source of wisdom in something divine and mysterious rather than in experience and human investigation. This did, in fact, come to be the common persuasion in Israel's wisdom tradition, and it is reasonable to suppose that Isaiah's influence was at work here.

We would expect that Isaiah's teaching in this area would be taken up and reflected first of all by his own disciples. Although there is no direct witness to the activity of these disciples, there is a widespread persuasion that much of the non-Isaianic material in Isa 1-66 stems from the "school of Isaiah," i.e., from his immediate disciples and those who succeeded them; although this persuasion can hardly be provided with certain proof, neither is it pure conjecture.[34] Some of the later passages in the Isaiah collection reflect the teachings we have been discussing and it is worth referring to them briefly as evidence of the continuation of Isaiah's influence in this area.[35]

Isa 30:20f. seems to speak of Yahweh as a Teacher,[36] promising that He will be visible and that His instruction will be given audibly:

> While from behind you a voice will sound in your ears:
> "This is the way; walk in it,"
> When you would turn to the right or to the left.

[34]See the discussion of McKenzie, *Second Isaiah*, XXI-XXIII.

[35]Wisdom glosses (such as Hos 14:10; Mic 6:9b; and, probably, Isa 3:10f.; 31:2) which are the work of editors do not enter into consideration here.

[36]In spite of the plural form of *môrèkā*, this is the interpretation usually adopted—and it is difficult to see how any other would make sense. See Duhm, *Das Buch Jesaia*, 223; Marti, *Das Buch Jesaja*, 225; Fischer, *Das Buch Isaias*, 203f.; Fohrer, *Das Buch Jesaja*, II, 101-104.

God Himself is the teacher and instructs concerning "the way." In 33:5f. Yahweh is depicted as enthroned, filling Zion with right and justice; included in the saving riches bestowed are *ḥokmâ*, *da'at*, and *yir'at yhwh*. The gifts obviously recall those bestowed on the future king in 11:2, only here they are given directly by Yahweh to (the inhabitants of) Zion.

Deutero-Isaiah reflects in a general way some of the elements of Isaiah's teaching that we have invesigated. In 40:13f. the prophet insists that Yahweh's spirit has never had need to be counseled or instructed by any other; Yahweh, obviously, is the possessor *par excellence* of such skills. In 44:25 (somewhat as in 29:14) Yahweh brings to naught the *ḥăkāmîm*, who here, however, are Babylonians and are classified with diviners. In 47:10 Daughter Babylon is reproached for thinking she has *ḥokmâ* and *da'at* that enables her to say "I, and no one else"; only Yahweh can speak in this manner (see 45:6 and 46:9 for similar uses of *'epes*), and the reproach suggests that wisdom and knowledge can be claimed by Yahweh alone. In 48:17 Yahweh is introduced as the one who teaches (piel participle of *lmd*) what is profitable (hiphil of *y'l*) and who shows them the right "way" (*madrîkăkā bᵉderek tēlēk*); the picture is that of a wisdom teacher and the text is reminiscent of 2:3 and 30:20f. In 53:11 the Servant of Yahweh is said to justify by his knowledge (*da'at*); many wish to adopt a different reading, but the term can make good sense on the supposition that the author is here adapting to the Servant some of the things said of the Davidic king in 11:1-9.[37] Finally, in 54:13 it is said:

> All your sons shall be taught by the Lord,
> and great shall be the peace of your children.

This passage combines the themes of instruction from God and peace that we have seen to be so closely related in Isaiah.

Turning from such passages, which may have come from circles that consciously carried on Isaiah's teachings, to compositions that spring directly from the wisdom tradition, the situation is more complicated. We have already noted that the conception that God is the source of wisdom was widespread in the ancient Near East;[38] on the other hand, Israel seems to have been reluctant to call Yahweh "wise" or to attribute wisdom directly to Him.[39] Passages in the wisdom books which speculate about the source or nature of wisdom are generally considered late compositions. If the Isaian authorship of 11:1-9 be conceded, there is no reason to doubt that it, as well as other Isaian passages which relate to the theme of wisdom and which effectively see Yahweh as its only source, exercised considerable influence in this development. The process by which wisdom is directly related to the

[37]The suggestion is equally valid if the line arrangement of BHS be adopted.

[38]See above, pp. 47, 60f.

[39]See above, Ch. 3, n. 19.

spirit of Yahweh had to begin somewhere, and it makes at least as good sense to suppose that Isaiah originated it as to hold that, since the relation of wisdom to spirit generally comes in late passages, Isa 11:1-9 must be dated late.[40] If, furthermore, a given wisdom passage seems to reflect the Isaian passage in terminology and/or theme, there is still more reason to suppose that wisdom has been influenced by prophecy. We will, therefore, look briefly at a few passages that may reflect such influence.

Speculation on the source and nature of wisdom is a major concern in Prov 1-9; we may point to the following passages in particular: 1:20-33; 2:1-11; 3:13-20; 4:5-9.10-13; 8:1-36; 9:1-6.11. Only once in these passages is *rûaḥ* used, namely, in 1:23; here it is Wisdom personified that speaks and is the one who will pour out her spirit; this is a new twist on the theme of God pouring out His spirit, but the intended result is probably the same: the recipient acquires wisdom as a divine gift. In the second of the passages listed (2:1-11) it is said that the one who seeks Wisdom personified (vss. 1-4) will understand *yir'at yhwh* and *da'at 'ĕlōhîm*, that Yahweh gives *ḥokmâ* and from his mouth come *da'at* and *tᵉbûnâ*; we have here three of the six "gifts" bestowed by the spirit of Yahweh in Isa 11:2. If we regard the etymological connection between *bînâ* and *tᵉbûnâ*, only the pair *'ēṣâ* and *gᵉbûrâ* is not represented. Within the long development in Prov 8 the passage consisting of vss. 12-16 almost certainly reflects Isa 11:1-5. Lady Wisdom (*ḥokmâ*) recounts her qualities, and they include *da'at mᵉzimmôt*, *'ēṣâ*, *bînâ*, and *gᵉbûrâ*. The only item of the six in Isa 11:2 that is missing here is *yir'at yhwh*—which is no doubt why a glossator thought it should be supplied. The context confirms the suggestion that these qualities of wisdom come from Isa 11:2,[41] for they are immediately identified as the means by which kings (and

[40]Van Imschoot, "Sagesse et esprit dans l'Ancien Testament," 23-49, observes that never in the collections of Prov, the wisdom psalms, Job 28, Eccl, Bar, or the wisdom passages in Tob is wisdom related to the spirit of God; the same is not true of the historical and prophetic books, where they are often related, and he thinks this was made possible because wisdom was conceived of as a divine prerogative, communicated to men, a mysterious force analogous to the spirit of Yahweh. His evidence for the relationship of wisdom and spirit in the historical books, however, consists mainly of texts in which they are in fact not related and rather late texts in which they are (e.g., Dt 34:9—usually assigned to P); one early text, however, is Gen 41:38f. In the prophetic books it is really only Isa 11:2 that relates wisdom to God's spirit, and this text van Imschoot accepts as early, even seeing influence from it in Prov 8:14f. (see below). Vriezen, "RuachYahweh (Elohim) in the Old Testament," 56, says that wisdom and spirit are connected explicitly only in Isa 11 and Gen 41:38f. and that "all other evidence of a connection between *ruach* and *chokma* is of a more recent date." The fact that Isa 2:2-4; 9:1-6; and 11:1-9 are closely related in thought has been widely recognized; taken as a whole, it would be difficult to find a more satisfactory historical and theological context than the ministry of Isaiah. That Isaiah concerned himself with wisdom traditions has been clearly established; but where and when would we look to find a comparable interest in wisdom *and* in the Zion tradition, in Davidic messianism, and in universal peace?

[41]Van Imschoot, "Sagesse et esprit dans l'Ancien Testament," 40.

other officials) rule; *ṣedeq* appears here (vs. 15), as it does in Isa 11:4.5. The author of this piece thinks of these qualities as necessary for *all* rulers; this is in profound accord with Isaiah's thought, for the prophet described the ideal in terms of what was needed but lacking in the historical models.

The connection between *rûaḥ* and *ḥokmâ* in Prov 1-9 does not rest only on the one occurrence of *rûaḥ* in 1:23. In 8:23 Lady Wisdom says "From of old I was poured forth (*nsk*)." The expression almost certainly means that Wisdom is here conceived of as a spirit; cf. the similar statement in 1:23, where spirit is "poured out" (hiphil of *nb'*, "to bubble"). The suggestion finds confirmation in Isa 29:10, where *nsk* is used with *rûaḥ*. Thus it seems very likely that one of the most significant OT passages concerning the nature and origin of wisdom draws something from the thought of Isaiah.

Surprising as it may be, spirit and wisdom are but seldom related in the Hebrew canon. Prov 1:23 is the *only* text in Prov in which *rûaḥ* refers to God's spirit. Job very possibly owes something to Isaiah in the description of God's wisdom in 12:13:

'immô ḥokmâ ûgᵉbûrâ lô 'ēṣâ ûtᵉbûnâ

If *tᵉbûnâ* be allowed to stand for *bînâ*, four of the six items from Isa 11:2 are present; in this case four is the maximum possible, for *da'at wᵉyir'at yhwh* could not be predicated of God. In Job God's *rûaḥ* appears more frequently than in Prov, but usually as a destructive force (4:9; 26:13) or as that which gives life to man (27:3; 33:4). Only in 32:8, in Elihu's discourse, is God's *rûaḥ* related to wisdom:[42]

> But it is a spirit (*rûaḥ*) in man,
> the breath of the Almighty, that gives him understanding.

Qoheleth never speaks of God's spirit, and the relatively few references in the Pss usually designate God's wind, etc. Only 51:13; 139:7; 143:10 suggest something deeper; only the last of these speaks of instruction from God, and *ḥokmâ* does not appear.

Later movements in this line are likely to reflect the developments we have already discussed. Thus Sir 1:8 is very much in the line of Prov 8:22-26; Solomon's prayer for "the spirit of Wisdom" in Wis 7:7 probably reflects both 1 Kgs 3:6-14 (or 2 Chr 1:10-12) and Isa 11:2. When Wis 9:17 asks:

> Or who ever knew your counsel, except you had given Wisdom
> and sent your holy spirit from on high?

[42]The *rûaḥ* whose visit Eliphaz describes in 4:15 is a personal being distinct from God.

it is closer to Isa 11:2 than to any other passage. In the light of the evidence of such passages, it can be asked whether even such references to "the spirit of wisdom, understanding, and knowledge" (*ḥokmâ*, *t^{e}bûnâ*, and *da'at*) as Ex 31:3; 35:31 (of Bazalel, artisan for the Tabernacle) and 1 Kgs 7:14 (of Hiram, architect of the Temple) and to "the spirit of wisdom" (of Joshua) as Dt 34:9 are not also to be attributed ultimately to the influence of Isaiah.

The final conclusions of this study may be summarized as follows. Isaiah's use of *tôrâ*[43] terminology indicates an attempt to situate all wisdom in Yahweh and to derive all wise instruction from Him alone; this is not for the sake of condemning the empirical approach but for the sake of insisting that God's will, when known through religious tradition or revelation, must be allowed to overrule human calculations. Isaiah's description of the ideal king of the future in 11:1-9 indicates that the wisdom which is Yahweh's comes to man only as a charismatic gift. These two teachings, that all true wisdom is from God and that man can possess it only as a charismatic gift, became common coin in Israel's later wisdom tradition; there are some texts, at least, which indicate that Isaiah's influence in this development was considerable.

[43]If it be asked why Isaiah used this term rather than *mûsār*, *tôkaḥat*, or *miṣwâ*, terms which figure largely in the wisdom tradition for the teacher's instruction, it is probably because of their overtones of chastisement, rebuke, and precept, respectively; *tôrâ* on the other hand, means simply "instruction."

BIBLIOGRAPHY

N.B. Many relevant works of a more general nature, even though cited in the preceding pages, are omitted from this bibliography.

Ackroyd, Peter R. "Historians and Prophets," *SEA* 33 (1968) 18-54.

Ahlström, G. W. "Oral and Written Transmission: Some Considerations," *HTR* 59 (1966) 69-81.

Albright, William F. "The Names 'Israel' and 'Judah' with an Excursus on the Etymology of *TÔDÂH* and *TÔRÂH*," *JBL* 46 (1927) 151-85.

———. "Some Canaanite-Phoenician Sources of Hebrew Wisdom," *VTSup* 3 (1955) 1-15.

Alonso-Schökel, Luis. "Motivos sapienciales y de alianza en Gn 2-3," *Bib* 43 (1962) 295-315.

Alt, Albrecht. "Zur literarischen Analyse der Weisheit des Amenemope," *VTSup* 3 (1955) 16-25.

———. "Die Weisheit Salomos," *TLZ* 76 (1951) 139-44.

Anderson, Bernhard W., and Harrelson, Walter, eds. *Israel's Prophetic Heritage. Essays in Honor of James Muilenburg*. New York: Harper & Row, Publishers, 1962.

Anderson, R. T. "Was Isaiah a Scribe?" *JBL* 79 (1960) 57f.

Baltzer, Klaus. "Considerations Regarding the Office and Calling of the Prophet," *HTR* 61 (1968) 567-81.

Bauer-Kayatz, Christa. *Einführung in die alttestamentliche Weisheit. BibSt* 55. Neukirchen-Vluyn: Neukirchener Verlag, 1969.

Baumgartner, Walter. *Hebräisches und aramäisches Lexikon zum Alten Testament*. Lieferung I. Leiden: E. J. Brill, 1967.

———. *Israelitische und altorientalische Weisheit*. Sammlung gemeinverständlicher Vorträge und Schriften aus dem Gebiet der Theologie und Religionsgeschichte 166. Tübingen: J. C. zb. Mohr, 1933.

———. "Die israelitische Weisheitsliteratur," *ThRu* N.F. 5 (1933) 259-88.

———. "The Wisdom Literature," *The Old Testament and Modern Study*. Ed. H. H. Rowley. London: Oxford University Press, 1961 (c1951), 210-37.

Becker, Joachim. *Gottesfurcht im Alten Testament*. Rome: Pontifical Biblical Institute, 1965.

Beecher, Willis J. "*Torah*: A Word-study in the Old Testament," *JBL* 24 (1905) 1-16.

Begrich, Joachim. "Die priesterliche Tora," *BZAW* 66 (1936) 63-88.

Bergmeier, Roland. "Zum Ausdruck *'ṣt rš'ym* in Ps 1:1; Hi 10:3; 21:16 und 22:18," *ZAW* 79 (1967) 229-32.

Blanchette, Oliver. "The Wisdom of God in Isaia," *AER* 145 (1961) 413-23.

de Boer, P. A. H. "The Counsellor," *VTSup* 3 (1955) 42-71.

Boston, James R. "The Wisdom Influence Upon the Song of Moses," *JBL* 87 (1968) 198-202.

Boström, Gustav. *Proverbiastudien: Die Weisheit und das fremde Weib im Spr. 1-9. LUA* N.F. Avd. 1. Bd. 30. Nr. 3. Lund: C. W. K. Gleerup, 1935.

Bourke, Joseph. "The Wonderful Counsellor," *CBQ* 22 (1960) 123-43.

Braulik, Georg. "Die Ausdrücke für 'Gesetz' im Buch Deuteronomium," *Bib* 51 (1970) 39-66.

Brongers, H. A. "Le crainte du Seigneur (*Jir'at YHWH, Jir'at 'Elohim*)," *OTS* 5 (1945) 151-73.

Brunner, Hellmut. *Altägyptische Erziehung.* Wiesbaden: O. Harassowitz, 1947.

__________. "Der freie Wille Gottes in der ägyptischen Weisheit," *Les Sagesses du Proche-Orient ancien* (see under Colloque de Strasbourg), 103-120.

__________. "Gerechtigkeit als Fundament des Thrones," *VT* 8 (1958) 426-28.

Buber, Martin. *The Prophetic Faith.* Tr. C. Witton-Davies. New York: Harper & Row, Publishers, 1960 (c1949).

Buchanan, George W. "Eschatology and the 'End of Days'," *JNES* 20 (1961) 188-93.

Budde, Karl. "Über die Schranken, die Jesajas prophetischer Botschaft zu setzen sind," *ZAW* 41 (1923) 165-77.

Cazelles, Henri. "Les débuts de la sagesse en Israël," *Les Sagesses du Proche-Orient ancien* (see under Colloque de Strasbourg), 27-40.

Cheyne, T. K. *The Prophecies of Isaiah.* Vol. I. London: Kegan Paul, Trench, & Co., 1889.

Childs, Brevard S. "The Enemy from the North and the Chaos Tradition," *JBL* 78 (1959) 187-98.

__________. *Isaiah and the Assyrian Crisis. SBT* 2/3. London: SCM Press Ltd., 1967.

Clements, Ronald E. "Deuteronomy and the Jerusalem Cult Tradition," *VT* 15 (1965) 300-312.

__________. *Prophecy and Covenant. SBT* 1/43. Naperville, Ill.: Alec R. Allenson, Inc., 1965.

Clifford, Richard J. "The Use of *HÔY* in the Prophets," *CBQ* 28 (1966) 458-64.

Colloque de Strasbourg 17-19 mai 1962. *Les Sagesses du Proche-Orient Ancien.* Bibliothèque des Centres d'Études supérieures specialisés. Paris: Presses Universitaires de France, 1963.

Couroyer, H. P. "Le chemin de vie en Égypte et en Israël," *RB* 56 (1949) 412-32.

__________. "Idéal sapiential en Égypte et en Israël," *RB* 57 (1950) 174-79.

Couturier, Guy. "Sagesse babylonienne et sagesse israélite," *Sciences ecclesiastiques* 14 (1962) 293-309.

Crenshaw, J. L. "Amos and the Theophanic Tradition," *ZAW* 80 (1968) 203-215.

__________. "The Influence of the Wise upon Amos: The 'Doxologies of Amos' and Job 5:9-16; 9:5-10," *ZAW* 79 (1967) 42-51.

__________. "Method in Determining Wisdom Influence upon 'Historical' Literature," *JBL* 88 (1969) 129-42.

Cross, Frank M., Jr. "The Divine Warrior in Israel's Early Cult," *Biblical Motifs: Origins and Transformations.* Ed. Alexander Altmann. Cambridge: Harvard University Press, 1966, pp. 11-30.

__________, and Freedman, David. N. "The Blessing of Moses," *JBL* 67 (1948) 191-210.

Dahood, Mitchell. "Some Ambiguous Texts in Isaias," *CBQ* 20 (1958) 41-49.

Delcor, M. "Les attaches littéraires, l'origine et la signification de l'expression biblique 'Prendre à temoin le ciel et la terre'," *VT* 16 (1966) 8-25.

Derousseaux, Louis. *La crainte de Dieu dans Ancien Testament*. Paris: Les Éditions du Cerf, 1970.

Dhorme, E. "Prêtres, devins et mages dans l'ancienne religion des Hébreux," *RHR* 108 (1933) 113-43.

Donner, Herbert. *Israel unter den Völkern. Die Stellung der klassischen Propheten des 8. Jahrhunderts v. Chr. zur Aussenpolitik der Könige von Israel und Juda. VTSup* 11. Leiden: E. J. Brill, 1964.

Driver, G. R. " 'Another Little Drink'—Isaiah 28:1-22," *Words and Meanings. Essays Presented to David Winton Thomas.* Ed. P. R. Ackroyd and B. Lindars. Cambridge University Press, 1968.

________. "Isaiah I-XXXIX: Textual and Linguistic Problems," *JSS* 13 (1968) 36-57.

Dubarle, A. M. *Les sages d'Israël. Lectio Divina* 1. Paris: Les Éditions du Cerf, 1946.

________. "Où en est l'étude de la littérature sapientielle?" *ETL* 44 (1968) 407-419.

Duesberg, H., and Fransen, I. *Les scribes inspirés*. Rev. ed. Maredsous: Éditions de Maredsous, 1966.

Duhm, Bernhard. *Das Buch Jesaia. HKAT* III, 1. 4th ed. Göttingen: Vandenhoeck und Ruprecht, 1922.

Dürr, Lorenz. "Das Erziehungswesen im AT und im antiken Orient," *MVAG* 36 (1932) 1-160.

Eichrodt, Walther, *Der Heilige in Israel: Jesaja 1-12 übersetzt und ausgelegt.* Stuttgart: Calwer Verlag, 1960.

Eissfeldt, Otto. "Sohnespflichten im alten Orient," *Syria* 43 (1966) 39-47.

Elliger, Karl. "Prophet und Politik," *ZAW* 53 (1935) 3-22.

Engnell, Ivan. "The Call of Isaiah: An Exegetical and Comparative Study," *UUA* 1949:4. Uppsala: A.-B. Lundequistska Bokhandeln, 1949.

________. *Studies in Divine Kingship in the Ancient Near East.* Oxford: Basil Blackwell, 1967.

Evans, D. Geoffrey. "Rehoboam's Advisers at Shechem and Political Institutions in Israel and Sumer," *JNES* 25 (1966) 273-79.

Fensham, F. Charles. "Widow, Orphan, and the Poor in Ancient Near Eastern Legal and Wisdom Literature," *JNES* 21 (1962) 129-39.

Fey, R. *Amos und Jesaja. WMANT* 12. Neukirchen-Vluyn: Neukirchener Verlag, 1963.

Fichtner, Johannes. *Die altorientalische Weisheit in ihrer israelitisch-jüdischen Ausprägung. BZAW* 62. Giessen: Verlag Alfred Töpelmann, 1933.

________. "Jahwes Plan in der Botschaft des Jesaja," *ZAW* 63 (1951) 16-33.

________. "Jesaja unter den Weisen," *TLZ* 74 (1949) 75-80.

________. "Zum Problem Glaube und Geschichte in der israelitisch-jüdischen Weisheitsliteratur," *TLZ* 76 (1951) 145-50.

________. "Die 'Umkehrung' in der prophetischen Botschaft: Eine Studie zu dem Verhältnis von Schuld und Gericht in der Verkündigung Jesaja," *TLZ* 78 (1953) 459-66. Reprinted in *Gottes Weisheit.* Ed. K. D. Fricke. Stuttgart: Calwer Verlag, 1965, pp. 45-51.

Fischer, Johann. *Das Buch Isaias, I. Teil: Kapitel 1-39.* Bonn: Peter Hanstein Verlagsbuchhandlung, 1937.

Fohrer, Georg. "Action of God and Decision of Man in the Old Testament," *Biblical Essays 1966. Proceedings of the Ninth Meeting of "Die Ou-Testamentiese Werkgemeenskap in Suid-Afrika."* Potchefstroom: Pro Rege-Pers Beperk, 1967.

________. *Studien zur alttestamentlichen Prophetie (1949-1965). BZAW* 99. Berlin: Verlag Alfred Töpelmann, 1967.

________. *Das Buch Jesaja.* 2 vols. *Zürcher Bibelkommentare.* Zurich: Zwingli Verlag, 1960.

________. "Prophetie und Geschichte," *TLZ* 89 (1964) 481-500.

Gamper, Arnold. *Gott als Richter in Mesopotamien und im Alten Testament: Zum Verständnis einer Gebetsbitte.* Innsbruck: Universitätsverlag Wagner, 1966.

Gampert, August. *La thora; Étude historique sur ses origines et son développement.* Geneva: Imprimerie Romet, 1895.

Gemser, Berend. "The Importance of the Motive Clause in Old Testament Law," *VTSup* 1 (1953) 50-66.

________. "The Instructions of 'Onchsheshonqy and Biblical Wisdom Literature," *VTSup* 7 (1959) 102-128.

________. *Sprüche Salomos. HAT* 16. Tübingen: J. C. B. Mohr, 1963.

Gerstenberger, Erhard. "Zum alttestamentlichen Weisheit," *Verkündigung und Forschung* 14 (1969) 28-44.

________. *Wesen und Herkunft des "apodiktischen Rechts".* Neukirchen: Neukirchener Verlag, 1965.

________. "The Woe-Oracles of the Prophets," *JBL* 81 (1962) 249-63.

Gese, H. *Lehre und Wirklichkeit in der alten Weisheit.* Tübingen: J. C. B. Mohr, 1958.

Ginsberg, Harry L. "Some Emendations in Isaiah," *JBL* 69 (1950) 51-60.

Goedicke, H. "Die Lehre eines Mannes für seinen Sohn," *Zeitschrift für ägyptische Sprache und Altertumskunde* 93 (1966) 62-71.

Gordis, R. "The Social Background of Wisdom Literature," *HUCA* 18 (1944) 77-118.

Gordon, Edmund. "A New Look at the Wisdom of Sumer and Akkad," *BO* 17 (1960) 122-52.

________. "Sumerian Animal Proverbs and Fables: 'Collection Five'," *JCS* 12 (1958) 1-21, 43-75.

________. *Sumerian Proverbs: Glimpses of Everyday Life in Ancient Mesopotamia.* University Museum Monographs. Philadelphia: The University Museum, 1959.

Gottwald, Norman. *All the Kingdoms of the Earth: Israelite Prophecy and International Relations in the Ancient Near East.* New York: Harper & Row, Publishers, 1964.

Gray, George B. *A Critical and Exegetical Commentary on the Book of Isaiah, I-XXXIX.* Vol. I. New York: Charles Scribner's Sons, 1912.

Gray, John. "Kingship of God in the Prophets and Psalms," *VT* 11 (1961) 1-29.

Gressman, H. *Israels Spruchweisheit im Zusammenhang der Weltliteratur.* Berlin: Karl Curtius, 1925.

Gunkel, Hermann. "Aegyptische Parallelen zum alten Testament," *ZDMG* 63 (1909) *531-39.*

Gutbrod, Walter. "The Meaning of *tôrâ*," *TDNT*, IV, 1044-47.

Habel, N. "The Form and Significance of the Call Narrative," *ZAW* 77 (1965) 297-323.

Haldar, Alfred. *Associations of Cult Prophets among the Ancient Semites.* Uppsala: Almquist & Wikells Boktryckeri Ab, 1945.

Hammershaimb, E. "On the Ethics of the Old Testament Prophets," *VTSup* 7 (1959) 75-101.

Harrelson, Walter. "Nonroyal Motifs in the Royal Eschatology," *Israel's Prophetic Heritage* (see under Anderson, Bernhard W.), pp. 147-65.

Hartman, Louis F. "Daniel," *JBC* 26:1-38.

Harvey, J. "Le 'Rîb-Pattern', réquisitoire prophetique sur la rupture de l'alliance," *Bib* 43 (1962) 172-96.

Hayes, John H. "The Tradition of Zion's Invulnerability," *JBL* 82 (1963) 419-26.

Heaton, E. W. *The Hebrew Kingdoms.* New Clarendon Bible. Vol. III. London: Oxford University Press, 1968.

Hempel, Johannes. *Das Ethos des Alten Testaments. BZAW* 67. Berlin: Verlag Alfred Töpelmann, 1964.

Hermisson, Hans-Jürgen. *Studien zur israelitischen Spruchweisheit. WMANT* 28. Neukirchen: Neukirchener Verlag, 1968.

Herntrich, Volkmar. *Der Prophet Jesaja: Kapitel 1-12. ATD* 17. 2nd ed. Göttingen: Vandenhoeck & Ruprecht, 1954.

Herrmann, Siegfried. *Die prophetischen Heilserwartungen im Alten Testament: Ursprung und Gestaltwandel.* Stuttgart: W. Kohlhammer Verlag, 1965.

Hertzberg, H. W. "Die Entwicklung des Begriffes *mšpṭ* im AT," *ZAW* 41 (1923) 16-76.

Holladay, William L. "Isa. III 10-11: An Archaic Wisdom Passage," *VT* 18 (1968) 481-87.

__________. *The Root šûbh in the Old Testament.* Leiden: E. J. Brill, 1958.

Honeyman, A. M. "Isaiah I 16 *hizzakkû*," *VT* 1 (1951) 63-65.

L'Hour, Jean. "Les interdits *to'eba* dans le Deutéronome," *RB* 71 (1964) 481-503.

Huffmon, H. B. "The Covenant Lawsuit in the Prophets," *JBL* 78 (1959) 285-95.

Humbert, Paul. *Recherches sur les sources égyptiennes de la littérature sapientiale d'Israël.* Mémoires de l'Université de Neuchâtel: Neuchâtel. Secretariat de l'Université, 1929.

Hyatt, J. Philip. "Torah in the Book of Jeremiah," *JBL* 60 (1941) 381-96.

van Imschoot, Paul. "Sagesse et esprit dans l'Ancien Testament," *RB* 47 (1938) 23-49.

Janzen, Waldemar. "*'ǍSRÊ* in the Old Testament," *HTR* 58 (1965) 215-26.

_________. *Mourning Cry and Woe Oracle*. *BZAW* 125. Berlin: Walter de Gruyter, 1972.

Jasper, F. N. "Reflections on the Moral Teaching of the Prophets," *SJT* 21 (1968) 462-76.

Jenni, Ernst. "Jesajas Berufung in der neueren Forschung," *TZ* 15 (1959) 321-39.

Jeshurun, George. "A Note on Isaiah 9:5," *JBL* 53 (1934) 384f.

Johnson, Aubrey R. *The Cultic Prophet in Ancient Israel*. Cardiff: University of Wales Press, 1962.

Kaiser, Otto. *Isaiah 1-12*. Tr. R. A. Wilson (from 2nd ed. of *ATD* 17, 1963). Philadelphia: The Westminster Press, 1972.

Kayatz, Christa. *Studien zu Proverbien 1-9: eine form- und motivgeschichtliche Untersuchung unter Einbeziehung ägyptischen Vergleichsmaterials*. *WMANT* 22. Neukirchen-Vluyn: Neukirchener Verlag, 1966.

Kingsbury, Edwin C. "The Prophets and the Council of Yahweh," *JBL* 83 (1964) 279-86.

Kissane, Edward J. *The Book of Isaiah*. Vol. I. Dublin: The Richview Press, 1941.

Knierim, Rolf. "The Vocation of Isaiah," *VT* 18 (1968) 47-68.

Köhler, Ludwig. *Deuterojesaja (Jesaja xl-lv) stilkritisch untersucht*. *BZAW* 37. Berlin: Verlag Alfred Töpelmann, 1923.

Kramer, S.N. "Gilgamesh and the Land of the Living," *JCS* 1 (1947) 3-46.

_________. *History begins at Sumer*. Garden City, N. Y.: Doubleday & Company, Inc., 1959 (c1956).

_________. "Sumerian Wisdom Literature: A Preliminary Survey," *BASOR* 122 (Apr. 1951) 28-31.

Kuschke, Arnulf. "Zu Jes 30:1-5," *ZAW* 64 (1952) 194f.

Lambert, W. G. *Babylonian Wisdom Literature*. Oxford: Clarendon Press, 1960.

Leclant, Jean. "Documents nouveaux et points de vue récents sur les sagesses de l'Égypte ancienne," *Les Sagesses du Proche-Orient ancien* (see under Colloque de Strasbourg), pp. 5-26.

Lescow, Theodor. "Die dreistufige Tora: Beobachtungen zu einer Form," *ZAW* 82 (1970) 362-79.

Lindars, Barnabas. "Torah in Deuteronomy," *Words and Meanings: Essays Presented to David Winton Thomas*. Ed. P. R. Ackroyd and B. Lindars. Cambridge: Cambridge University Press, 1968, pp. 117-36.

Lindblom, Johannes. *Prophecy in Ancient Israel*. London: Basil Blackwell, 1962.

_________. "Wisdom in the Old Testament Prophets," *VTSup* 3 (1955) 192-204.

Lipiński, E. "*b'ḥryt hymym* dans les textes préexiliques," *VT* 20 (1970) 445-50.

_________. "Macarismes et Psaumes de congratulations," *RB* 75 (1968) 321-67.

von Loewenclau, Ilse. "Zur Auslegung von Jesaja 1, 2-3," *EvT* 26 (1966) 294-308.

Lohfink, Norbert. *Das Hauptgebot: Eine Untersuchung literarischer Einleitungsfragen zu Dtn 5-11*. *AnBib* 20. Rome: Pontifical Biblical Institute, 1963.

_________. *Lectures in Deuteronomy*. Rome: © Norbert Lohfink, 1968.

McKane, William. *Prophets and Wise Men. SBT* 1/44. London: SCM Press, 1965.

————. *Proverbs: A New Approach.* Philadelphia: The Westminster Press, 1970.

McKenzie, John L. "The Elders in the Old Testament." *BibOr* Vol. 1. *AnBib 10.* Rome: Pontifical Biblical Institute, 1959, pp. 388-406.

————. "Royal Messianism," *CBQ* 19 (1957) 25-52.

————. Second Isaiah. AB *20.* Garden City, N.Y.: Doubleday& Company, Inc., 1968.

Malamat, Abraham. "Kingship and Council in Israel and Sumer: A Parallel," *JNES* 22 (1963) 247-53.

Malfroy, Jean. "Sagesse et loi dans le Deutéronome," *VT* 15 (1965) 49-65.

Marti, Karl. *Das Buch Jesaja. Kurzer Hand-Commentar zum Alten Testament* X. Tübingen: J. C. B. Mohr, 1900.

Martin-Achard, Robert. "Ésaïe et Jérémie aux prises avec les problèmes politiques; Contribution à l'étude du thème prophétie et politique," *RHPR* 47 (1967) 208-224.

————. "Sagesse de Dieu et sagesse humaine chez Ésaie," *maqqēl shâqēdh, La branche d'amandier: Hommage à Wilhelm Vischer.* Montpellier: Causse, Graille, Castelnau, 1960, 137-44.

Minette de Tillesse, Georges. "Sections 'tu' et sections 'vous' dans le Deutéronome," *VT* 12 (1962) 29-87.

Miller, P. D., Jr. "The Divine Council and the Prophetic Call to War," *VT* 18 (1968) 100-107.

Montgomery, John Warwick. "Wisdom as Gift. The Wisdom Concept in Relation to Biblical Messianism," *Int* 16 (1962) 43-57.

Moran, William. "Some Remarks on the Song of Moses," *Bib* 43 (1962) 317-27.

Moriarity, Frederick. "Isaiah 1-39," *JBC* 16:1-66.

Müller, Hans-Peter. "Der Begriff 'Rätsel' im Alten Testament," *VT* 20 (1970) 465-89.

————. *Ursprünge und Strukturen alttestamentlicher Eschatologie. BZAW* 109. Berlin: Verlag Alfred Töpelmann, 1969.

Murphy, Roland E. "Assumptions and Problems in Old Testament Wisdom Research," *CBQ* 29 (1967) 407-418.

————. "The Concept of Wisdom Literature," 46-54. *The Bible in Current Catholic Thought.* Ed. John L. McKenzie. New York: Herder and Herder, 1962.

————. "Form Criticism and Wisdom Literature," *CBQ* 31 (1969) 475-83.

————. "The Interpretation of Old Testament Wisdom Literature," *Int* 23 (1969) 289-301.

————. "Introduction to Wisdom Literature," *JBC* 28:1-40

————. *A Study of the Hebrew Root yrh.* Unpublished M.A. Dissertation. Washington, D. C.: The Catholic University of America, 1948.

Napier, B. D. "Isaiah and the Isaian," *VTSup* 15 (1966) 240-51.

Noth, Martin. "Die Bewährung von Salomos 'Göttlicher Weisheit'," *VTSup* 3 (1955) 225-37.

Nougayrol, Jean. "Les sagesses babyloniennes: Études récentes et textes inédits," *Les Sagesses du Proche-Orient ancien* (see under Colloque de Strasbourg), pp. 41-51.

Östborn, Gunnar. *Tōrā in the Old Testament: A Semantic Study*. Lund: Håken Ohlssoms Boktryckeri, 1945.

Pfeiffer, R. H. "The Fear of God," *IEJ* 5 (1955) 41-48.

Porteous, Norman W. "Royal Wisdom," *VTSup* 3 (1955) 247-61.

Posener, Georges and Garnot, Jean Sainte Fare. "Sur une sagesse égyptienne de basse epoque." *Les Sagesses du Proche-Orient ancien* (see under Colloque de Strasbourg), pp. 153-57.

Preuss, Horst Dietrich. "Erwägungen zum theologischen Ort alttestamentlicher Weisheitsliteratur," *EvT* 30 (1970) 393-417.

Pritchard, James, ed. *Ancient Near Eastern Texts Relating to the Old Testament*. 2nd ed. Princeton, N.J.: Princeton University Press, 1955.

_________. *The Ancient Near East: Supplementary Texts and Pictures Relating to the Old Testament*. Princeton, N.J.: Princeton University Press, 1969.

Procksch, Otto. *Jesaia I. KAT* IX. Leipzig: A. Deichertsche Verlagsbuchhandlung, 1930.

von Rad, Gerhard. "The City on the Hill," *The Problem of the Hexateuch and other essays*. Tr. E. W. T. Dicken. New York: McGraw-Hill Book Company, 1966, pp. 232-42.

_________. "Job XXXVIII and Ancient Egyptian Wisdom," *ibid.*, 281-91.

_________. "The Joseph Narrative and Ancient Wisdom," *ibid.*, 292-300.

_________. *Der Heilige Krieg im alten Israel*. Zurich: Zwingli Verlag, 1951.

_________. *Old Testament Theology*. Tr. D. M. G. Stalker. 2 vols. New York: Harper & Row, Publishers, 1962-65.

_________. *Studies in Deuteronomy*. Tr. D. M. G. Stalker. *SBT* 1/9. London: SCM Press, 1953.

_________. *Wisdom in Israel*. Tr. J. D. Martin. Nashville: Abingdon Press, 1972.

_________. "Das Werk Jahwes [*ma'ăśeh/pō'al*]," *Studia Biblica et Semitica*. Ed. W. C. van Unnik and A. S. van der Woude. Wageningen: H. Veenman, 1966, pp. 290-98.

Rankin, O.S. *Israel's Wisdom Literature: Its Bearing on Theology and the History of Religion*. New York: Schocken Books, 1969 (c1936).

Rengstorf, K. H. "*mathētēs*: The Term in the Old Testament and Judaism," *TDNT* IV, 426-41.

Richter, Wolfgang. *Recht und Ethos. Versuch einer Ortung des weisheitlichen Mahnspruches. StANT* 15. Munich: Kosel-Verlag, 1966.

Robert, A. "Les attaches littéraires bibliques de Prov. I-IX," *RB* 43 (1934) 42-68, 172-204, 378-84; 44 (1935) 344-65, 502-525.

_________. "Le Psaume CXIX et les sapientiaux," *RB* 48 (1939) 5-20.

_________. "Le sens du mot loi dans le Psaume CXIX," *RB* 46 (1937) 182-206.

Robinson, H. W. "The Council of Yahweh," *JTS* 45 (1944) 151-57.

Rowley, H. H. "The Nature of Old Testament Prophecy in the Light of Recent Study," *The Servant of the Lord and other Essays on the Old Testament.* 2nd ed., rev. Oxford: Basil Blackwell, 1965, pp. 95-134.

__________, ed. *Studies in Old Testament Prophecy.* Edinburgh: T. & T. Clark, 1946.

__________. *Worship in Ancient Israel: Its Forms and Meaning.* Philadelphia: Fortress Press, 1967.

Rylaarsdam, J. Coert. *Revelation in Jewish Wisdom Literature.* Chicago: University of Chicago Press, 1946.

Scheepers, Johannes Hendrich. *Die Gees van God en die Gees van die Mens in die Ou Testament.* Kampen: J. H. Kok, 1960.

Schmid, Hans Heinrich. *Wesen und Geschichte der Weisheit: Eine Untersuchung zur altorientalischen und israelitischen Weisheitsliteratur. BZAW* 101. Berlin: Verlag Alfred Töpelmann, 1966.

Scott, R. B. Y. "Priesthood, Prophecy, Wisdom, and the Knowledge of God," *JBL* 80 (1961) 1-15.

__________. *Proverbs, Ecclesiastes. AB* 18. Garden City, N. Y.: Doubleday & Company, Inc., 1965.

__________. "Solomon and the Beginnings of Wisdom in Israel," *VTSup* 3 (1955) 262-79.

Skehan, Patrick W. "Isaias and the Teaching of the Book of Wisdom," *CBQ* 2 (1940) 289-99. (Reprinted in *CBQMS* 1, 162-71.)

__________. "The Seven Columns of Wisdom's House in Proverbs 1-9," *CBQ* 9 (1947) 190-98. (Revised, *CBQMS* 1, 9-14.)

__________. "A Single Editor for the Whole Book of Proverbs," *CBQ* 10 (1948) 115-30. (Revised, *CBQMS* 1, 15-26.)

__________. "Some Textual Problems in Isaia," *CBQ* 22 (1960) 47-55.

__________. "Wisdom's House," *CBQ* 29 (1967) 468-86. (Revised, *CBQMS* 1, 27-45.)

__________. *Studies in Israelite Poetry and Wisdom. CBQMS* 1. Washington, D. C.: The Catholic Biblical Association of America, 1971.

Skladny, Udo. *Die ältesten Spruchsammlungen in Israel.* Göttingen: Vandenhoeck & Ruprecht, 1962.

Smith, Louise Pettibone. "The Use of the Word *twrh* in Isaiah, Chapters 1-39," *AJSL* 46 (1929) 1-21.

Smith, W. S. "The Relationship between Egyptian Ideas and Old Testament Thought," *JBR* 19 (1951) 12-15.

Staerk, W. "Der Gebrauch der Wendung *b'ḥryt hymym* in alttestamentlichen Kanon," *ZAW* 11 (1891) 247-53.

Story, C. J. K. "The Book of Proverbs and Northwest Semitic Literature," *JBL* 64 (1945) 319-37.

Terrien, Samuel. "Amos and Wisdom," *Israel's Prophetic Heritage* (see under Anderson, Bernhard W.), pp. 108-115.

Toy, Crawford H. *A Critical and Exegetical Commentary on the Book of Proverbs.* New York: Charles Scribner's Sons, 1899.

Vattioni, F. "Studi sul libro dei Proverbi," *Augustinianum* 12 (1972) 121-68 (contains extensive bibliography on many aspects of wisdom studies).

Vawter, Bruce. "Apocalyptic: Its Relation to Prophecy," *CBQ* 22 (1960) 33-46.

__________. *The Conscience of Israel.* New York: Sheed & Ward, 1961.

__________. "Introduction to Prophetic Literature," *JBC* 12:1-25.

__________. *"Social Justice" in the Prophet Isaiah.* Denver, Colo.: St. Thomas Seminary, 1958.

Vergote, Joseph. "La notion de Dieu dans les livres de sagesse égyptiennes." *Les Sagesses du Proche-Orient ancien* (see under Colloque de Strasbourg), pp. 159-90.

Vollmer, Jochen. "Zur Sprache von Jesaja 9:1-6," *ZAW* 80 (1968) 343-50.

__________. "Jesajanische Begrifflichkeit?" *ZAW* 83 (1971) 389-91.

Volten, Aksel. "Der Begriff der Maat in den Ägyptischen Weisheitstexten." *Les Sagesses du Proche-Orient ancien* (see under Colloque de Strasbourg), pp. 73-101.

Vriezen, Th. C. "Essentials of the Theology of Isaiah," *Israel's Prophetic Heritage* (see under Anderson, Bernhard W.), pp. 128-46.

__________. "Prophecy and Eschatology." *VTSup* 1 (1953) 199-229.

__________. "Ruach Yahweh (Elohim) in the Old Testament." *Biblical Essays 1966. Proceedings of the Ninth Meeting of "Die Ou-Testamentiese Werkgemeenskap in Suid-Afrika."* Potchefstroom: Pro Rege-Pers Besperk, 1967, pp. 50-61.

van de Walle, Baudoin. "Problèms relatifs aux méthodes d'enseignement dans l'Égypte ancienne." *Les Sagesses du Proche-Orient ancien* (see under Colloque de Strasbourg), pp. 191-207.

Weinfeld, Moshe. "The Dependence of Deuteronomy upon the Wisdom Tradition" (Hebr.), *Kaufmann Jubilee Volume.* Jerusalem: Magnes Press, 1960, pp. 89-108.

__________. "Deuteronomy—The Present State of Inquiry," *JBL* 86 (1967) 249-62.

__________. "The Origin of the Humanism in Deuteronomy," *JBL* 80 (1961) 241-47.

__________. *Deuteronomy and the Deuteronomic School.* Oxford: Clarendon Press, 1972.

Weiser, Artur. *Introduction to the Old Testament.* Tr. D. A. Barton. London: Darton, Longman & Todd, 1961.

__________. *The Psalms: A Commentary.* Tr. H. Hartwell. Philadelphia: The Westminster Press, 1962.

Westermann, Claus. *Basic Forms of Prophetic Speech.* Tr. H. C. White. Philadelphia: The Westminster Press, 1967.

Whedbee, James William. *Isaiah and Wisdom.* Nashville: Abingdon Press, 1971.

Whybray, Roger N. *The Succession Narrative: A Study of II Sam. 9-20 and I Kings 1 and 2. SBT* 2/9. London: SCM Press Ltd., 1968.

__________. *Wisdom in Proverbs: The Concept of Wisdom in Proverbs 1-9. SBT* 1/45. London: SCM Press Ltd., 1965.

Wildberger, Hans. *Jesaja: I. Teilband, Jesaja 1-12. BKAT* X; Neukirchen: Neukirchener Verlag, 1965-72.

__________. "Jesajas Verständnis der Geschichte," *VTSup* 9 (1963) 83-117.

———. "Die Thronnamen des Messias," *TZ* 16 (1960) 314-32.

———. "Die Völkerwallfahrt zum Zion: Jes. II 1-5," *VT* 7 (1957) 62-81.

Wilder, A. N. "The Nature of Jewish Eschatology," *JBL* 50 (1931) 201-206.

Wolf, C. Umhau. "Traces of Primitive Democracy in Ancient Israel," *JNES* 6 (1947) 98-108.

Wolff, Hans Walter. *Amos' geistige Heimat*. Neukirchen-Vluyn: Neukirchener Verlag, 1964.

———. *Frieden ohne Ende: Jesaja 7.1-17 und 9.1-6 ausgelegt*. Neukirchen: Neukirchener Verlag, 1962.

———. *Dodekapropheten 1, Hosea*. *BKAT* XIV/1. Neukirchen: Neukirchener Verlag, 1961.

Worrell, John. "*'ṣh*: 'Counsel' or 'Council' at Qumran?" *VT* 20 (1970) 65-74.

Wright, G. E. "The Lawsuit of God. A Form-Critical Study of Deuteronomy 32," *Israel's Prophetic Heritage* (see under Anderson, Bernhard W.), pp. 26-67.

Würthwein, Ernst. "Jesaja 7, 1-9. Ein Beitrag zum Thema 'Prophetie und Politik'," *Theologie als Glaubenswagnis. Festschrift für Karl Heim*. Hamburg: Furche-Verlag, 1954, pp. 47-63.

———. *Die Weisheit Ägyptens und das Alte Testament*. Marburg: Schriften der Philipps-Universitat Marburg, 1960.

Zimmerli, Walther. *The Law and the Prophets: A Study of the Meaning of the Old Testament*. Tr. R. E. Clements. Oxford: Basil Blackwell, 1965.

———. "The Place and Limit of the Wisdom in the Framework of the Old Testament Theology," *SJT* 17 (1964) 146-58.

———. "Zur Struktur der alttestamentlichen Weisheit," *ZAW* 51 (1933) 177-204.

Zuch, R. B. "Hebrew Words for 'teach'," *BS* 121 (1964) 228-35.

INDEX OF MODERN AUTHORS

Ahlström, G. W., 20
Albright, W. F., 4f., 34, 35
Alonso-Schökel, L., 98
Alt, A., 32, 33, 36, 62
Anderson, B. W., 16
Anderson, G. W. 16
Anderson, R. T., 45
Baumgartner, W., 33, 78, 81
Becker, J., 46, 128
Beecher, W. J., 3, 6, 68, 89
Begrich, J., 6, 8, 9, 10, 12-14, 25, 65, 69, 89
Bentzen, A., 7, 9, 16, 25
Blanchette, O., 46, 126
Blenkinsopp, J., 17
de Boer, A. H., 52
Boston, J. R., 18
Bourke, J., 126
Bowden, J. S., 7
Braulik, G., 19
Bright, J., 20, 22
Brongers, H. A., 47
Brunner, H., 47
Buber, M., 57, 108
Buchanan, G. W., 88
Budde, K., 107, 108
Burrows, M., 84
Cazelles, H., 30, 46, 50
Cheyne, T. K., 85, 88, 92, 93, 101, 102, 105, 106, 112, 113, 124
Childs, B. S., 35, 46, 52, 53, 86, 113
Clamer, A., 5
Clements, R. E., 10, 17, 85, 87, 90
Clifford, R., 101
Cody, A., 110
Couroyer, H. P., 33, 37, 44
Crenshaw, J. L., 36, 46, 118
Cross, F. M., Jr., 6, 7, 17
Dahood, M., 120
Delitzsch, F., 3, 4
Derousseaux, L., 17, 47, 68, 129
Donner, H., 52, 53, 67, 112, 114
Driver, G. R., 49, 127
Driver, S. R., 3, 6
Dubarle, A. M., 35
Duesberg, H., 27, 34, 37
Duhm, B., 69, 85, 95, 98, 106, 107, 110, 111, 112, 113, 117, 124, 131
Eichrodt, W., 69, 85, 87, 88, 91, 96, 106, 124
Eissfeldt, O., 6, 10, 16, 17, 35, 50, 69, 85, 86, 112
Engnell, I., 3, 4, 61
Evans, D. G. 52
Fensham, F. C., 82
Fey, R., 46
Fichtner, J., 1, 37, 40, 41, 43, 44, 45, 50, 51, 54, 58, 85, 91, 99, 103, 121, 124, 126
Fischer, J., 84, 85, 88, 96, 104, 106, 112, 113, 124, 131
Fohrer, G., 14, 46, 50, 51, 57, 60, 65, 69, 71, 80, 85, 86, 103, 105, 106, 107, 112, 113, 114, 115, 116, 124, 126, 127, 129, 131
Fransen, I., 27, 34, 37
Freedman, D. N., 6, 7, 17
Gampert, A., 3
Gemser, B., 32, 35, 36, 39, 41, 44, 66
Gerstenberger, E., 26, 46, 60, 61, 81, 101, 103
Gesenius, W., 3, 5
Gordon, E. I., 30, 50, 110
Gottwald, N. K., 60, 85, 87, 88, 89, 108, 112
Gray, G. B., 27, 69, 85, 88, 93, 96, 106, 108, 110
Gray, J., 16, 19
Gressman, H., 8
Gunkel, H., 33
Gutbrod, W., 3, 6, 18, 20
Habel, N., 57
Haldar, A., 4, 18, 25, 69
Hammershaimb, E., 69, 83, 124, 127
Harrelson, W., 124, 127
Hartman, L. F., 22
Harvey, J., 26
Hayes, J. H., 53, 86
Heaton, E. W., 29, 35, 46, 49, 52, 53, 60, 62, 68
Hempel, J., 73
Hermisson, H.-J., 35
Herntrich, V., 84, 85, 96, 100, 106, 124
Herrmann, S., 87
Honeyman, A. M., 78
Horst, F., 18
L'Hour, J., 18, 76
Huffmon, H. B., 26
Humbert, P., 33, 76
Hyatt, J. P., 20, 22
van Imschoot, P., 49, 62, 126, 133
Janzen, W., 101
Jasper, F. J., 66
Jenni, E., 57, 99
Jeshurun, G., 127
Johnson, A. R., 58
Joüon, P., 110, 128
Kaiser, O., 46, 124
Kapelrud, A. S., 87
Kayatz, C. 42, 44
Kingsbury, E. C., 63
Kissane, E., 69, 85, 96, 105, 113f., 124

Knierim, R., 57, 64
Koch, K., 101
Koch, R., 124
Köhler, L., 7
Kramer, S. N., 30, 31, 63
Kraus, H.-J., 14, 83
Lambert, M., 4
Lambert, W. G., 29, 30
Leclant, J., 30, 32, 34, 62
Lescow, T., 68
Lindars, B., 3, 5, 6, 7, 9, 11, 15, 17, 20, 23, 27, 29, 66, 67, 85, 96, 117
Lindblom, J., 18, 25, 28, 45, 50, 52, 62, 68, 69, 85, 96, 106, 108
Lipiński, E., 88, 101
von Loewenclau, I., 46, 49, 50, 118
Lohfink, N., 17
McCarthy, D. J., 61
McKane, W., 29, 35, 36, 39, 40, 42, 44, 46, 47, 50, 54, 55, 56, 58, 59, 75, 76, 96, 100, 103, 121, 123, 126, 127, 129
McKenzie, J. L., 23, 52, 124, 131
Malamat, A., 52
Malfroy, J., 18
Marti, K., 69, 85, 86, 92, 93, 95, 101, 106, 108, 112, 113, 115, 131
Martin-Achard, R., 45, 126
Meyer, R., 78
Minette de Tillesse, G., 17
Mitchell, H. G., 24
Mowinckel, S., 25, 83, 87, 88, 125
Müller, H.-P., 87
Murphy, H. G., 4, 5, 8, 35, 49, 80, 83, 84, 90, 91, 92, 128
Murphy, R. T., 20
Napier, B. D., 60
Noth, M., 7, 11, 49, 52, 62
Nougayrol, J., 30
Nowack, W., 16
Östborn, G., 3, 5, 9, 18, 27, 28, 62, 90
Pedersen, J., 18, 96
Pfeiffer, R. H., 47
Porteous, N. W., 62, 126
Procksch, O., 69, 85
von Rad, G., 8, 10, 25, 35, 36, 37, 47, 49, 53, 56, 63, 65, 69, 85, 86, 87, 88, 89, 96, 112, 121, 124, 125
Rankin, O. S., 33, 66, 73, 85, 124
Rengstorf, K. H., 110
Richter, W., 18, 26, 35, 46, 50, 52, 60, 71, 81, 103
Ringgren, H., 124
Robert, A., 41, 99
Robinson, H. W., 7, 18, 64
Rost, L., 45
Rowley, H. H., 20, 23, 25, 33, 84, 85, 88
Scheepers, J. H., 129
Scott, R. B. Y., 10, 11, 18, 27, 35, 36, 39, 40, 45, 46, 50, 52, 103, 126
Sellin, E., 14
Skehan, P. W., 35, 36, 44, 46, 106
Skinner, J., 5, 22, 27
Skladny, U., 35
Schmid, H. H., 30, 32, 33, 35, 46, 47, 50, 61, 62
Smith, G. A., 85
Smith, L. P., 7, 14, 20, 24, 65, 69
Smith, W. S., 33
von Soden, W., 4
Speiser, E. A., 5
Staerk, W., 86
Stuhlmueller, C., 24
Terrien, S., 46, 118
Thomas, D. W., 39
Toy, C., 38, 39, 40, 41
de Vaux, R., 5, 27, 28
Vawter, B., 10, 87, 96, 124
Vergote, J., 47, 62
Vollmer, J., 127, 130
Volten, A., 30, 47
Vriezen, T. C., 49, 63, 65, 85, 87, 124, 133
van de Walle, B., 34
Weill, R., 34
Weinfeld, M., 18, 81
Weiser, A., 10, 16, 78, 80, 83, 84, 89, 90, 91, 92, 124, 128
Wellhausen, J., 3, 4, 5, 7
Westermann, C., 69, 72, 79, 112
Whedbee, J. W., 46-49, 50, 52, 53, 56, 58, 61, 63, 66, 101, 102, 116, 121, 123, 124, 126
Whybray, R. N., 34, 36, 42, 46
Wildberger, H., 28, 46, 49, 50, 54, 60, 63, 67, 69, 72, 75, 76, 77, 83, 85, 86, 88, 89, 94, 95, 96, 98, 99, 100, 103, 104, 105, 106, 108, 109, 126, 127, 129, 130
Wilder, A. N., 87
Wilson, J. A., 32, 74
Wolf, C. U., 52
Wolf, H. M., 109
Wolff, H. W., 46, 53, 57, 70, 80, 85, 108, 118, 130
Würthwein, E., 53
Zimmerli, W. 69

INDEX OF SCRIPTURE REFERENCES

Genesis

2-3 98
4:23 98
12:6 5, 7f., 27
18:4 78
18:18 88
19:2 78
24:14 90
41:38f. 133
43:24 78
43:31 78
43:32 74, 76
46:34 74, 77
49:2 70
49:17 94
50:20 47

Exodus

2:5 78
8:22 77
13:9 6
13:16 44
15-17 119
16:4 6
18 27
18:13-23 7
18:16 6
18:20 6
19:13 4
22 74
22:20-23 81
23:1 38
23:6-9 81
23:6-8 104
23:7 38
23:8 66
24:12 6
27:20 78
28:30 8
30:34 78
31:3 135
35:31 135

Leviticus

6:2 11
6:7 11
6:18 11
7:1 11
7:11 11
7:23 13
7:25 13
7:27 13
7:37 11
11:46f. 9
11:46 11
12:7 11
13:59 11
14:2 9
14:8f. 78
14:32 9
14:54 9
14:57 9
15:13 78
15:32 9
16:8 7
17:1 76
18:22 76
18:26f. 76
18:29f. 76
18:30 76
19:5 13
20:13 76
23:19 76
24:2 78
24:7 78
26:15 97
26:43 97

Numbers

11:17 125
14-17 119
14:11 99
14:23 99
16:30 99
19:2 11, 28
26:55f. 7
27:21 7
31:21 11, 28
33:54 7
34:13 7
35:31 38
36:2f. 7

Deuteronomy

1:5 15, 17
4:1-40 17
4:5-8 15
4:8 17
4:26 110
4:44-11:32 17
4:44 15, 17
5:32 29
6:8 44
7:25 74, 76
8:5 15
10:18 81
11:18 44
12:31 74
14:3-20 9
14:29 81
16:11 81
16:12 81
16:14 81
16:19 66
17:1 74, 76
17:8-13 8
17:11 15, 17, 27, 95
17:18f. 17
18:9 110
18:12 74, 76
19:14 81
21:3 127
21:6 78
21:18-21 50
21:20 39
22:5 74, 76
23-25 18
23:19 74, 76, 77
24:4 74, 76
24:17 81
25:1f. 38
25:13-16 81
25:16 74
26:12f. 81
27:3 17
27:8 17
27:15 74
27:19 81
27:26 17
28:1 117
28:20 96
28:58 15, 17
28:61 15, 17
28:63-68 17
29:20 15, 17
29:28 15, 17
30:10 15, 17
30:19 110
31:9-13 15
31:9 17
31:11f. 17
31:12 117
31:16 96
31:20 99
31:24-29 15
31:24-26 17
31:28 110
32:1f. 70

Deuteronomy (Cont'd)

32:2 43, 98
32:5 119
32:19 99
32:34 106
32:46 17
33 6f.
33:4 17
33:8-11 6f., 8
33:9 98
33:10 6f., 17, 89
34:9 133, 135

Joshua

1:7 17
1:8 17
7:14-18 7
8:31f. 19
8:31 17
8:32 17, 113
8:34 17
9:18 119
10:24 71
14:2 7
15:1 7
17:1 7
18:6ff. 7
18:6 8
22:5 17
23:6 17, 19
24:16 96
24:20 96
24:26 17, 19

Judges

2:12 96
3:10 125
5:3 70
6:34 125
9:37 7
10:1-5 7
10:6 96
10:10 96
11:6 71
11:11 71
11:29 125
12:7-15 7
13:25 125
14:19 125
15:14 125
18:5f. 7
19:21 78
20:9 7

Ruth

3:3 78
4:7 106, 110

1 Samuel

2:17 99
6:7 127
8:8 96
10:10 125
11:6 125
12:10 96
14:36-42 7
15:23 19, 97
15:26 19, 97
16:1-7 19
16:13 125
23:6-12 7
25:41 78
28:6 7
30:7f. 7

2 Samuel

7:19 17
11:8 78
12:14 99
12:20 78
13:12 66
14:17 62
15:3 118
15:12 109
15:32-37 36
16:23-17:14 36
16:23 59
17:1-14 54, 63, 123
17:14 47, 59
17:23 63
22:27 119
22:29 127
22:31 98

1 Kings

2:3 17, 19
3:4-14 62
3:4-12 36
3:6-14 134
3:12 90
3:16-28 36
3:28 62, 90
4:3 36
5:9-14 36, 62
7:14 135
8:36 92
9:9 96
10:1-13 36, 62
12:4 127
12:6-15 36
12:8 38
12:9 127
12:11 127
12:13 38
12:14 59, 127
13:30 101
16:20 109
18:18 37
21:8 105
22:19-23 63f.
22:38 78

2 Kings

5:10 78
5:12f. 78
10:31 17, 19
11:14 109
12:21 109
14:6 17, 19
14:9 109
15:15 109
15:30 109
17:4 109
17:13 17, 22
17:15 19, 97
17:16 37
17:34 17
17:37 17
18:20 59, 127
19:29 123
20:8-11 123
21:8 17
21:22 96
22:8 17
22:11 17
22:17 96
23:24f. 17
23:25 19

1 Chronicles

5:18 110
6:27 92
25:8 110

2 Chronicles

1:10-12 134
7:19 37
10:13 38
10:14 38
12:1 37
19:9 128
23:13 109
25:27 109

Ezra
2:63 7
9:10 37

Nehemiah
7:65 7
10:1-2 105
13:3 117

Esther
8:8 105
8:10 105

Job
4:2 72
5:9-16 46
5:13 59
5:17 40, 97
6:18 94
8:2 72
8:6 78
9:5-10 46
9:30 78
10:3 59
11:2 72
11:4 43, 78, 98
12:13 127, 134
13:6 70, 72
13:17 70
14:17 105
15 126
15:2 72
15:14 79
15:15 78
17:12 102
16:17 78
16:21 90
17:16 120
18:2 72
19:2 72
19:23 113
21:2 70, 72
22:2 72
25:4 79
25:5 78
27:13 46
28 126
28:28 80
29:6 78
29:21 59
32:12 90
33:1 70
33:9 78
34:2 70
34:16 70, 72
36:16 120
36:22 91
37:14 72
38 126

Psalms
1:1 40, 59
1:6 93
2 126
2:8 93
2:9 89
10:3 99
10:13 99
12:7 98
15 13, 25
17:6 98
18 126
18:27 119
18:29 127
18:31 98
19:8-15 128
19:10 128
20 126
21 126
24 25
24:3-6 13
25:4 91, 92, 93, 94
25:5 93
25:8-12 91
25:8ff. 92
25:8 91, 93
25:10 38
25:12 91, 93
25:13 29
25:14 91
26:6 78, 79
27:11 92, 93, 94
32:1f. 92
32:3-7 92
32:8-11 92
32:8 92, 93
32:9 92
34 128
34:12-22 80
34:12 128
34:15 80
36 84, 89
36:1-4 80
36:4f. 98
36:4 80
36:5 98
37:3 29
37:9 29
37:11 29
37:22 29
37:29 29
37:34 29
45 126
46 88
46:10f. 88
48 88f.
49:2f. 72
49:2 51, 71
49:4f. 72
49:14 46
50 69, 83f.
50:1 71
50:4 84
50:5 84
50:7 84
50:8-15 84
50:14 84
50:16-21 84
50:16 84
50:23 84
51:4 79
51:6 79
51:9 79
51:13 134
58:11 78
59:16 119
72 126
72:4 83
72:12-14 83
73:13 79
76 88
76:11 88
78:1 70, 71
78:7 38
86:11 92, 93
87 88, 89
89 126
89:31 37
94:8-11 90
94:10 90, 93
94:12 40, 93
94:16 93
101 126
101:4 119
105:45 38
106:3 41
106:35 110
107:11 99
110 126
110:6 89
111:10 128
112:1 40
119 38, 98f.
119:1f. 40
119:9 79
119:33 93
119:53 37

Psalms (cont'd)

119:87 37
128:1 40
132 126
138:2 98
139:7 134
143:10 134
147:15 98

Proverbs

1-9 28f., 41-44, 75, 133, 134
1 126
1:5 43, 98
1:7 128
1:8-19 44, 73
1:8f. 44
1:8 34, 39, 41, 43, 70, 71, 117, 118
1:9 44
1:10-19 39
1:10-18 44
1:10-14 44
1:15 44, 109
1:16 44
1:19 44
1:20-33 133
1:22 115
1:23 133, 134
1:25 59, 117
1:29 128
1:30 59, 99, 117
2 126
2:1-11 133
2:1-8 38
2:1 42
2:5 128
2:8 38, 93, 94
2:9 42
2:11 38
2:12 109
2:13 38, 94
2:15 119
2:20 37, 94
2:21 29
3:1-4 42
3:1 34, 38, 43, 70
3:2 44
3:6 94
3:7 103
3:9 67
3:11 97
3:13-20 133
3:16 44
3:18 40
3:21-24 42
3:21 38
3:31 109
3:32 39, 74, 119
4:1-4 38
4:1f. 42, 71
4:1 34, 39, 70, 118
4:2 34, 38, 43, 98
4:4 37, 44
4:5-9 133
4:6 38
4:9 134
4:10-13 38, 133
4:10-12 42
4:10 39
4:11 92
4:13 38
4:14 81, 94, 109
4:20-22 38, 42
4:20 37
4:21 37
4:23 38
5:1f. 38, 42
5:1 51, 70
5:2 38
5:7 39
5:12 99
5:13 39
6:1-19 75
6:6-8 50
6:7 71
6:16-19 75, 76
6:16f. 77
6:16 74
6:20-24 38
6:20-22 42
6:20 34, 38, 41, 43, 68, 70, 71
6:23 34, 43, 68
7:1-5 38
7:1-3 42
7:1 37, 70
7:2 34, 37, 43, 44
7:3 44
7:21 43, 98
7:22 50
7:24 39, 70, 109
8:1-36 133
8:6 39
8:7 74, 75
8:8f. 118
8:8 119
8:12-16 126, 133
8:13 128
8:14f. 133
8:14 56, 59
8:22-26 134
8:23 133
8:29 29
8:32f. 39
8:32 37, 40, 93
8:33 118
9:1-6 133
9:6 38, 81
9:7f. 90
9:9 43, 98
9:10 126, 128
9:11 44, 133
9:15 94
10-31 44
10:1-22:16 35
10 126
10:11 44
10:17 34, 37, 38
10:27 44, 128
10:30 29
11:1 74, 75, 79
11:20 40, 74, 75, 119
11:30 44
12:15 39, 59, 118
12:22 40, 74, 75
12:28 94
13:1 39
13:3 38
13:6 38
13:13 68
13:14 37
13:18 37
13:19 74
13:20 39
14:2 119
14:4 50
14:26 128
14:27 128
14:31 67f., 82
15 126
15:4 44
15:5 37, 99
15:8f. 74
15:8 40, 74, 75, 77
15:9 40
15:10 38
15:16 128
15:18 37
15:19 94
15:25 82
15:26 74, 75
15:31f. 39
15:31 118
15:33 128
16 35, 126

Proverbs (cont'd)

16:2 78
16:5 40, 74, 76
16:6 128
16:9 47
16:12 74
16:13 34
16:21 43, 98
16:22 34
16:23 43, 98
16:33 7
17:15 38, 74, 75, 77, 104
17:20 119
19:1 119
19:5 90
19:8 37
19:16 37, 68
19:17 82
19:20f. 59
19:20 39, 118
19:21 47, 48, 54
19:23 128
19:26 50
19:27 34, 38, 39, 118
20:1 104
20:5 59
20:9 79
20:10 74, 75, 77, 79
20:11 78
20:18 59
20:23 74, 75, 79
20:24 47
20:26 38
20:28 38
21:3 41, 73, 77, 83
21:7 74
21:8 78
21:12 38
21:17 104
21:27 40, 74, 75, 77
21:30f. 47
21:30 59
22:4 128
22:5 109, 119
22:9 82
22:17-24:22 33, 82
22:17 37, 39, 43, 51, 118
22:18 37
22:22f. 82
23 126
23:10f. 82
23:12 34
23:15 38
23:17 128
23:19f. 38
23:19 39, 81
23:20f. 39
23:22 39, 50
23:26 38, 50
23:29-35 104
24:9 74
24:22 43
24:24 104
24:26 118
25:1-29:27 35
25 35
25:5 38
25:15 71
26:3 50
26:5 103
26:11 50
26:12 103
26:13 134
26:17 50
26:25 74
27:3 134
27:8 50
27:9 59
27:11 38
28:1 50
28:4 37f.
28:6 119
28:7 37, 38f.
28:9 37, 39f., 74, 75, 77, 117
28:11 103
28:16 44
28:25 37
29:3 39
29:8 115
29:9 120
29:14 82, 83
29:18 37, 40f.
29:22 37
29:27 74
30 126
30:3 110
30:5 98
30:8 29
30:18f. 50
30:24-31 50
31:1-9 43
31:1 41
31:4f. 104
31:15 29
31:26 34, 37, 41
32:8 134
33:4 134

Ecclesiastes

4:6 120
6:5 120
7:10 93
9:17 120
10:16 101

Wisdom

6:1f. 71
7:7 134
9:17 134f.

Sirach

1:8 134
4:18 81
6:22 118
11:19 120
11:21 118
12:11 120
16:23 46
18:33 104
19:2 104
24:22 44
31:21 120
38:24-39:11 34
31:25-31 104
33:19 71
34:8 119
39:27 46
48:15 71

Isaiah

1-66 94, 131
1-41 94
1-39 57, 85, 96, 124
1-12 46
1:2f. 46, 49f., 51, 57, 58, 118, 122
1:2 60, 70
1:3 50, 60
1:4 60, 83, 95, 96, 99
1:7 83
1:8 86
1:10-17 12, 14, 24, 25f., 28, 68, 69, 83f., 124
1:10 26, 51, 67, 68-84, 95, 120
1:11-15 79
1:11 72
1:13 74-77
1:14 96
1:15 24, 75, 77, 78
1:16f. 79-83, 98
1:16 78f.
1:17 24, 77, 110
1:18-20 26, 68
1:19 114, 117

Isaiah (Cont'd)

1:23 24
1:25 127
1:26 127, 131
1:27 86
1:28 96
2:1-5 86, 93
2:2-4 19, 62, 84-89, 95, 130, 131, 133
2:3 12, 65, 67, 68, 84-95, 132
2:4 72, 90, 110, 130
2:6-21 53
2:12 53
3:3 51
3:6f. 71
3:10f. 131
3:10 101
3:12 81, 94
3:16f. 86
5 52
5:1-7 46, 131
5:8-10 46
5:8f. 100
5:9 53
5:11-13 46, 100
5:13 128
5:18-24 100, 104, 126, 131
5:18-23 102, 104
5:18f. 103
5:18 102
5:19-24 100
5:19 49, 54, 56, 102, 103
5:20f. 102f.
5:21 36, 49, 51, 55, 103, 126
5:22-24 104, 124
5:22f. 101, 103
5:22 104
5:23 103, 104
5:24 19, 65, 68, 95-104, 121
5:29 56
5:30 104
6:1-8:18 108
6:1-8:15 107, 108, 112
6 53, 64
6:1-13 108
6:1 62
6:5 62
6:8 64
6:9f. 57
6:9 58, 117
6:10 56
6:11f. 53
6:11 57
6:12 96
7:1-8:18 108
7 108
7:1-17 53, 57
7:1-9 52, 53
7:3 109
7:4-9 57
7:4 113, 130
7:5 49, 55
7:7 49, 53, 55
7:9 113
7:10-20 52
7:11 56, 57f.
7:14-8:22 109
7:14f. 109
7:15 98
8:1-8 57
8:1-4 52, 108, 109
8:1f. 110
8:1 109, 113
8:2 110
8:5-8 52, 108
8:6 130
8:9f. 108
8:10 55, 59
8:11-15 108, 109
8:11 109, 110
8:12f. 111, 129
8:13 109
8:16-20 106
8:16-18 106-110, 113
8:16 65, 67, 68, 104-112, 115, 117, 120
8:17f. 106
8:18 86, 107
8:19f. 106, 107
8:20 65, 67, 68, 104, 105, 106f.
9:1-6 53, 58, 127, 130, 133
9:4f. 89
9:5 62, 127
9:6 107, 108
9:15 81
10:1-4 52, 100
10:1-3 100
10:1f. 46
10:3 96
10:5-15 63
10:5ff. 100
10:11 100
10:12 86
10:13 51
10:14 96
10:15 46
10:18-24 100
10:21f. 100
10:24 86
10:32 86
11 133
11:1-9 58, 95, 124, 126, 127, 130, 131, 132, 133, 135
11:1-5 126, 128, 133
11:1 127
11:2f. 128
11:2 51, 62, 124-30, 132, 133, 134, 135
11:3f. 72, 83, 90
11:4 90, 130, 134
11:5 134
11:9 89
14:24-27 49, 55
14:24 53, 55
14:27 55
16:3 59
17:2 96
17:9 96
19:11f. 51
20:1-6 52
22:3 71
24:5 68
26:7f. 94
26:10 118
28-30 113
28:1-4 100
28:7-13 115
28:7 55
28:9 67, 91, 116, 117
28:12 113, 114, 117, 130
28:14-22 53, 115
28:16f. 86
28:16 113
28:22 53, 116
28:23-29 46, 49f., 63, 115
28:23 70, 98, 99
28:26 59, 67, 91, 116
28:29 49, 56, 58, 127
29:1ff. 100
29:4 98
29:8 86
29:9f. 117
29:10 134
29:11 105
29:13f. 115
29:13 67f., 129
29:14f. 49

Isaiah (Cont'd)

29:14 36, 51, 55, 56, 58, 126, 127, 132
29:15f. 46, 53, 55, 63, 100, 115
29:15 59, 120
29:24 43, 98
30:1-5 100, 116
30:1 49, 55, 59, 60, 118, 120
30:7 113
30:8-17 112, 113, 116, 120
30:8-14 112
30:8 113, 114
30:9f. 114
30:9 60, 66f., 68, 112-120
30:10f. 117, 118
30:10 114
30:11 94, 117
30:12 59, 118, 119
30:13f. 120
30:15-17 112
30:15 112, 113, 115, 117, 119f., 127, 130
30:18 101, 112
30:20f. 131f.
30:20 91
31:1-3 53, 100, 116
31:2 49, 52, 58, 131
31:4 86
31:9 86
32:9 70, 98
32:20 101
33:1ff. 100
33:5f. 132
33:6 128
33:8 94
33:14-16 13, 25
36:5 56, 127
37:30 123
38:7f. 123
38:22 123
39:1-17 53
40:13f. 132
40:14 94
41:3 94
42:1-4 23
42:4 23
42:18-25 23
42:21 23
42:24 23
44:25 132
45:6 132
45:9f. 100
46:9 132
47:10 132
48:17 132
49:1 70
49:16 113
50:4 111
51 86
51:4f. 23
51:4 23, 70, 71
51:6-8 23
51:7 23
53:11 132
54:13 111, 132
56:1-8 25, 26
56:2 101
57:2 118
59:7 44
59:14 118
60:14 99
66:2-3 12

Jeremiah

2:6 127
2:8 20
2:22 79
4:14 79
6:16 22
6:17 22
6:18 71
6:19 20, 21, 22, 97
7:5-12 101
7:8f. 101
7:10f. 101
8:8 20
8:9 36, 97
9:12 20, 21, 22, 37
10:2 110
11:9 109
13:15 70
13:23 111
14:21 99
15:19 39
16:11 20, 21
17:15 54
18:18 6, 20, 36
22:3 81
22:15f. 83
23:1-4 100
23:5 62
23:17 99
26:4f. 21f.
26:4 20, 21f.
31:33 20, 21
31:34 21
32:10f. 105
32:10 110
32:14 105
32:23 20, 21
32:25 110
32:44 105, 110
33:24 99
35:6-19 60
35:14 29
35:16 29
35:18 21, 29
44:10 20, 21, 22
44:23 20, 21

Lamentations

1:11 39
2:6 99
2:9 62
4:7 78

Baruch

4:1 44

Ezekiel

5:6 97
7:26 6, 22
12:22 54
13:3ff. 100
13:18-21 100
19:3 110
19:6 110
20:13 97
20:16 97
20:24 97
22:26 9, 22
23:14 113
34:2ff. 100
43:11 22
43:12 22
44:5 22
44:23 9

Daniel

9 15
9:4-20 22
9:10 22, 24
9:11 24
9:13 24
10:14 88
11:18 71
12:4 105
12:9 105

Hosea

4:1 97, 128
4:6 6, 10, 11, 19, 97, 128

Hosea (Cont'd)

5:1 70
6:6 12, 14, 128
8:1 10, 11, 19
8:2 11
8:11 12
8:12 11f., 19
8:13 12
14:10 131

Joel

1:2 71
2:7 94

Amos

2:4 19, 97
3:1 70
3:10 118
3:13 70
4:1 70
4:4f. 12, 14
5:4f. 12, 14
5:14f. 14, 80
5:18-20 100
5:21-24 12, 14
6:1-7 100
7:16 70

Micah

1:2 70, 71
2:1-3 100
3:1-4 83
3:1 71, 73
3:2 71
3:9-12 83
3:9 71
3:10 71
3:11 6, 8, 19
3:12 86
4:1-4 84, 86
4:2 12, 19, 94
4:3 90, 110
6:1-8 26
6:2 70
6:6-8 13, 25, 26
6:9 51, 131
6:11 79

Nahum

3:1-7 100

Habakkuk

1:4 19f.
2:6-8 100
2:9-11 100
2:12-14 100
2:15-17 100
2:19f. 100
2:19 8, 20, 27

Zephaniah

2:5-7 100
3:1-5 100
3:4 9, 19

Haggai

2:10-14 13
2:11-14 9
2:11 9, 24, 27

Zechariah

7:1-14 24f.
7:1-7 25f.
7:1-3 9
7:7 25
7:12 24f., 117
8:18f. 9
11:7 100

Malachi

1:10 12
2:6-9 24
2:7 9
3:22 24

Matthew

5:3-12 101
13:51f. 93

Luke

6:20-26 101

1 Corinthians

1:17-25 58